LAST RIDE OF THE IRON HORSE

HOW LOU GEHRIG FOUGHT ALS TO PLAY ONE FINAL CHAMPIONSHIP SEASON

DAN JOSEPH

Mechanicsburg, PA USA

Published by Sunbury Press, Inc.
Mechanicsburg, Pennsylvania

www.sunburypress.com

ISBN: 978-1-62006-232-6 (Trade Paperback)

Library of Congress Control Number: Application in Process

FIRST SUNBURY PRESS EDITION: May 2019

Product of the United States of America
0 1 1 2 3 5 8 13 21 34 55

Set in Bookman Old Style
Designed by Crystal Devine
Cover by Terry Kennedy
Edited by Lawrence Knorr

Continue the Enlightenment!

Contents

Acknowledgments

There was a time when researching a book like this required trekking to various libraries and archives to spin through reels of microfilm and flip through thick, musty books of bound newspapers. No more. Ninety percent of the research for *Last Ride of the Iron Horse* was done online. So I would be remiss if I did not start by acknowledging the websites that made my work possible: newspapers.com, newspaperarchive.com, genealogybank.com, fultonhistory.com, proquest.com, archive.org, lantern.mediahist.org, and ancestry.com. These sites and the people behind them give users quick access to thousands of newspapers, magazines, books, government records and other printed matter from both past and present. Less legwork, more finger tapping. This makes the research of one's book less of a "journey" (pardon the use of that overused word) but you reach your destination in a shorter time with a bigger, richer vat of information. Hopefully, that leads to a better book.

That said, I do have a list of individuals to acknowledge as well. Without their kind assistance, this book would be missing key details.

Thanks to:

- Cassidy Lent at the National Baseball Hall of Fame in Cooperstown, for answering numerous questions, and providing me with a partial copy of Lou's March 1940 appearance on radio's *Chase and Sanborn Show* (aka the Edgar Bergen and Charlie McCarthy Show).

- Linda Kocis at the Public Library of Cincinnati & Hamilton County, who provided me with *Cincinnati Post* articles about the 1938 All-Star Game.

- Derek Long at the Marr Sound Archives at the University of Missouri-Kansas City, who sent me the rare recording of Gehrig's appearance on *Gang Busters*.
- Doak Ewing of Rare Sports Films Inc., from whom I purchased an excellent DVD containing several programs and films on Gehrig's life.
- Jacob Pomrenke of the Society for American Baseball Research, who sent me some of SABR's oral interviews with old-time ballplayers before all the interviews were made publicly available.
- The staff in the Recorded Sound Center at the Library of Congress, who enabled me to hear Gehrig's radio appearances in connection with the 1939-40 World's Fair, the complete Bergen/Gehrig show, and NBC's broadcasts from the 1938 World Series.
- The staff at the Archives Center at the National Museum of American History, who helped me find the text of Gehrig's speech to the 1938 *Herald Tribune* forum.
- Two Voice of America colleagues: Elizabeth Arrott, who provided feedback on the manuscript and encouragement (as always), and Marissa Melton, who pointed me toward history resources in Jefferson City, Tennessee. It's always helpful to know somebody from the town where the subject of your book crashed his car.
- Al Lang and Linda Gass in the Stephens-Burnett Memorial Library at Carson Newman University, who helped me track down local articles on Gehrig's December 1937 car crash in Jefferson City, Tennessee.
- Wayne Roberts, the director of the Jefferson County Archives, who found and sent me the judge's ruling that Gehrig should be reimbursed for the crash.
- Tanya Elder, senior archivist at the American Jewish Historical Society, who discovered that Gehrig spoke at not one but two major fundraising events to benefit Jews fleeing the Nazis.

- To Dr. Richard Bedlack at Duke University, who shared his thoughts and insights into Gehrig's illness and ALS in general. Let's hope that soon, the work of ALS researchers like him bears fruit.
- To Brian Frederick, executive vice president for communications at the ALS Association, for sharing his thoughts on whether ALS will always remain "Lou Gehrig's Disease."

Special thanks goes to Lawrence Knorr, the chief of Sunbury Press, a fellow baseball history lover who jumped on the book immediately when I pitched it to him. More thanks of the special variety goes to Terry Kennedy, who designed the cover, and Crystal Devine, who handled the inside design and photo section.

Final thanks goes to my wife, Yoni, and our two sons, Sammy and Elani. They've all been very patient while I worked on this book and the previous one, *Inside Al-Shabab*. (Yes, totally unrelated topic.) I think I'm done writing for now, guys. Let's go outside and play ball.

Introduction

In 1938, Lou Gehrig put together the most extraordinary . . . no, jaw-dropping season of any player in baseball history.

Gehrig, all-star slugger and first baseman for the New York Yankees, was starting to suffer from ALS—amyotrophic lateral sclerosis. The crippling disease would force him to retire one year later and kill him within three. And yet, he remained one of the best players in the American League. He started every game on the Yankee schedule, including a stretch where the team played six doubleheaders in seven days. He placed in the league's top ten for home runs, extra-base hits, walks, on-base percentage, runs scored, and runs batted in. And thanks in part to his heavy hitting, the Yankees ran away with the AL pennant and swept the Chicago Cubs in the World Series to become baseball's champions for the third straight year.

Think about it and you can't help but wonder . . . how in God's name did he *do* that?

ALS is a disease without mercy or a cure. It destroys the nerve cells that enable people to control their muscles; as the cells shut down, the muscles do too, making it harder and harder for the victim to move, speak, eat, and breathe. One ALS sufferer, historian Tony Judt, described the disease as "progressive imprisonment without parole. First, you lose the use of a digit or two; then a limb; then and almost inevitably, all four." In the bestseller *Tuesdays with Morrie,* writer Mitch Albom likened ALS to a lit candle that "melts your nerves and leaves your body a pile of wax."

The disease has only one mixed blessing: it doesn't affect the brain. Most victims remain lucid and able to think for themselves. But they are brutally aware that their body is dying, and that with each passing week they lose a little more function and freedom.

Early ALS symptoms are usually mild, allowing many sufferers to keep working for a time, often with accommodations from his or her employer. But professional athletes don't get that luxury. Tim Shaw had spent six years in the NFL, playing special teams and linebacker, when he noticed his right arm growing weaker before the 2013 season. When he lifted weights it wouldn't go up as fast as his left arm; on pull-ups, his right hand kept slipping off the bar. During a preseason game, Shaw recalled, he found himself in perfect position to tackle the ball carrier at the line of scrimmage. He hit the guy hard, like a linebacker should . . . only to see the runner slip free because his right arm couldn't hang on. The Tennessee Titans released Shaw a week later. Doctors diagnosed him with ALS the following spring.

So for Gehrig to play an entire season with the disease, and to play at such a high level, is nothing short of astounding. Yankee general manager Ed Barrow said as much when he learned of Gehrig's ALS diagnosis in June 1939. "Imagine what kind of constitution he has, to have played all last year," Barrow said.

This book expands on Barrow's thought. Early chapters chronicle how Gehrig sensed a defect in his swing even before the '38 season began, and fell into one of the deepest slumps of his career. He pulled out of it, but for months he struggled to hit and play up to his usual standard. Some newspaper columnists demanded he leave the lineup. Finally, as the Yankees hit the hardest stretch of their season in August, Lou began pounding home runs like his old self—a turnaround that was hailed at the time and which in hindsight looks truly miraculous. It may have been a case of temporary "ALS reversal," a rare phenomenon that researchers are still trying to document and understand.

Besides examining his last full season in the lineup, *Last Ride of the Iron Horse* sheds light on the rest of Gehrig's life at the time, starting with a car crash in which he was lucky to escape injury. Even without his battle against ALS, 1938 would have been a momentous year for "Larrupin' Lou." In January, he starred in a Hollywood movie. That spring, the Yankees gave him the highest salary in baseball. In May, he stretched his famous consecutive game streak past the two-thousand mark. In October, he spoke at a forum on the nation's issues alongside figures like Eleanor

Roosevelt. And in November he publicly denounced the rising menace of Nazism—no small gesture for a man with deep ethnic German roots, who was also baseball's most famous active player.

The year turned out to be Gehrig's final hurrah. That winter he grew strangely clumsy—dropping teacups, tripping over curbs. At spring training in 1939, teammates noticed the lack of coordination in his movements, the absence of power in his swing. The Yankees stuck by him for eight games of the regular season before a struggling and perplexed Gehrig benched himself on May 2nd, not wanting to do his team any further harm. His consecutive games streak and career were over, and he had but two years to live.

But nearly a century after his passing, his legacy lives on. ALS is still known in many quarters as "Lou Gehrig's Disease" or in the shorthand of the twenty-first century, Lou. His poignant farewell address on July 4th, 1939—"*Today, I consider myself the luckiest man on the face of the Earth*"—remains one of the most memorable and iconic speeches in the history of sports. The 1942 biopic *Pride of the Yankees* (not a favorite of mine, but mine is a minority opinion) cemented his place in history and continues to get showings on TV, introducing new generations to his story.

Books about Gehrig and/or the Yankees—and there are dozens—usually treat his '38 season as a prelude to tragedy. But this work takes a different path, presenting Lou's last full season as something to be marveled at and studied. After all, there is no greater example in baseball history, maybe in all of sports history, of an athlete overcoming a great misfortune to keep playing, and keep performing like a champion.

Dan Joseph, May 2019

1

Lou Gehrig Crashed Here

There would have been no ALS diagnosis, no "luckiest man" speech, no classic tearjerker starring Gary Cooper had a December 1937 car crash in Jefferson City, Tennessee turned out a little uglier.

The driver of one car was a woman from the nearby town of Greeneville, population sixty-two hundred. Ricie Stogner was driving east on the Andrew Johnson Highway—a simple two-lane road, despite the presidential name—when her car skidded on pavement made slick by morning rain. The car veered into the other lane and struck an oncoming convertible, which careened off the road and plowed through a roadside hedge, into a Jefferson City family's back yard. There it came to rest with unsightly body damage, most notably some ripped off fenders and a broken running board.

The occupants of that car were a husband and wife who lived outside New York City, population seven and a half million. They emerged from the car shaken but unhurt and commenced chatting with a resident of the house, who happened to be a part-time reporter for *The Journal*, a newspaper in nearby Knoxville. The couple explained they were driving through the area on a trip to southern California. The man planned to attend the Rose Bowl game, Cal versus Alabama, that coming Saturday. Then he was due to start shooting a movie, a real Hollywood Western starring Smith Ballew, one of those singing cowboy types who had become so popular. Maybe there was a garage nearby that could fix the car? They only had four days left to get to Los Angeles.

The reporter, Clara Park, might have been skeptical of these claims except for one thing: the man helping to explain them was one of the most famous athletes in America, Lou Gehrig.

In 1937, one did not have to be a baseball fan to recognize Gehrig's name or face. Even in rural east Tennessee, hundreds of miles from any major-league ballpark, images of Lou swinging a bat and bashing hits for the mighty New York Yankees could turn up anywhere—magazine covers, the daily sports pages, the newsreels shown at movie theaters, ads for cigarettes, shaving cream and athletic gear, or the back of a cereal box on someone's breakfast table. Some Americans had even heard his prominent New Yawk accent on the popular evening radio programs. And what Lou was telling Park was true. Through the efforts of his publicity agent, he had landed a co-starring role in a movie to be released by Twentieth Century Fox. That had been in the papers too; the film's producer said if the first picture did well, he'd put Gehrig in a series of adventure movies.

Of course, Lou knew the only reason Hollywood beckoned was his prowess with a baseball bat. He was only thirty-four but already, many considered him the best first baseman in the game's history. He ranked second on the all-time home run list, trailing only his legendary former teammate, Babe Ruth. He sat high in the top ten counts for batting average, runs scored and runs batted in (RBI), the other numbers that mattered in that era of simpler, hand-tallied statistics. In recent years, he had added something extraordinary to his résumé almost every season. In 1931, he set the American League RBI record. In '32, he became only the second player to hit four home runs in a game. In '34, he won the Triple Crown, leading the AL in homers, RBI and batting average. And in 1936, he put it all together, capturing the home run title and the Most Valuable Player award as the Yankees won the World Series.

Not many noticed then, but he also led the American League in walks several times. Pitchers feared him, and many preferred to give him a pass and try their luck with other Yankee sluggers than allow one of the bullet-like line drives that flew off Lou's bat.

"He was perfectly built for power," wrote the East Tennessee-born and raised Grantland Rice, the most prominent sportswriter of Gehrig's time. Rice once compared him to a character from a

Rudyard Kipling poem—"Hans the blue-eyed Dane, bull-throated, bare of arm." Lou was actually of German descent, but at six-foot-one, 210 pounds, with tree trunk legs, muscles rippling from his arms and back, dark wavy hair, and a pair of watchful blue eyes, he evoked the mighty figure that Kipling described.

What really set Gehrig apart, in the eyes of the public and his peers, was "The Streak." For over a dozen seasons, going back to June 1st, 1925, Lou had appeared in every regular season game for the Yankees, over nineteen-hundred games in all to that point. This was a feat that appealed to the baseball cognoscenti and the casual fan alike. Everyone could admire the sheer will and physical endurance it took never to miss a day of work year after year after year after year. Admiring sportswriters ensured the public knew about the illnesses and injuries Gehrig soldiered through to stay on the field, including the flu, severe back pain, shoulder and hamstring injuries, bone chips in his elbow, broken fingers, and two pitches that struck him on the head, both of which knocked him unconscious.

In the early part of his career, sportswriters nicknamed him Columbia Lou, after the university he attended, and Larrupin' Lou, after a nineteenth-century verb that means "to beat or thrash." But as time went on, Gehrig gained new handles inspired by his streak. Some writers called him the Iron Man; others waxed poetic and referred to him as the Iron Horse, a name coined for the first train locomotives a hundred years before.

Famed *Los Angeles Times* columnist Jim Murray once wrote: "I don't suppose I ever saw a better baseball player than Lou Gehrig. But he was more than a player. He was a symbol of indestructibility. He was Gibraltar in cleats, a mass of muscular power. He looked immortal."

Until the accident, the trip west had been uneventful for Lou and his wife of four years, Eleanor. The two were making a cross-country drive rather than travel by train or plane, the latter an expensive and still somewhat risky proposition in 1937. Driving coast to coast in that era meant a weeklong trek on roads of variable quality, some made of soft macadam material, others made of old-fashioned dirt. But the Gehrigs were going in style. Their Packard 8 convertible was a luxury vehicle, a steel behemoth over sixteen feet long, with an eight-cylinder engine (thus the name) and a top speed of about ninety miles per hour. Lou had paid two thousand dollars for the Packard in late 1936, three times the average cost of a car in that mid-Depression year. Starting from their home in New Rochelle, New York, the couple made their way south and got on US Route 70, one of the earliest national highways, running from North Carolina to southern Arizona. The road then and now crosses through Jefferson County, Tennessee; the Gehrigs were driving through the area on December 27th when they encountered Ricie Stogner.

"I saw her coming down the highway, weaving back and forth," Lou told the *Journal*, "and I knew we were going to collide, so I pulled my car as far over as I could to the side, but we bumped anyhow." The word "bumped" sounds like an understatement given the damage to the Packard and the hedge. Clara Park credited her five-foot high shrubs with preventing the car from turning over and causing the Gehrigs serious injury. Stogner also escaped without injury, a fortunate break considering the heft of the Packard.

It was not every day that a star of Gehrig's magnitude passed through little Jefferson City, population twenty-five hundred. So within a short time of the crash, a good number of the townspeople had gathered outside the house where Park lived with her husband Frank, his mother and two of Frank's siblings. The Yankee first baseman took it all in stride, reported Park, spending three hours talking to the gawkers. "He probably sprained his wrist autographing pads, books and scraps of paper shoved at him," she wrote. Smiling genially, he also invited the townsfolk to see the Yankees' next exhibition game in the area. Major league teams played spring training games throughout the South in those years; the Yankees had stopped in Knoxville each of the last four springs and no doubt Gehrig knew they would play there again in April.

Amid the hubbub, the Gehrigs determined that Jefferson City lacked the facilities to repair their car. For that, they'd have to take it to Knoxville, about thirty miles to the southwest. Somebody called Cowan Rodgers Jr., president of a well-known Knoxville car dealership. Rodgers drove out and guided the Gehrigs and their ailing vehicle to a garage on Knoxville's West Cumberland Avenue. In two hours, mechanics returned the car to roadworthy shape, and by late afternoon, the Gehrigs had resumed their trip west, with another two thousand miles of driving ahead.

If life was like a 1930s Western that would be the end of the story, with the cowboy-to-be shaking a few hands, waving goodbye, and riding off into the sunset. However, life rarely turns out like the movies and is especially loath to follow the script of a Western.

The Associated Press picked up Clara Park's report on the crash and distributed it to papers nationwide. But what should have been a small feather in her cap turned to embarrassment when an Associated Press sportswriter noted that Park's initial report referred to Lou as the first baseman for the New York Giants, the team the Yankees beat in the World Series three months earlier. That item appeared in many newspapers too, leaving Park with a tarnished reputation as well as tire tracks and a ruined hedge in her yard.

Meanwhile, sometime after the accident, possibly as he stopped in Knoxville while driving home in February, Lou pressed Ricie Stogner for damages. A local justice of the peace ruled that Stogner had to pay for the repairs to the Packard, a cost of two hundred and fifty-six dollars, big money in 1937, when the average American worker earned less than two thousand dollars per year. Stogner and her husband Walter balked, and the case went to court, with Lou hiring Knoxville attorney H.H. McCampbell to represent him. A case involving a surety bond—a guarantee from a third party that Gehrig would get paid—made its way to the Circuit Court of Jefferson County. A hearing was scheduled for July 1938 but a Jefferson City newspaper reported Gehrig "will be unable to attend due to the tight race in the American League." Judge W.P. Monroe would finally issue a ruling on November 22nd, affirming the justice of the peace's ruling and awarding Lou the full amount of damages, plus court costs.

It is not known if Lou ever collected the money. He had acquired a new car by that time and was facing a more existential threat, one that made the accident in East Tennessee seem like a faint blip in the rearview mirror.

He had also gone through a very full year, one filled with exhilarating highs, depressing lows, and some unusual in-betweens, starting from the moment he arrived in sunny southern California.

2

Hollywood

There must have been hundreds, maybe thousands of American boys in 1938 who would have forked over a full year's allowance, or their entire baseball card collection, if they could spend an afternoon hanging out with their athletic idol, Lou Gehrig. How strange then that on the first day of the new year, Lou found himself parked next to a youngster who, by all available evidence, would have paid dearly to be somewhere else.

Lou was just trying to pay back a favor to Christy Walsh—his publicity agent, and the man who launched his budding movie career. Sixteen months earlier, Walsh heard that producer Sol Lesser had obtained the rights to the cinematic Tarzan franchise and was looking for a new face to play the jungle hero role made famous by Olympic swimmer Johnny Weissmuller. Walsh—a hustler by nature, and always one to think big—envisioned Lou in the part and offered the first baseman's services after securing his approval. "I got in touch with [Lesser] and asked how about Gehrig? I pointed out that Lou was the iron man of baseball, a good-looking fellow with a splendid physique with plenty of sex appeal for the box office," the agent told reporters.

To prove the last point, Walsh convinced his client to don a leopard-spot caveman outfit for some beefcake publicity photos. In a couple, Gehrig mimicked the famous *ahhhh-eeeyah-ahhhh* Tarzan yell; in others, he stripped down to caveman undies to peer amorously at the camera and show off his muscular biceps and chest.

Meeting with newspaper reporters in Walsh's Manhattan office, Lou acknowledged the thought of him as Tarzan might seem "screwy" to some. But in his own self-deprecating way, he insisted he could do the job. "I'm not an actor, but I could learn. I photograph well, much better than I look. I've talked on the radio a lot and I was a success. So why couldn't I play Tarzan?" he said.

The newspaper guys treated, or more accurately, tortured their readers with jungle and monkey jokes over the next few days. One said Lou might go on a diet of raw meat; another said the next time he got walked, he'd amble down to first on all fours. Syndicated columnist Henry McLemore, who was more of a cynic, wrote that the proposed movie should end with Gehrig giving Walsh a ten percent commission, followed by "a kick in the pants for allowing him to make such a durn fool of himself." But Walsh and Gehrig had the last laugh because Lesser decided that Lou had real potential in the movie biz and asked him to come to California in March 1937 for a screen test and contract talks.

Gehrig made the trip—and that's where the *quid pro quo* began.

Walsh, as it turned out, wanted the fledgling actor's help. For two years, he had battled his ex-wife, Madaline, for custody of their only child, Christy Walsh Jr. In court, the sides battled to a draw; a Los Angeles Superior Court judge awarded each parent six months' custody per year. But on a day to day basis, Walsh was losing. Despite the court order, the boy spent most weeks with his mother and was growing more hostile toward his dad. In one embarrassing incident, reported by the Los Angeles newspapers, Christy Jr. said in court that he disliked his father. He couldn't give the reason why. "I guess it's just instinctive," he said.

Christy Sr. didn't believe that for a second but felt he needed to counteract what he saw as Madaline's manipulation of their son. So he turned to his clientele. Walsh had made his name as one of the most successful, certainly the most famous publicity man in the world of sports. Over the years he had raised the profiles and incomes of some true legends, including Notre Dame football coach Knute Rockne, auto racing champ-slash-World War I flying ace Eddie Rickenbacker, and a dugout's worth of baseball stars, including Dizzy Dean, Walter Johnson, and Ty Cobb.

Exactly the kind of people who might impress a pre-teen boy like Christy Jr., one might say.

His first move was to draw on his ties to George Herman Ruth—the Babe.

Walsh had signed Ruth as his first major client in 1921, supposedly after he finagled a meeting with the slugger by posing as a Prohibition-era beer delivery man. Ruth—whose booming home runs ended baseball's low-scoring Deadball Era, whose drawing power more than doubled attendance at Yankee games, whose whirl-around swings and misses were almost as entertaining as his long hits, whose bottomless appetites for food, drink, women and attention made him the personification of America's "Roaring Twenties"—did not need publicity, per se. What Walsh did for the Babe was to monetize his popularity. At first, he sold ghostwritten newspaper articles that were published under Ruth's byline, a common if unethical ruse in the days before radio gave the public a glimpse at players' real voices and thoughts. He began doing the same for other stars under the banner of the "Christy Walsh Syndicate." But soon Ruth soared to a higher level of celebrity, allowing Walsh to set up product endorsements, films, vaudeville appearances, and other lucrative projects for the Sultan of Swat. One of their most profitable ventures was a three-week, cross-country exhibition tour that Ruth undertook after the 1927 season with a teammate and youngster named Gehrig.

Over seventeen years with Walsh, the Babe raked in about a half-million dollars beyond his baseball salary, huge money for the times. So if his agent needed a favor, Ruth was glad to lend a hand. Soon after Christy Jr. was enrolled at a Catholic military academy in the fall of 1935, he got a letter of encouragement from his dad's most famous associate. Somewhat counter to his reputation for alcoholic and sexual gluttony, in this letter Ruth touted the benefits of religious education. "When I was a young boy I attended St. Mary's School in Baltimore, where the good Brothers were very patient with me and helped me a lot toward future life. I'm sure the Sisters at St. John's will help you," read the letter, referencing Ruth's childhood in a Catholic orphanage.

The note was typewritten, raising the possibility of a ghostwriter, most likely Christy Jr.'s own father. It did have the Babe's distinctive signature, with its fat capital B and tall, sweeping R, grandiose in a manner befitting baseball's home run king.

The letter may have impressed the boy's classmates, but none of Ruth's glory seemed to rub off on the elder Walsh, who remained in his son's doghouse. So he turned to his other superstar Yankee client.

Lou had signed on with Walsh during his breakout year, the magic '27 season when he and Ruth staged a season-long, seesaw battle for the American League home run crown. At the start of the year, Gehrig was considered a fine young player, full of promise. But a rush of early-season homers, starting with a pair he smashed on Easter Sunday in front of a home crowd of thirty-five thousand, transformed him into a fan favorite and Ruth's first real rival in the round-tripper department. By June, the dizzying array of newspapers which New York boasted in that era—the *Times, Post, Sun, Daily News, American, Graphic, World-Telegram, Herald Tribune* and *Daily Mirror*, among others—made it headline news each time one of the "home run twins" pulled ahead or pulled even in their duel.

"Who Is This Lou Gehrig?" one paper finally asked in twenty-four-point type. Walsh saw an opportunity and hired a ghostwriter who interviewed Lou and cooked up a thirty-part series on his still-brief baseball career. "There was a ready market at boom prices for the autobiography of this clean-living, level-headed son of a poor New York family," Walsh later wrote in a self-published memoir. Ruth won the home run title, setting a record with sixty. But Gehrig finished with a higher batting average, racked up one hundred seventy-five RBI and won the league MVP award. Meanwhile, the Yankees won a hundred and ten games, swept the World Series and earned lasting renown as the greatest team in baseball history. In their post-season exhibition tour, the more established Ruth took the bulk of the proceeds but Walsh paid Lou a hefty ten thousand dollars, a sum greater than his Yankee salary for the year. Gehrig used the money from the ghostwriting and the tour to buy his first house in affluent New Rochelle, north of the city.

Big money, a home, entry into Hollywood . . . Christy Walsh had done a lot for Lou Gehrig. Now in return, Walsh asked Gehrig to help him win back his son's love.

Lou flew out to Los Angeles on March 3rd, 1937, during a contract dispute with the Yankees that had delayed his arrival at spring training. One afternoon, between meetings with Lesser, he and Walsh drove up to Madaline's new place, a five-bedroom house in tony Hollywood Hills she had inherited from her father. The plan was for Lou to have a friendly chat with the boy, whom he had met before. But no chatting materialized. When Gehrig entered his room, Christy Jr. didn't talk, didn't even stand up; instead, he "sat and played with a pussy cat," according to the senior Walsh.

At a court hearing a few weeks later, Walsh cited his son's disinterest in Gehrig, and sports in general, as evidence that Madaline was making him unmanly. After an acrimonious private meeting with Christy Jr., judge Goodwin Knight agreed, saying in court that no boy should lead a "cream puff existence," and adding that Christy Jr. needed a good spanking. But his words amounted to empty bluster, as the judge left the boy in his mother's care.

Walsh wasn't done playing the Gehrig card. In December 1937, Lou informed Walsh he'd be coming west again to make his movie. Around the same time, organizers of college football's Rose Bowl invited two undefeated teams, the California Bears and Alabama Crimson Tide, to play in the annual New Year's Day game, then the number one event on America's winter sports calendar. Walsh had a brainstorm: why not take his son *and* Gehrig to the game? Lou would probably enjoy the experience; he had played football at Columbia University. And maybe Christy Jr. would get excited too. What American boy wouldn't want to watch the Rose Bowl sitting between his dad and one of baseball's greatest superstars? Surely, this combination would win Walsh some goodwill from his son, maybe break the ice and get him to pull away from his mother a bit.

That was how Lou found himself driving up to Madaline's house on Ponet Drive on the morning of January 1st, 1938. It was a nice day for a football game—sunny, not humid, temperature rising to the mid-sixties. It may not have been the best day for Gehrig, who had just wrapped up a three thousand mile trek across the country. And there are no good days to be pulled into a custody dispute. But Lou was nothing if not a good sport. In Walsh's memoir, he described Gehrig as "the easiest figure it has been my pleasure to manage." To secure Lou's presence, it could be that Walsh simply had to ask.

A wire service story described the scene at Madaline's home: "Tickets to the game were scarce. Every boy in that neighborhood who heard that Christy Jr. was going to the game envied him. And when they saw him leave in the company of Lou Gehrig, they stood agape."

But, the report noted, "Christy Jr. merely scowled." To his father's dismay, the scowl stayed in place all afternoon, even as father, son, and Iron Horse sat among ninety thousand fans in Pasadena cheering on California to a 13–0 victory. Lou attempted to engage Christy Jr. in conversation—about baseball, football, school, anything. All he got in return was stony silence.

It was the last time Walsh tried to use his connections to win his son's heart. Later that month, he signed papers that gave Madaline full custody of the boy. He said the Rose Bowl outing convinced him that his life, that of sports and men who achieved fame in the field, meant nothing to his son. "If my removal from his boyhood will give him a normal life," he said, "I am content to make the sacrifice and let his maturing intellect and his father's record take care of the future."

Gehrig never spoke of his New Year's Day experience, or the Walshes' ordeal. It was a peculiar way to begin the year, and with day one of his film shoot on the horizon, he evidently put the incident out of his mind. It certainly wasn't bothering him on January 3rd when met a few of the Rose Bowl-winning Bears in person, including future Philadelphia A's outfielder Sam Chapman, and posed for photos with the players and child actor Bobby Breen, another fledgling star in Lesser's stable.

He also chatted that day with some Hollywood reporters about his budding movie career. Lou admitted he might have difficulties filming a Western; I'm not too good at riding horses, he said, and I'm no better at shooting a gun. Then there was the fact Gehrig, who was known for his shyness around women, was uncomfortable kissing anybody but his wife. There would be a female lead in the movie, and audiences expected movie actors to kiss their female co-stars, even in Westerns.

"Maybe I won't have to kiss her," he said to Lesser's assistant who was watching over the interview.

"Oh yes, you will," the assistant replied. "You can start practicing on her as soon as we get her cast."

Lou wasn't ready to give up the point. "Maybe you won't be able to find a girl," he said. "Maybe it would be a good idea to have an all-man show, like in baseball."

Lesser's man laid down the law. "Got to have a girl. You've got to kiss her," he said.

* * *

Whether or not to kiss a beautiful actress in his cinematic debut—if this was to be Lou Gehrig's main problem as 1938 unfolded, then the year would be a good one, not unlike the twenty or so preceding it. To this point, Gehrig had lived a life that could rightfully be described as charmed, and he knew it. "When I tell people I'm just a big lucky guy they don't seem to believe it," he said early that year to *World-Telegram* columnist Joe Williams, one of his closest pals in the press. "They put it down to modesty and persist in asking how I got where I am in baseball. But I'm not trying to be modest or anything like that; I've been lucky."

Luck was not so obviously present when the boy dubbed Henry Louis Gehrig entered the world in New York City on June 19th, 1903. He was the second of four children born to Heinrich and Christina Gehrig, two immigrants from Germany who came to the United States seeking a better life than what their native land could offer. As of mid-1903, they hadn't found it. The couple lived in a low-rent, no-frills tenement building on Manhattan's Upper East Side, one of the hundreds in the city that housed working-class transplants from Europe like themselves. Heinrich had a skill—ornamental metal work, pounding patterns into sheets of iron—but didn't make much money, partially because of shaky health, partially because at heart he was a man of leisure, one who preferred spending time with friends in a bar or a card game instead of doing physical labor. Lou once estimated that his father brought home eight to ten dollars a week, low wages even for the early 1900s. "Lou's family was just plain poor," Eleanor later wrote.

The poverty put stress on the Gehrigs' marriage, which endured other strains from the start. When they met in 1901, Heinrich was thirty-four years old and had been in the U.S. for fourteen years; Christina was twenty and just a year off the boat. Neither one ever explained the circumstances of their meeting or attraction. What's known is that when they tied the knot, in November 1901, Christina was already three months pregnant. She gave birth the following May to a girl they named Anna. Unfortunately, the baby died in September, a little over three months old.

Before Anna passed, the family moved into the tenement now immortalized as Lou Gehrig's birthplace: 1994 Second Avenue. The only known photos of the long-demolished structure, taken in 1940 for city tax records, show a light-colored, five-story brownstone, one of eight built in a block. The photos highlight the fact that Gehrig was born into the most urban of environments. All of the buildings have fire escapes dangling from their façades. Not a single tree nor blade of grass can be seen. And across the street, some forty feet from the tenement windows, stand tracks for the elevated trains that rumbled up and down the avenue for eighteen hours a day. Every few minutes, when a train rushed by, people in the tenements were subjected to an ear-splitting roar, a cacophony of wind, engine and wheel noise that reverberated off the streets and buildings below.

Even when the tracks were quiet, tenement life was hard. Buildings such as the Gehrigs' were notorious for cramped apartments, dark, dirty hallways, an absence of ventilation or private bathrooms, and a tendency for dangerous germs to breed. Pneumonia, tuberculosis, diphtheria, scarlet fever, typhoid—these illnesses were still leading causes of death in New York as the twentieth century dawned. Poor Anna could have come down with any of them. The doctor who signed her death certificate didn't specify her illness but wrote that she had suffered from "convulsions."

The Gehrigs would endure the loss of two other children: daughter Sophie, who died of diphtheria in 1906 before her second birthday, and an apparently short-lived and unnamed boy, whose birth in 1905 was not recorded by the city. "We were a sickly lot and caught everything," Lou later said. "Although mother did everything possible, I alone survived."

From the start, however, it was clear Lou was more robust than his siblings. Famed baseball writer Fred Lieb, who knew the Gehrig family well, wrote that Lou weighed a robust fourteen pounds at birth. Mother ensured that child maintained the weight. "I believe in food—lots of it," Christina once said. "Lou started in as a baby to eat all he could hold. He didn't become an athlete on spinach."

And Christina was always cooking because as Heinrich lazed away the hours, she assumed the role of breadwinner. The neighborhood of Lou's early childhood, variously defined as Yorkville or Lower Harlem, contained both tenements and mansions. The mansion-owners hired tenement-dwellers to cook their meals, clean their homes and wash their laundry. Christina did all three, though her specialty was preparing hearty, heavy, meaty meals. It helped that she was blessed with workhorse energy and unusual strength, the latter most visible in her man-like forearms, not much smaller than those of her famous son. She also had a strong drive to lift the family out of poverty, and to ensure that Lou—her pride, her joy, and increasingly the reason she lived and breathed—got an education and made something of himself.

The future Iron Horse picked up his mother's priorities and work ethic early on. "Lou told me that he never played hooky or missed a day through eight years of grade school, even with a mild case of pneumonia," Eleanor later wrote. When not in school, he served as Christina's assistant, helping her lug baskets of laundry and food to customers, and being rewarded with helpings of her roast beef, pies, and other delicacies. The time and attention Christina showered on him made Lou into an all-star level mama's boy, a quality that would profoundly affect his life, even after he became a Yankee and a star.

The little family moved further north in Manhattan when Lou was five, finding an apartment in the growing Washington Heights area. Lou entered Public School 132, a massive four-story, red brick building that kids still attend more than a hundred years later. There, the child of German immigrants was Americanized—making friends, learning playground games, getting his first taste of baseball and football, and shedding his accent. At various times, he had to endure taunts of "Fatty," for his size, and "Krauthead," for his ethnicity. But the insults faded away as the other kids noticed their target growing unusually tall and strong. They also noticed that when he hit a baseball, it went far.

This became even more evident in his teens when, at his parents' behest, Lou enrolled in the High School of Commerce, a specialty school focused on job skills. Christina harbored dreams of her son becoming an engineer or architect. Instead, Commerce became a springboard for his athletic career. He played soccer, and the school team won three straight city championships. He played football and led the squad in touchdowns. He played baseball, and in his senior year propelled the team to a city title and a trip to Chicago for a one-game "High School World Series." Reporters often misspelled his name—Gherig and Gehring were frequent corruptions—but they got it right that at-bat he possessed exceptional power. One out-of-town writer who witnessed him play in May 1920 put it this way: "He can hit a ball harder than any prep man I have seen. Looks like he may be a Babe Ruth someday."

Most budding sluggers in Gehrig's time went straight from high school to baseball's minor leagues. But Christina still saw college in her son's future. A few years earlier, she had taken a job cooking meals at the Sigma Nu Theta fraternity house at Columbia University. Lou would come by after school, help her serve dinner, and wash dishes. Columbia's athletic director, Bobby Watt, got wind that the cook's assistant was the same kid getting mentioned in the sports pages and gave Gehrig an athletic scholarship. Lou struggled to stay afloat academically, and almost lost his eligibility when he let the New York Giants talk him into playing pro ball one summer in Hartford, Connecticut under an assumed name. But after sitting out his freshman year as punishment, Gehrig became the instant star of the Columbia team in the spring of 1923. In one not atypical contest against Fordham, he hit a three-run homer into the center-field stands *and* pitched a complete game, striking out twelve in an 8–2 victory. For the season, his batting average was .444, with seven homers in nineteen games.

Yankee scout Paul Krichell came calling that June, offering Lou a fifteen-hundred-dollar bonus to sign with the club. Lou, tired of seeing his mother slave to pay the bills, accepted. "I needed the money badly," Gehrig said years later. "Baseball offered the one way to financial security for me and my own." The Yankees farmed him out to Hartford for most of the '23 and '24 seasons, letting him gain experience, but it was only a matter of time before he made the big club. In a year and a half of minor-league ball, he averaged a home run every eight at-bats.

Still only twenty-one, Gehrig made the Yankees' opening day roster in 1925. The Streak began a few weeks later, on June 1st, when he pinch-hit and flied out in a loss to the Senators. With the team languishing in seventh place, manager Miller Huggins revamped his lineup the next day, benching three regulars, including first baseman Wally Pipp. Baseball lore holds that Pipp complained of a headache before the game and that Huggins told him to rest. A contemporary *Daily News* article suggests otherwise, saying Pipp was benched due to "feeble hitting." Whatever the case, Lou whacked out three hits that day as the Yankees broke a five-game losing streak. Huggins made an abrupt but indisputably correct decision; first base belonged to the kid from Columbia. He would not leave the lineup for fourteen years.

Most of those years can be considered prime. At Gehrig's real peak, between 1927 and 1937, he averaged thirty-nine homers and one hundred fifty-four RBI per season. His batting average over that span was .350. He walked twice as often as he struck out. He led the American League three times in homers, four times in runs scored, five times in RBI, five times in on-base percentage. With Gehrig in the lineup, the Yankees won seven pennants and six World Series. And in the Series, Gehrig was at his best, batting .361 with ten homers over thirty-four games.

As early as 1932, when Lou was only twenty-nine, Grantland Rice called him the most valuable first baseman in baseball history. The compliment came after the Yankees crushed the Chicago Cubs in the World Series, with Lou bashing nine hits and three homers in a four-game sweep. "It was Gehrig's first home run that shot poison in the souls of Cub pitchers," Rice wrote. "From that point on they seemed to sense the approach of certain doom. The Hammer of Thor was hanging above their heads."

If Gehrig was Thor, however, Babe Ruth was the incredible Hulk—a little bit stronger and a much greater spectacle. At one point, Lou finished second to Ruth in the AL home run race four years in a row. In the 1928 World Series, Gehrig torched the St. Louis Cardinals for four home runs and nine RBI during a four-game sweep, but Ruth captured the headlines with a grand three-homer day in the finale. In 1932, Lou's hot hitting decimated the Cubs, but Ruth created one of baseball's enduring legends with his "called shot" in game three when he allegedly pointed to Wrigley Field's center-field seats and blasted the next pitch to that exact spot.

That sense of theater, along with his great abilities, kept Ruth at center stage and Gehrig a step or two off to the side. For the most part, Lou was fine with that. "Some people thought Lou was jealous because Babe was number one with the public and with the paymaster, but that was nonsense," Eleanor wrote. Fred Lieb confirmed, "It was commonly said at the time that Gehrig lived in Ruth's shadow. Such talk never bothered Lou. 'It's a pretty big shadow,' he said. 'It gives me lots of room to spread myself.'"

However, the situation changed as Ruth grew older and fatter and Lou grew more confident. He had taken a monumental leap forward in September 1933 when he married Eleanor Grace Twitchell, a woman from Chicago with a petite build, sophisticated tastes, and an assertive streak. She needed the latter to deal with Christina Gehrig. Throughout his twenties, Lou lived with his parents in New Rochelle and built his life around his mother, who cooked his meals, came to most of his games, and even accompanied him to spring training in Florida. More than once he told a reporter he would never marry, that "Mom makes a home comfortable enough for me." Mom had tried to preserve her status by badmouthing potential Mrs. Gehrigs. But with a determined Eleanor on his side, Lou could finally cut the umbilical cord. His new wife expanded his worldview, introducing him to opera, Broadway theater, and the idea of travel for pleasure, not just baseball.

She also encouraged him to claim his rightful place in the spotlight. "Eleanor worked hard, through philosophy and persuasion, to break down his inbred inferiority complex," wrote Lieb. "Ruth was fading, and she wanted Lou to take Babe's place as the outstanding figure in baseball."

Gehrig got his chance when the Yankees released the aging Ruth before the 1935 season and appointed Lou as team captain. He turned in a good year—.329 average, thirty homers, one hundred twenty RBI. But the numbers were a comedown after his '34 Triple Crown season, and the Yankees missed the postseason for the third consecutive year. For the '36 season, the team brought up a rookie from the Pacific Coast League, one with a power stroke almost equal to Lou's, a huge range in center field and a rare athletic elegance that brought droves of new fans to Yankee Stadium. With Joe DiMaggio in the lineup, the Yanks steamrollered to the pennant and an easy victory in the World Series over the Giants. DiMaggio got much of the credit and adulation, even though Gehrig crushed forty-nine homers and won the MVP award.

"Curious how Gehrig, one of the greatest ballplayers the game has ever known, has had to walk in someone's shadow ever since he has been with the Yankees," Frank Graham of the *Sun* wrote in one of his columns. "First it was Babe Ruth whom the Iron Horse followed. Now it is DiMaggio."

Those kinds of comments may be why Lou's ears perked up when Christy Walsh suggested he take a fling at the silver screen. The agent clearly did not have to do much persuading. "I'm dead serious about the whole thing," Gehrig told reporters. "This is a new field and I'm willing to take a whirl at it. In fact, anxious." Asked about the Tarzan photos, he said, "I guess the public is entitled to see my body." These were very un-Gehrig like things to say. But together, they indicate that Lou was tired of being eclipsed. On some level, the shy mama's boy wanted to be the brightest star in the Yankee sky.

* * *

Technically speaking, "Rawhide" would not be Gehrig's first appearance in a major motion picture. In 1927, Babe Ruth played a small role as himself in *Speedy*, a film by silent movie comedy star Harold Lloyd. In the film, Lloyd plays a taxi driver who Ruth flags down for a lift to Yankee Stadium. The Babe spends the next few minutes hanging on for dear life as Speedy carelessly zooms through New York traffic, barely missing collisions with streetcars, lamp posts, fire trucks, people and the occasional horse. When they arrive at the Stadium, Ruth shouts at the driver (via on-screen text), "If I ever want to commit suicide, I'll call you!" But just before he speaks, a man wearing a bow-tie walks behind the cab and looks at the camera through the windows. There, on screen for about three seconds, is the young Lou Gehrig, doing a cameo inside Ruth's cameo.

By the time Gehrig prepared to make his real film debut in late 1937, he was one of three Yankees dabbling in the movie biz. Ruth, who had acted in two baseball-themed dramas in the 1920s, returned to the screen in January with a nine-minute short called *Home Run on the Keys*. The film consists of three brief scenes. In the first, Ruth tells some hunting buddies about his alleged "called shot" in the 1932 World Series. In real life, multiple witnesses have said Ruth was pointing at hecklers in the Cubs' dugout, not the center-field stands. But this film is not about reality, as proven in scene two, where Ruth, who was not known for his musical abilities, is struck with inspiration at the piano and convinces his film friends, who just happen to be professional songwriters, to compose an instrumental called—what else?—"Home Run on the Keys." The short wraps up with a tuxedoed Ruth "conducting" an orchestra through the tune on a radio show.

Joe DiMaggio took his own turn before the cameras in August 1937, appearing briefly in a Republic Pictures musical entitled *Manhattan Merry Go Round*. In his two short scenes, filmed over one morning in New York, DiMaggio is somehow mistaken for a singer by the Italian-born owner of a nightclub. He is pushed onstage and stiffly warbles two lines of a ditty before the owner stops him and explodes: "You tenor? No! You baritone? No! You basso profundo? No! What are you?" DiMaggio replies: "I'm a center fielder." An uncomfortable DiMaggio required twelve takes to complete his parts and expressed no further desire for a movie career. "The toughest part about this whole business of acting is being nonchalant. That's a pretty tough thing to be," he said.

Gehrig, in contrast, approached his newfound career with serious intent. During his first meeting with Sol Lesser in March 1937, he took a screen test. Lesser paired him with a veteran bit-part actor, Edward Keane, to read a scene set in a doctor's office. Lou's acting was hammy—one newspaper report said he gave his "histrionic all" during the test—but he had his lines down cold, and could cue Keane when the latter forgot his dialogue. Lesser signed him to a contract the next day, with Walsh looking over Lou's shoulder. A showbiz paper reported that he would earn twenty-five hundred dollars per week while filming. At a luncheon to introduce Lou to the Hollywood press, Lesser downplayed talk of his rookie actor playing Tarzan but expressed the conviction that Gehrig could make a splash in the movie world. "I believe we will hit a home run at the box office," he said.

Not everyone agreed with Lesser's prediction. For years, sportswriters had chastised Lou for an alleged lack of "color," that amorphous, you-know-it-when-you-see-it quality that has been prized by journalists and sportswriters since the invention of ink. The charge was true in the sense that Lou did not have a charismatic personality like Ruth or the boyish likability of DiMaggio. "When it comes to that personal magnetism, you've either got it or you ain't," wrote *New York Daily News* columnist Jack Miley the day after Gehrig signed his movie contract. "Roosevelt has it, Hoover hasn't. Dempsey has it, but not Tunney. DiMaggio, like Ruth, has; but not Gehrig . . . I think Gehrig's advisors are making a great mistake in trying to create synthetic fame for him via the movies, Tarzan yelling and such hokus pokus."

Putting aside the fact that Gehrig had already achieved great fame and popularity without Hollywood's help, Miley's assessment of Lou's personality was fundamentally wrong. Lou's friends and teammates never described him as bland or boring. The word most often used was *reserved*. "He had a tremendous personality. It wasn't as outgoing as much as Babe's was," said Hall of Fame Yankee pitcher Lefty Gomez. "He loved to play bridge; he and [fellow Yankees] Bill Dickey and Red Rolfe and Jesse Hill, they played a lot of bridge. Gehrig would read the best-sellers, go to the symphony and the opera. Just a wonderful guy, after you got to know him. But he wasn't easy to meet, you know what I mean?"

"Because Gehrig was quiet, sometimes moody, the impression prevailed that he was what ballplayers call a loner. Far from it," wrote reporter Tom Meany, who covered the Yankees for many years. "He was a good bridge player and loved to play, but bridge isn't the kind of noisy, roistering game that poker and hearts are. Lou loved to fish and you don't fish in front of crowds. He also liked to play billiards and it was something to see that huge frame sprawled over a table, those big paws hiding a cue, and Lou nursing the balls in straight rail with a truly deft touch."

"Lou didn't lead by being talkative, I'll tell you that," recalled Yankee outfielder Tommy Henrich. But lead he did. "Every time I faced a new pitcher I went to him and boy, he would give me the best advice he could, 'cause he found about what kind of hitter I was, a fastball hitter. And being able to talk with Lou and have him take an interest in me, I never forgot that, because I felt very close to him."

Christy Walsh may have summed it up best in his self-published memoir. "Modesty," he wrote, "is the main thing preventing Lou from being the dominating personality in the world of sport today."

Initially, Lou was slated to act in a movie called *The Trail Blazers*, described in press reports as either a nineteenth-century pioneer story or a drama about the building of Boulder Dam. When that didn't work out, he was ticketed for a role as "comedy relief" in a movie titled *Laughing Senor*. But that project was shelved too, and it wasn't until late 1937 that Lesser decided Gehrig would make his film debut in a modern-day Western, eventually entitled *Rawhide*. His co-stars would be actress Evalyn Knapp and singer-turned-actor Smith Ballew, who had previously teamed in another Sol Lesser production, *Hawaiian Buckaroo*, a musical Western oddly transplanted to the islands. Ballew would also serve as Knapp's love interest, sparing Lou the embarrassment of a kissing scene.

In terms of its script and production values, *Rawhide* is the epitome of a 1930s grade-B cowboy flick. The plot: baseball star Lou Gehrig, playing himself, tells a gaggle of New York reporters he's through with the game and is moving out West to find peace on a ranch. But upon arrival, he and his sister, played by Knapp, run into a gang using threats and violence to extort "protection" fees from local ranchers. Teaming with a local attorney, played by Ballew, Lou and some townsfolk shut down the scheme and put the bad guys in jail, engaging in the requisite fist fight, cowboy songs, chase scene, and bloodless gun battles along the way. The movie ends with Gehrig sitting on his porch, preparing for a long rest—only to leap out of his chair and declare he's heading home after his club (presumably the Yankees) sends a telegram saying it'll pay the salary he wants.

By the standards of the genre, the movie is entertaining stuff and gives Lou a couple of moments to shine. The first time he approaches a horse, a ranch hand tells him, "Just walk right up to him like you wasn't afraid." Lou laughs and replies, "I couldn't be that deceitful." The most exciting scene is the bar fight, where Gehrig and Ballew tussle with a half-dozen bad guys before Gehrig knocks them out one by one—not with punches, but by hurling pool balls at their heads. It was Lou's favorite moment in the film, perhaps because he got to shatter some windows, a mirror and several shot glasses behind the bar with supposedly errant throws. "Lou never had more fun in his life than when he was throwing those pool balls," Eleanor told a reporter the following month.

In fact, Gehrig relished the entire three-week film shoot, done largely at the Morrison Ranch, a site in the San Fernando Valley often used for Westerns. "This is more fun than even the World Series," he told one reporter during the shoot, borrowing a line from the script. He wouldn't give up baseball for pictures, he added, but liked the notion of playing ball in the summer and making movies every winter. Nerves were not a problem, he insisted. "Strange as it may seem, I had absolutely no mike or camera fright. Acting came suspiciously easy to me," he later said.

Learning how to ride a horse was harder; Lou, a lifelong New Yorker, was used to getting around on foot or wheels. The film crew pranked him one day, outfitting his horse with bicycle handlebars. But within a few days, he picked up enough equestrian skills to get by. "Mrs. Gehrig razzed me for a week when I told her

I'd have to ride a horse," he said. "But I never did get a blister and my legs never did get sore."

That last comment touches on an issue that baseball fans and inquisitive neurologists have debated for years: when did Lou begin showing signs of ALS, and did he betray any hints of it with his performance in *Rawhide*?

In 1989, Dr. Edward Kasarskis, a professor of neurology at the University of Kentucky, published a paper in which he claimed to see evidence of Gehrig's early symptoms in the movie. Kasarskis wrote that in two scenes, Lou appeared to rely on his hands to lift himself from the ground. He said the movement—known as a partial Gowers maneuver—is common among people experiencing weakness in their legs. Kasarskis said he also spotted atrophy of small muscles in Lou's hands, a classic telltale sign of ALS. Another neurologist, Dr. Harold Klawans concurred with Kasarskis in a book eight years later. "His movement in getting out of a chair was not quite normal, either," Klawans wrote. "He had to use his hands to push down on his legs to straighten his hip joints. Normally, the leg muscles do this without help, but if those muscles become weak, the patient learns to cope in this characteristic manner."

In 2006, researchers Melissa Lewis and Dr. Paul Gordon took a fresh look at the movie. Lewis and Gordon examined all of Gehrig's scenes, paying special attention to the bar fight and the way he carried out routine activities like writing, chewing food, climbing stairs, and getting out of a car. Then, they graded him on the ALS Functional Rating Scale, a point system used by doctors to evaluate the physical abilities of ALS patients and track changes in their condition. The researchers concluded that Gehrig functioned normally in the film, scoring thirty-two out of a possible thirty-two points on a slightly modified scale. In fact, they said, Gehrig showed "exceptional strength and coordination" in the film, consistent with his reputation as a top athlete.

Who's correct? To the untrained eye, Lewis and Gordon's assessment seems closer to the mark. Someone experiencing ALS symptoms would likely have trouble staying atop a horse or would have complained about soreness afterward. In the bar fight scene, Lou handles all his own stunts, throwing punches and tossing aside combatants like a seasoned brawler. In his most impressive feat of strength, he lifts an average-sized man off the ground and raises him above his head. Watching the film at half-speed confirms that Gehrig himself performed the stunt in one sweeping motion, with no stunt doubles or camera tricks. Yes, the man was an extra allowing himself to be picked up. Lou is still lifting a grown man about six feet off the ground, and holding him almost horizontally.

Gehrig's movie career beyond *Rawhide* remains an unanswerable "what if" question. When the movie came out at the tail end of March 1938, reviewers were generally kind if slightly patronizing to the rookie actor. Many noted that he looked thrilled simply to be in the film—"like an overgrown kid in a Christmas cowboy suit," said one. But some newspapers gave him genuine praise, such as the *Post,* which said he showed "surprising poise," and *Daily News,* which said he "tosses off his lines as naturally as he walks to the plate and clouts out one of those home runs."

In fact, the showbiz newspaper *Variety* was downright enthusiastic about Lou's Hollywood prospects, stating that in time he could develop into a Bill Boyd or Buck Jones type, referring to two well-known Western movie actors of the era. "Photographing well, he has both the personality and the voice to ensure the stamp of approval by producers as well as audiences," said the unidentified reviewer. "The baseball star is more than window dressing for the picture . . . and if exploited properly, he should help make this one of the top money-getters of the season."

For the record, *Rawhide* performed only average or slightly above average at most theaters, according to the scattered box office returns reported in *Variety* and other Hollywood newspapers. Gehrig made a couple of personal appearances to promote the film, most notably the premiere in St. Petersburg, Florida, where the Yankees were in the thick of spring training. The debut on March 23rd was a gala affair, complete with a parade, fireworks, live radio coverage, and "hillbilly" music provided by St. Louis Cardinals outfielder Pepper Martin and Mud Cat Band. Thousands jammed the Capitol Theater to see the movie and its star. Among those present was Christy Walsh. A photo taken that night shows agent and client standing next to each other, both men smiling broadly. Lou looks especially happy. And why not? After all these years, he was finally the main star, the undisputed center of attention, not forced to share the spotlight with Ruth or DiMaggio or anyone else.

Asked to speak from the theater's stage, Gehrig returned to the theme of good fortune he had mentioned to Joe Williams. "People think I'm modest when I say I'm lucky," he said. "I'm not—I am lucky, and if anybody wants to argue with me about it, I'll stand and argue with him all day."

Little did Gehrig know that deep inside his body, his luck was starting to turn.

3

First Signs

Lou and Eleanor were making the long drive back from Hollywood when they stopped in Knoxville the morning of February 5th. The visit was probably so they could meet with a lawyer and discuss the December car crash in nearby Jefferson City—the Gehrigs, as noted, wanted to be reimbursed for the cost of repairs to their Packard. But Bob Wilson, sports editor of the *Knoxville News-Sentinel*, got word that they were in town and reached out to the Yankee star. Lou graciously agreed to an interview and a late breakfast in the coffee shop of the Farragut Hotel, a place he knew from the Yankees' annual stop in Knoxville during spring training tours of the South. On the last visit the previous April, the New Yorkers crushed the minor league Tennessee Smokies 14–5. Lou whacked three hits, including a three-run homer that broke open the game.

Lou was not always the best interview; his reserve usually got in the way, and he wasn't a natural quipster like Ruth or Lefty Gomez. (Gomez's best line, about slugger Jimmie Foxx: "He's so strong he has muscles in his hair.") But Wilson found his guest to be in an upbeat mood, eager to discuss his experiences in Hollywood. "I asked him about the movie before mentioning baseball, and the big fellow clapped his hands, leaned back in his chair, and started laughing," Wilson wrote. The reporter then listened as Lou ran through the entire plot of *Rawhide*, pausing only to laugh at certain bits or take a bite of his eggs and toast.

"You are going to like that picture," he boasted. "I think it's going to be a knockout." Wilson couldn't help but notice that his guest was dressed semi-Western style, wearing a brown checkered shirt and a handkerchief around his neck.

Lou became less gregarious when Wilson, switching to baseball, tried to pump him about his possible 1938 salary. The Yankees' other superstar, Joe DiMaggio, had made headlines a few weeks earlier when he demanded the team pay him forty thousand dollars, a huge figure for the time, one that would make him the best-paid player in all of baseball. The Yankees, along with many sportswriters, noted that DiMaggio was entering only his third year in the majors; Gehrig, who was entering his sixteenth, had yet to reach that salary plateau.

Lou backed his teammate's push, saying "Joe's a great kid. I hope he gets what he's asking for. He's a great ballplayer and deserves what he can get." But he was evasive when Wilson asked Lou about his own contract demands. "I don't know what salary I will get," he said. "I never worry a great deal about that."

That last statement, as Wilson likely knew, was a long way from the truth. *All* professional athletes worry about their salary. They are forced to, having just a few years to maximize earnings before the ravages of time and injuries force them to retire. A 2007 study by three University of Colorado demographers detailed the stark reality. The researchers looked at the careers of nearly six thousand twentieth-century major league baseball players, excluding pitchers, who are more injury-prone, and "cup of coffee" guys who appeared in only a game or two. They found the average player lasted in the majors a shade over five and a half years. Most players' careers ended before age thirty. In Gehrig's time, when there were only sixteen teams and doctors were less able to fix torn rotator cuffs and ACLs, the average major league stay was even shorter, lasting less than four and a half years. Had ALS not struck him in 1938, Gehrig, entering his mid-thirties, might have declined anyway. In baseball terms, he was overdue.

Gehrig and his contemporaries had other reasons to worry about their pay. Players of the era had no union, no pension, and were barred from using agents in salary talks. They also had to deal with the reserve clause, the language found in every player's contract which allowed a team to own his rights in perpetuity unless that team chose to trade, sell or release him. Club owners had imposed the clause decades earlier, arguing it was necessary to keep salaries manageable. But players were stuck with a system that gave them almost no negotiating leverage. Pittsburgh Pirates first baseman Elbie Fletcher hoped for a nice raise after driving in a career-high one hundred four RBI in 1940. Instead, he recalled, Pirates owner Bill Benswanger gave him an edict: "At the end of the season Benswanger said, 'Tell you what I'll do—if you sign right now, I'll give you ten thousand dollars. If you don't, when you get your contract [in the mail], it'll only be for nine.'"

"What the hell could you do? They used to tell you what you're gonna make, and if you don't like it, stay home," Fletcher added. The reserve clause would withstand numerous legal challenges until arbitrator Peter Seitz ruled it null and void in 1975, opening the door to players earning salaries in the millions, then tens of millions of dollars per year.

Players of the '30s faced a whole other obstacle unique to their time—the Great Depression. Led by the Yankees, total major league attendance had climbed steadily during the previous decade, reaching a new high of ten million-plus in 1930. Despite the reserve clause, wages crept upward too, and by the '30 season, a record sixty-four players were earning "five-figure" salaries of at least ten thousand dollars, topped by Ruth, who pulled down eighty thousand. But as unemployment soared, banks collapsed and shantytowns popped up across the country, fans stopped coming to baseball games. Overall attendance plunged forty percent, leaving most teams operating in the red. Clubs didn't hesitate to slash wages, recalled Hall of Fame manager Al Lopez, a catcher with the Brooklyn Dodgers during Gehrig's glory years. "It was really, really rough in the Depression, especially when Roosevelt came in and closed all the banks," he said. "Your bargaining power went out the door, because the argument the ballclubs had is, 'We don't know how far we can go, cause if the banks are not open, we won't be able to operate, and nobody would come out here, 'cause they don't have any money to come to the park.'"

Fortunately for Gehrig, if there was one team owner immune to the Depression, it was the Yankees' Jacob Ruppert Jr. Ruppert was the mustachioed, *bon vivant* scion of one of New York's wealthiest families. His father, Jacob Sr., made a fortune brewing beer, the go-to beverage for millions of German immigrants who poured into the U.S. during the late 1800s. Jacob Jr. began working at the family brewery at age eighteen in 1885 after his father steered him away from aspirations to attend West Point and become a soldier. At first, father assigned son to menial tasks like driving the horse-drawn wagons that delivered beer to saloons across New York. But within a decade the bright, driven Ruppert Jr. was running the company. Under his reign, the brewery's flagship product, Knickerbocker lager, became one of the best-selling beers in the city and would remain so well into the twentieth century.

In fact, Jacob Ruppert succeeded at almost anything he tried. In his twenties, he volunteered for the state National Guard and rose to the rank of colonel. In his thirties, he won four terms in the U.S. House of Representatives. Even in his rich man hobbies like dog breeding and horse racing, he tended to come out on top. One of his prize St. Bernards won "best of breed" at the 1919 Westminster Kennel Club Dog Show. One of his thoroughbreds ran in the 1893 Belmont Stakes, although in that case, the Ruppert touch didn't work—the horse finished last.

But no other activity captured Ruppert's heart like baseball. He played the game as a youth and inquired about buying major league teams as early as the 1890s. He finally entered the game in 1915, when he and a newfound business partner, Tillinghast L'Hommedieu "Cap" Hutson, purchased the Yankees. To that point, the Yanks were a poor, losing ballclub. Three years earlier they had lost the lease to their stadium, Hilltop Park, forcing them to rent space from the National League's Giants at the Polo Grounds in Harlem. But Ruppert and Huston laid out big bucks to purchase players, with the biggest outlay—a then-staggering one hundred thousand dollars cash plus a three hundred thousand dollar loan—going to the Boston Red Sox in January 1920 for the services of Babe Ruth. With Ruth planting home run balls and fans in the seats like no man before him, the Yankees captured three straight AL pennants in the early twenties and became the first team to draw more than a million fans per year. In 1923, the newly-flush club opened its own ballpark in the Bronx, majestic

Yankee Stadium. The long Yankee dynasty was born, and Ruppert installed himself as sole patriarch by buying out his partner.

Because of Ruppert's riches, Gehrig did better in the salary department than most of his peers. After he won his first MVP award in 1927, the Yankees more than tripled his salary, to twenty-five thousand dollars per year, and gave him a three-year contract, a true rarity in baseball then. Ruppert kept Lou at that salary or near it for seven years afterward, even as many other players saw their paychecks shrivel. Lou, thankful for his good fortune in life, aware that most Americans were struggling to put food on the table, seemed content. "Lou is not the sort that holds out [for more money]" wrote his pal Joe Williams in a January 1932 column. "And he believes that Colonel Jake has a fatherly interest in him. Lou is impressed with the fact that Ruppert has done pretty well by him thus far."

But after Gehrig's own Triple Crown season in 1934, he pressed for a fatter paycheck, partly at the urging of his wife. "You know I've got a new manager now," he told reporters in February 1935, smiling at Eleanor in case anyone missed the point. He refused to declare himself a holdout, but warned, "I'm going to want a lot more money than I got last year. I'm worth it." After some hesitation, Ruppert gave in and boosted Lou's salary above thirty thousand dollars for the first time.

After winning the MVP award in 1936, Lou staged his first real holdout, asking the Yankees to pay him fifty thousand dollars for the '37 season, a figure that only Ruth and Ty Cobb had previously reached. This time, Ruppert not only said no, he said hell no, initially refusing Gehrig any sort of raise at all. The two were soon engaged in a war of words through the press. Lou was polite but firm, noting the Yankees had not needed a backup first baseman for a dozen years and stating, "I am only asking what I believe to be my value to the club." Ruppert was more blustery, telling reporters, "There isn't a man on the team who can't be replaced"—as if the Yankees could easily land another first baseman guaranteed to rack up one hundred fifty RBI per year.

Ruppert even tried using Lou's movie deal as a negotiating tool. "Why do you think they want you out in Hollywood?" he told his first baseman via the papers. "They want you because you're a ballplayer . . . Quit playing ball and you couldn't get a job as a prop boy out there."

After missing three weeks of spring training, Gehrig ultimately signed for thirty-six thousand dollars—a five-thousand dollar raise, but well short of what he wanted, or deserved. Had he suspected the misfortune that lay ahead, he might have pushed harder for his true worth.

* * *

Contract talks for the 1938 season began the day after Lou and Eleanor finished their post-Hollywood drive back east. Upon arriving home in New Rochelle, Lou called Ruppert and requested a meeting to talk salary. Come down to the brewery, he was told. Reporters who got word of the impending chat, presumably from the Yankees, called Lou and asked what kind of money he was seeking. Forty thousand, maybe? Lou refused to name his price, deflecting the conversation toward his movie. "Wait till you see me riding that horse," he said.

Dressed in a gray pinstriped suit, eschewing a winter coat or hat as per his custom, Lou drove down to the Jacob Ruppert Brewery on the morning of February 8th. A brewery was an unusual place to conduct baseball business, but as more than one observer noted, Ruppert's offices didn't look like they belonged in a brewery. "I certainly expected to see some beer. . . . But there was none on display. There were large mahogany desks, white-marbled walls, and obsequious clerks," wrote Joe Williams after a visit in the early '30s. After a renovation in 1937, the offices became even more ostentatious, with oak paneling, stained glass windows, and a private elevator to take guests up to Ruppert's private dining room. Will Wedge of the *New York Sun* labeled Ruppert's suite "luxurious"—so luxurious that he thought it unwise for the Yankee owner to discuss contracts there. "The ascending note is the motif of the whole establishment, so no wonder ball players decide to go up in their demands as they go up to see the Colonel," he wrote.

Lou entered this lap of luxury at ten-thirty that morning and went into a closed-door, one-on-one meeting with his boss. There, he unveiled his demand—forty-one thousand, four hundred dollars. It was precisely a fifteen percent raise from his '37 salary. It was also a little more than what DiMaggio wanted for the coming year.

However, Ruppert again declined to offer Lou even a token raise. The men negotiated for an hour before declaring an impasse and coming out to face the media. Lou shook hands with his boss for the photographers but could not entirely contain his irritation. "Why should I take the same money as last year?" he asked. Ruppert was also annoyed. "There's the two-gun man, boys. Maybe you can handle him. Looks like I can't," he ruefully told reporters.

When he said "handle," Ruppert meant "push him into line." Forty-one thousand dollars was a huge salary in the late 1930s—twenty times what the average newspaperman earned, and more than thirty times the income of a typical factory worker. Some people harbored wage envy toward stars like Gehrig, and Ruppert may have hoped that sportswriters would paint his first baseman as selfish and unreasonable. It had happened before. When Lou held out in 1937, an *Atlanta Constitution* columnist implied none too subtly that he was overpaid for easy work: "Lou Gehrig was offered thirty-six thousand dollars for one season of six months' play. That happens to be six thousand dollars per month. The hours are two to four each afternoon."

But during Lou's '38 holdout, the columnists laid off the snark. In fact, the sportswriting fraternity came down strongly on Gehrig's side.

> "As a rule, baseball's holdouts leave me very chilly, particularly at this time of year, when the Internal Revenue department wants to know all about your business. But if there is one of the current holdouts with evidence to back his demands, it is Louis Henry Gehrig [sic]."—Francis J. Powers, *Chicago Daily News*.

> "When one considers the years of consistently high-class playing of Gehrig . . . it must be agreed he rates a salary of forty thousand per season."—George Barton, *Minneapolis Star-Tribune*.

> "If ever a ballplayer deserved an annual increase in salary that man is Lou Gehrig. . . . Gehrig is entitled to more consideration than the average star who holds out because of his phenomenal record for continuous service on the diamond."—Braven Dyer, *Los Angeles Times*.

So strong was Lou's iron man reputation that despite his age, not one writer suggested the end of his reign as Yankee first baseman was near. "The chances are Gehrig can keep his peak for three more years. He might even be good for four or five more," wrote Will Wedge in the *Sun*.

Lester Rodney of the *Daily Worker*—a communist newspaper, but one with a sports section—concurred with Wedge and then some: "Let's assume Gehrig will be one of the rare players who keep going until forty, which is possible as he is an extremely well-kept young man," he wrote. "Figuring on living until seventy, that will give Lou some thirty years in the future to worry about."

Ruppert probably hoped the consecutive-games streak would undermine Lou's resolve. The day of the brewery meeting, AP quoted an unnamed observer: "This guy has played nineteen hundred sixty-five straight games up to now, and I'd like to see anybody keep him from making it two thousand without using a gun." But as February ended and the Yankees reported to spring training in St. Petersburg, Lou remained a holdout.

Negotiations didn't resume until March 8th, when Gehrig drove down to the brewery for another meeting. Ruppert raised his offer to thirty-nine thousand. Not good enough, said Lou—he wanted forty. The men talked for an hour, unable to bridge the gap. Ruppert said he had made his final offer: "I went more than halfway with Gehrig. That's absolutely as far as I will go." When a reporter caught him at home the next day, Lou sounded the same adamant tone. "The next move is up to Colonel Ruppert. I'm making no plans to leave for Florida," he said.

But in reality, his will was weakening. A reporter noted three days later that Gehrig had been seen swinging baseball bats and suggested he was "getting that old feeling." He gave in on the 12th, signing his contract at Ruppert's figure. Even at that number, he would be baseball's highest-salaried player for the second straight year.

An unbylined item in the *Post* said Gehrig's signing meant "a long summer of hibernation" and inactivity for the Yankees' backup first baseman, Babe Dahlgren. "There's no future being Gehrig's understudy," it said.

Lou was brimming with confidence as he and Eleanor boarded a train at Penn Station on the evening of March 13th for the thirty-six-hour ride down to St. Petersburg. When a reporter asked who would capture the American League flag that year, he replied, "I can't see anybody but us—can you?" He acknowledged the Cleveland Indians could pose a challenge, but added, "for some reason, I've never been able to take the Indians seriously in the past." Asked if he had worked out during the winter, Lou acknowledged he hadn't. "After eight months of nervous and physical strain, a man is entitled to a little rest. Besides, I'm never far out of shape anyhow," he said.

He didn't voice it, but in all likelihood, he was dying to get back into action. The movies were great fun, but baseball was the thing that defined him. It had been more than five months since he faced live pitching, and that was far too long.

* * *

Lou arrived at the Yanks' spring training headquarters within an hour of stepping off the train in St. Pete and jumped into hitting and fielding drills with nary a warm-up except for some light running. It may not have been the best decision. He struggled in batting practice, hitting mostly pop-ups and foul balls into the dirt around home plate. And he called it quits after only an hour, complaining of the Florida heat and soreness in his hands. No one worried though; most hitters, even the great ones, need a few days of spring training to recapture their timing after the winter layoff. Yankee manager McCarthy put him in the lineup for the next day's exhibition game against the Boston Bees, and Lou played all nine innings, notching a single and double as the Yankees won 2–0.

For ten days thereafter, there were no obvious signs of anything wrong with the Yankee captain. He played in every game, hit the ball hard, got some hits—though no home runs—and focused on getting ready for the season. None of his teammates criticized him about the holdout, although he had to endure plenty of razzing about the movie. The first day he entered the clubhouse, Lefty Gomez morphed into a mock Hollywood director, barking instructions through a newspaper rolled up like a megaphone: "Very good, Mr. Gehrig! You and the horse looked fine in that last scene. Now in this one, I want you to come out shooting with both hands." A couple of days later, Lou stepped onto the field to find right fielder George Selkirk riding a mule, wearing a cowboy hat and carrying a toy pistol in each hand. Around his neck hung a sign that said "GEHRIG MODEL." A smiling Lou posed with Selkirk for a goofy photo that ran in a handful of newspapers.

In retrospect, there were a few minor warning signs mixed in with the hilarity. During a practice, Gehrig stumbled rounding first after a single. A few days later, the same thing happened during a game against the Cardinals and he was tagged out. In her memoir, Eleanor recalled that during that spring, Lou "did admit to me privately that his legs didn't feel so strong or springy, and they hadn't since he turned thirty."

But tired legs are hardly uncommon in older athletes. The real worry in the Yankee camp centered on DiMaggio, who remained a continent away in San Francisco, still holding out for a forty thousand dollar salary. Ruppert laid down the law: twenty-five thousand or nothing. General Manager Ed Barrow predicted the Yankees would win the pennant even if Joe sat out the whole season. "No one player ever made any ballclub," he said.

Then on March 26th, a cloud drifted over first base. The soreness in his hands Lou reported on his initial day in camp had grown worse, and now he had blisters and bruises on both palms. Batting gloves did not exist in 1938, so for that afternoon's game, he tried taping a piece of rubber to the bat handle, to ease the sting when he hit the ball. But it was no use. After three hitless at-bats against the Cardinals, he took himself out of the game. Exercising uncharacteristic caution, he sat out the next two, letting Babe Dahlgren take over his position.

This didn't affect his consecutive games streak, which included regular-season contests only. It was still unusual, as noted by

Rud Rennie of the *Herald Tribune.* "It is not the first exhibition game he has missed, but any time Gehrig does not play, it is interesting," Rennie wrote.

One contemporary writer suggested Lou had gone soft during the winter and was suffering from a case of "Hollywood hands." Jonathan Eig, the author of the 2005 Gehrig biography *Luckiest Man,* theorized that Gehrig was squeezing the bat extra hard to compensate for ALS draining strength out of his back, hips and legs, the parts of the body that supply most of the power when a batter strikes a ball.

Dr. Richard Bedlack, a neurologist and ALS researcher based at Duke University, says there's no way from today's vantage point to know for sure—but he agrees ALS caused Gehrig's hand problems. "It's highly plausible something was going on that caused him to grip the bat in a different way," he says. "I play golf, and I have a callous in one place on my hand because that's a pressure point for me, from playing golf for forty years the same way. You can imagine if I was injured and had to hold the club in a whole different way, I might get a blister because that part of my palm is not thickened up from years and years of use. [In Gehrig's case] it would be a new area that was feeling the contact of the bat."

The blisters and bruises were still bugging Lou when he returned to action on March 29th, and James Kahn of the *Sun* reported that "he can't clout a ball as solidly as he'd like to." He accepted three walks and knocked out one hit in that day's action. A day later, the Yankees broke camp in St. Petersburg to begin their annual exhibition tour, playing the organization's minor league teams. Joe McCarthy said Gehrig was "approaching form" but was not quite ready for the season.

Lou's performance over the next week and a half both proved and disproved his manager's observation. The Yankees trekked across the South, playing one or two games in cities like Tallahassee, New Orleans, Fort Worth and Atlanta. Each day, Lou punched out a hit or two, driving in an occasional run, coming around to score here and there. The writers traveling with the team soon noted that he had racked up a twelve-game hitting streak, pushing his spring batting average into the .350 range, best on the team. Only one problem—nearly every hit during the streak was a single. When Gehrig finally hit a double on April 10th in Little Rock, it was a fluke, a high fly ball down the line that the wind blew fair.

"Lou Gehrig has a good average, but he's not driving the ball as it were something shot out of a gun, as he does when he really is teeing off," wrote Stanley Frank of the *Post*, one of the reporters traveling with the team.

Lou later said he first sensed problems with his body during this period, specifically a "lack of power" in his swing. "It was quite mild at first," he told Grantland Rice in August 1939, "but even a year ago last spring I knew something was wrong . . . I knew there was no reason for this as I was still young enough and should have been strong enough. I knew I had kept myself in the best possible condition but lacked the old snap."

Not until the Yankees reached Knoxville on April 12th did Lou finally break loose, busting a home run in the second inning and a triple in the fifth as the Yankees walloped the minor-league Smokies, 19–4. The homer, a shot that traveled an estimated three hundred sixty feet, was to be the only one he hit in twenty-four preseason games. Still, it was enough to make some slightly nervous beat writers exhale. "Gehrig's contributions were particularly heartening, for the Iron Horse is the spiritual as well as the actual leader of this team," wrote Frank. Kahn chimed in a day later after Lou slammed a double and triple in Spartanburg, South Carolina. "The consistency of his hitting . . . is now being supplemented with that extra-base touch, and no misgivings are necessary now about how well that clean-up spot will be filled when the gong rings," Kahn wrote.

But Lou wasn't feeling quite as sanguine. He still thought the power was missing from his swing. The subject came up two days before the regular season began, as the Yankees, following a long train trip north, played a final preseason series against the Dodgers at Ebbets Field in Brooklyn. Hugh Bradley, the sports editor of the *Post*, was conducting brief interviews of various Yankee and Dodger players for his column. He approached Lou and asked about the dark background for hitters the Dodgers had installed in center field that spring. Lou said he liked it. Bradley then asked about Lou's winter experience in Hollywood. This question, Lou brushed off. He had something else on his mind.

"Sure, movies are swell, but this is baseball season," he said. "I got to do something about my hitting. I see the ball all right and take a proper cut and seem to connect like I want to, but somehow the ball doesn't seem to take the proper zoom. I've got to find out—"

Bradley interrupted to point out Gehrig was hitting .345 for the preseason.

"I didn't know my average was that good for the exhibitions," Lou said. "I still got to find out what's the matter, though."

The comments foreshadow a reported, oft-quoted observation from Kahn, who according to Eleanor's memoir said late in the '38 season he saw Lou timing pitches perfectly, meeting the ball squarely, but producing only soft, looping fly balls that barely cleared the infield. In April, Lou's hits still had some oomph, but not the amount he was accustomed to. Today's analysts would say his exit velocity was down; hits were leaving his bat at a slower speed than they usually did.

Lou couldn't have been encouraged when his hot streak came to a sudden end in Brooklyn. For the first time in two weeks, he was facing experienced major-league pitchers like Freddie Fitzsimmons and Waite Hoyt, not the Class A and Double A competition the Yankees had played across the South. In three games, he managed only two hits in twelve at-bats. Both hits were singles.

4

A Slow Start

Lou Gehrig's greatest season began on the dreariest of days—a wet, gray, windy afternoon in Boston, with the thermometer struggling to climb above forty-five degrees. If this hadn't been opening day, opined one local paper, "there wouldn't have been any ball game here at all." The Yankees and Red Sox played only at the insistence of Boston's management. A year earlier, opening weekend games between the teams drew crowds of twenty-five and thirty-five thousand to Fenway Park, big turnouts for the Depression era. On this April 18th, however, the weather held down attendance to a hardy ten thousand and change. Most were men bundled up against the cold, turning the stands into a sea of overcoats and snap-brim fedoras.

Early afternoon rain put a damper on the usual opening day festivities; pregame ceremonies were hurried, the players didn't take batting practice, and the Yankee players looked unhappy as they stood along the third-base line for the national anthem. The continued holdout of the Yanks' star center fielder hung in the air as well. When a newsreel reporter asked Joe McCarthy, "When is DiMaggio going to join up with the club?" the manager waved off the question and refused to utter a word. McCarthy likely didn't want to jinx the contract negotiations or rattle DiMaggio's substitute in center, backup outfielder Myril Hoag. Hoag turned out to have a fine day, rapping out two singles and driving in two runs. But Yankee starter Red Ruffing wasn't sharp, and the Red Sox knocked him out of the game during a six-run sixth inning.

Yankee comeback attempts fizzled, and the Sox emerged with a soggy 8–4 victory.

Nine innings of cold, wet baseball are not good for anybody's constitution and probably hurt Lou even more, given his short spring training and the early effects of ALS. But iron men let nothing stop them and Lou, wearing long sleeves, batting fourth, played the whole game. He helped spark the first Yankee rally, walking on four pitches and scoring minutes later on a hit from Tommy Henrich. After that, it was a quiet day—ground out, harmless walk, strikeout. The only moment of import for him came when he chased a foul pop-up that landed in the first-base stands. *Rawhide* had recently entered general release, and as Gehrig ran for the ball, several fans shouted, "Get a horse, Lou!" These were the first of many cowboy-themed catcalls Lou would have to endure during the '38 season because of his movie. Reporters chronicled them as the season went along. "Way to go, Two-Gun!" was one; "Hi-yo, Silver!"—a reference to the popular *Lone Ranger* radio show—was perhaps the most common.

He couldn't hear it, but Lou got a much warmer welcome in the Red Sox radio booth, where announcer Fred Hoey practically gushed with admiration for the Yankee captain. "On first base for the Yankees is the great Lou Gehrig, playing his nineteen hundred and sixty-sixth game," Hoey told listeners as Lou took the field. "After this game, thirty-four more games and he reaches two thousand consecutive great games. He started this wonderful run on June 1st, 1925." The comments reflected how much Lou had already become an icon, and how the streak, more so than his hitting accomplishments, had become his defining feature.

Hoey's remarks implied that the looming two-thousand milestone was a sure thing. But that certainty, shared by Lou's teammates, manager and millions of fans, evaporated in the following days as their hero fell not into a slump but a drought, a complete absence of offensive production. On day two of the season, the Yankees and Red Sox played a doubleheader to mark Patriots' Day, the Massachusetts state holiday. Gehrig went 0-for-4 with a strikeout in game one, 0-for-3 with a meaningless walk in game two. In the final game of the series, the Yankees faced Johnny Marcum, a journeyman pitcher who Lou had often tattooed for extra-base hits. On this day, he was 0-for-5. In three of those at-bats he came up with runners in scoring position; all three times he sat down without an RBI. The Yankees lost 3–2.

Almost immediately, newspaper scribes picked up on Lou's uncharacteristic struggles and speculated about the cause. One common theory was that the absence of DiMaggio's bat made Gehrig and the entire Yankee lineup more vulnerable. Lou seemed to endorse that view on Thursday, April 21st, the day DiMaggio finally ended his holdout and began a two-day, cross-country train ride from San Francisco to join his teammates. "I hope he's ready to play Saturday," Lou told a wire service. "We're not hitting and me, I'm the worst of the lot. No use talking, we haven't been right this spring."

At least one observer seemed to sense Gehrig's trouble ran deeper than the absence of his fellow star. Bill McCullough was a sportswriter for the *Brooklyn Daily Eagle* who covered all three New York-area teams but started the year on the Yankee beat. After the last Boston game, he wrote: "Lou doesn't look good at the platter. When he isn't tapping weakly to the infielders he is striking out. Twice yesterday Johnny Marcum whiffed him with a teammate on third." McCullough added a hopeful note, saying that the Yankees' return to the Bronx for the home opener might "help old Iron Horse regain his normal stride."

The comforts of home might have helped, except the Yankees' opening-day festivities were even more off-kilter than the ones in Boston. Morning rain held down the crowd to twenty-five thousand, about half of what was expected. Then, the players stood idle in center field for nearly twenty minutes before game time, waiting for a flag-raising ceremony, because New York's acting mayor Newbold Morris, filling in for the traveling Fiorello LaGuardia, initially refused to cross a union picket line to enter the stadium. After the flag was hoisted and Morris threw out the first pitch, Lou and the Yankees charged onto the field for the start of the game, only to be abruptly called back; baseball commissioner Judge Kenesaw Mountain Landis first wanted to hand out tokens commemorating the Yankees' 1937 world championship.

Eventually, the game got going and the Yankees crushed the Washington Senators 7–0 on the back of a four-hit shutout by

Ruffing. But Lou again was of no help, going 0-for-3, getting on base once when he was hit by a pitch. One paper said he looked "baffled" at the plate.

The next day, Lou finally connected for a base hit off the Senators' Wes Ferrell, a six-time twenty-game winner. But even this breakthrough was tainted. Batting in the first with two outs, Lou belted a four-hundred-foot drive that landed by the wall in deep right-center, scoring Red Rolfe to give the Yankees a 1–0 lead. He should have pulled into second with an easy double. But the hit-starved Gehrig wanted more. He charged past second base, gunning for third. The Senators' swift rookie center fielder, George Case, ran down the ball and made a strong, accurate throw. Lou slid, but the ball smacked into the third baseman's glove a split-second before his outstretched legs. Third out, end of the inning, end of the rally.

The Yankees lost 7–4. Then it was back to the drought: two more hitless games, one against the Senators, the other against the Philadelphia A's. In the A's game, Lou popped out with runners on second and third in the seventh, ending the Yankees' final chance for a comeback in a 6–1 loss.

Nearly every biography of Lou Gehrig notes that when he ended his consecutive games streak on May 2nd, 1939, he was batting just .143, having knocked out a mere four singles in the season's first eight games. What few people realize is that his start to the 1938 season was even worse. Eight games into the season, the mighty Gehrig, the model of Yankee power, was hitting a feeble .042, with one hit in twenty-four official at-bats. He had walked eight times, and come around to score twice. Other than that, he was an offensive zero.

After the A's game, new expressions of concern for Lou popped up in the newspapers. "[F]ans are beginning to wonder if the veteran first baseman has at last lost his eye," wrote Gayle Talbot of the Associated Press. "Any other Yank in a similar slump would have been pulled before this, but Manager Joe McCarthy is loath to break Lou's long record for continuous playing."

"[Gehrig] has been in slumps before, but this one is the worst ever," said a curiously unbylined article in the *Daily Eagle*. "From the stands, it appears as though Lou is out of physical condition.

His underpinning is weak. Three times during the Washington series he was thrown out when he should have made the base easily."

It's possible that Gehrig was out of condition after his shortened spring. But in all likelihood, his muscles were starting to feel the debilitating effects of ALS.

In a healthy nervous system, nerve cells known as motor neurons quickly and continuously transmit messages between the brain, the spinal cord, and muscles throughout the body. It's this system that allows a baseball player to carry out the dozens of split-second decisions he makes during a game, such as whether to charge a soft ground ball, dive for a sinking liner or swing at a bad curveball coming in flat and fat over the plate. In people with ALS however, the motor neurons inexplicably stop working and die, cutting off the flow of messages. There's not much physical pain involved, and usually no loss of cognitive functioning. But as more neurons perish, and signals from the brain become fewer and weaker, muscles become less and less responsive. Eventually, they stop working altogether, leaving the patient unable to move. Most patients survive only two to five years after diagnosis, with respiratory failure being the most common cause of death.

The initial effects of ALS are usually relatively minor—fatigue, muscle cramps or twitching, or stiffness or weakness in the arms, legs, and feet. For a time, some athletes can adjust to their new limitations, says Dr. Richard Bedlack. "It's not uncommon during the first year for people to be able to function at a pretty high level," he says. "I've had examples of patients who continue to do extraordinary things. They tell me, 'I'm a triathlete, and I knew something was wrong because my times weren't as good, but I continued to run triathlons.'"

But in sports like baseball where speed, coordination, and reflexes are paramount, even early ALS symptoms can be ruinous. One day an athlete's movements are smooth as silk and fast as lightning; eight or nine months later, it's like he's trying to play with lead weights strapped to his limbs.

ALS usually strikes people between forty and seventy, and the disease has cut down only a handful of professional athletes in their prime. Polish soccer player Krzysztof Nowak, a member of his country's national team, was diagnosed at age twenty-six and was forced to retire. He lived another four years. Former University of Washington basketball player Melissa Erickson developed ALS at age twenty-seven while playing professionally in Portugal. She lived for seven years. The disease hit at least two NFL players during their careers—Tennessee Titans linebacker Tim Shaw, who is still alive as of this writing, and Houston Oilers defensive lineman Glenn Montgomery, who lived only a year after being diagnosed in 1997.

Insight into what Gehrig experienced as a baseball player comes from the story of Pete Frates. Frates, a left-handed hitting first baseman like Gehrig, played NCAA Division I baseball for Boston College between 2004 and 2007, tying for the team lead in home runs during his senior season. One of his most cherished moments was hitting a homer in Fenway Park during a tournament. "I got a hanging curveball and put it in the bullpen," he said in 2013 before he lost his ability to speak. "That was really special, growing up a Red Sox fan and standing in the same batter's box as Ted Williams."

Frates (pronounced *fray*-tees) was never pursued by a major league team, but after college he continued to play in Boston-area competitive leagues and flourished, batting close to .400. In 2011, at age twenty-six, he felt his abilities had reached a new peak. But as that season progressed, he noticed changes in his body, starting with twitching in his upper body and arms. At first, he thought little of it, dealing with the problem by consuming extra Gatorade and bananas. Nevertheless, his bat speed slowed and baseball turned into a struggle. "I was striking out a ton and making average pitchers look like studs. I was normally one of the fastest guys in the league, but now I was lumbering around the basepaths, trying to get my legs moving," he said.

Frates' baseball career ended when he faced a University of Massachusetts pitcher known for throwing major-league velocity fastballs, ninety-plus miles per hour. After fouling off a few pitches, he swung at an inside fastball and was struck on the left wrist. There was no break, but the pain lingered for months, and in the process of seeing doctors and researching his symptoms

Frates realized he likely had ALS, a fact confirmed by doctors March 2012. His thoughts immediately went to Gehrig.

"Lou Gehrig now inspires me every day," Frates later wrote. "I have a poster of his speech on the wall of my garage. It is the last thing I see when I leave the house. I use his words to help me attack the day and keep up the fight against the beast that is ALS." And Frates knew how to fight, becoming one of the nation's foremost campaigners for ALS research. It was his Facebook campaign that turned an odd online fad—dumping buckets of ice-cold water on oneself for various charities—into a fundraising phenomenon that raised one hundred fifteen million dollars for the ALS Association in 2014. Twenty-three million was directed toward helping ALS patients and their families. Most of the rest was plowed into research on genes that might cause the disease, in hopes of finding a cure.

* * *

It's not known if Gehrig was feeling twitches, weakness or fatigue in April 1938. What's clear is that the horrible start pushed him into an emotional funk of roughly the same depth as his batting average. "The Yankee captain is down in the mouth over his protracted batting letdown. He doesn't know what to do about it," reported the *Daily Eagle,* which said he had been taking extra batting practice in vain. The *New York Times* reported that Gehrig looked mournful around Yankee Stadium, and said according to the "Gehrig homestead"—Eleanor, presumably—he was neither eating nor sleeping well.

Syndicated columnist John Lardner noted, accurately: "Lou takes these hitting slumps hard. He will be no fit company for man or beast until he begins to get hold of the ball and pull it sharp and clean to right."

As the drought continued, Gehrig very likely spent many a post-game brooding in the Yankee clubhouse. Joe DiMaggio once explained that on good days, Gehrig liked to shower and get out the clubhouse quickly. "But if he had a bad day, he'd stay longer, taking the blame. He really beat himself when something went wrong," DiMaggio said. The beatdown included indulgence in Gehrig's primary vice, smoking. "Lou loved his cigarettes," DiMaggio said. "Before the game, he'd have a cigarette or two and the same after the game. But on his bad days, he took more puffs."

The home fans did not take Gehrig's slump lying down. Fans handed him lucky charms at the ballpark and on the street—rabbit's feet, horseshoes, four-leaf clovers, old coins, even "Jewish prayer cylinders," according to the *New York Sun*. Other, less patient individuals showered him with boos and Bronx cheers. A particularly bad outbreak occurred April 28th after Gehrig popped out in the eighth inning of a 6–1 loss to the Red Sox at the Stadium. *Sun* writer James Kahn said the next day that Gehrig "has the look of a man searching for a good sharp knife, so he can cut his throat. He is down." Heckling on the road was to be expected. Getting it at home was a new phenomenon. The jeers were no doubt inspired by events beyond the slump, such as Gehrig's spring training holdout, his stab at movie stardom and the Yankees' lackluster play to start the season. The fans were booing DiMaggio too for his own extended holdout. The sounds still reached Gehrig's ears, and they had to hurt.

Gehrig finally got a few hits in the waning days of April and delivered his first game-winning blow of the season against Boston on April 29th, an RBI single in the sixth that broke a 4–4 tie. But McCarthy still felt compelled to defend his first baseman to the press the next day. "Lou is down in the dumps because he isn't hitting," the manager said. "But he hit two on the nose yesterday. His slump shouldn't be taken too seriously . . . He is an established ballplayer and one day he'll get going. He is far from washed up."

What the manager giveth, the manager taketh away. Two days after voicing his support for Gehrig, McCarthy dropped him from fourth to sixth in the lineup. No one questioned why. The day of McCarthy's comments, Gehrig had gone 0-for-5. The following day, he was 0-for-3 with two strikeouts in a 4–3 loss to the Senators. His batting average now stood at .109, with three RBIs. DiMaggio would now assume cleanup duties, with Bill Dickey hitting fifth. "Let Lou hit his way back into the clean-up spot,"

McCarthy told reporters, adding, "I just want to see how a few things work out."

A pair of Senators—two future Hall of Famers, in fact—seemed to go out of their way to rub in the embarrassment Gehrig was feeling. One was outfielder Al Simmons, who'd been in the American League almost as long as Gehrig and battered AL pitchers almost as hard. "Yeah, the Yankees are having trouble and I do love it," Simmons told a Cleveland reporter. "Wait till you see that Gehrig. He's got so he's changing his stance every time he comes to bat. And we're giving him the old cowboy yell and telling him that Hollywood has fixed him for good."

The other was the team's owner, sixty-nine-year-old Clark Griffith. Griffith, a top-notch pitcher during his playing career, ran the Senators for decades on a tight rein and a tighter budget. He is remembered in part for his lack of foresight; at various times, he took hard stands against nighttime baseball, the All-Star Game, farm systems, free agency, and integration. But speaking to the *Washington Evening Star* on second of May 1938, he sounded eerily prescient, as though he knew Gehrig's troubles were not the result of temporary factors like batting stance and lack of conditioning. Asked if he thought Gehrig was "rusting," Griffith replied: "Well, he ain't a-going to get better. He might be a worn-out piece of iron. Gehrig's taken an awful beating since 1925. He's been on a lot of pennant-winning teams and he's had to hustle every minute. I give him credit for that—he hustles. But he don't a-look like he's going to hit much, anymore. He's pushing at the ball now and not snapping his bat around like he used to."

Many observers would make similarly gloomy comments in 1939. Griffith was the only one making them this early.

McCarthy was certainly more hopeful than Griffith. In fact, his wife, Elizabeth, wrote Lou a cheer-up letter that month, telling him "don't get discouraged just because you are in a little slump," and assuring him that "Joe is as strong for you as he ever was." There is no evidence that McCarthy talked about benching Lou at this stage. But the thought must have crossed his mind. On May 1st, the Yankees had a 7–7 record and were in third place—not a cause for true alarm, but also not what Yankee fans expected after two straight romps to the American League pennant followed by crushing wins in the World Series. DiMaggio, Dickey, and Rolfe were hitting; it was Gehrig who was holding back the Yankee offense. Maybe a rest would do him some good?

The Yankees had added a competent backup first baseman to the club that spring, a twenty-five-year-old from San Francisco, Ellsworth Tenney Dahlgren, better known as Babe. Like many young baseball players, Dahlgren grew up idolizing Gehrig. "The story went back to my high school days. I carried a picture of Lou in my binder. He was more or less an inspiration to me, he and Babe Ruth," Dahlgren recalled. This younger Babe had spent his rookie year of 1935 as the Red Sox' regular first baseman, hitting .263 with nine home runs. However, he was benched the following year when Boston acquired two-time MVP Jimmie Foxx from the A's. When Lou staged his holdout in the spring of '37, the Yankees traded for Dahlgren and sent him down to the team's highest farm club, the Newark Bears. In a letter to a scout, Newark executive and future Yankees general manager George Weiss relayed Joe McCarthy's plans for the young first baseman. "He . . . states that he wants to be protected to bring back Dahlgren if anything happens to Gehrig," Weiss wrote.

Playing every day in Newark, Dahlgren excelled, batting .340 with eighteen home runs for a team that won the minor league World Series. Promoted to the Yankees in '38, Dahlgren was just happy to be back in the big leagues and had absolutely no designs on Lou's job. "I never did think for a moment—no, it would have seemed like the wildest dream that I would be the guy to replace him," he said. And at the moment, he wasn't. The Yankees, like the Red Sox before them, had doubts about Dahlgren's hitting, and in any case, Lou was not volunteering to give him a chance, the kind that Wally Pipp gave him in 1925.

* * *

Sometimes the best medicine for a struggling hitter is a really bad pitcher. On May 3rd, Lou got to face one, Jim Walkup of the St. Louis Browns. Walkup wasn't just a bad hurler; he was a guaranteed slump killer for the other team. In his first full season, 1935, he walked two batters for every one he struck out, led the Brownie staff in home runs allowed and finished the year with a 6.25 earned run average. After spending most of 1936 in the minors, he made the Browns' starting rotation the following year and rewarded them with even ghastlier pitching, racking up a 7.36 ERA, still one of the highest single-season marks for pitchers who threw at least one hundred fifty innings. He'd finally lose his starting spot in July '38 after starting the year with zero wins, ten losses, and an ERA rising like a helium-filled balloon. Walkup stayed in the majors as long as he did only because he played for the Browns, the American League's eternal weak sister, almost bereft of money and major-league talent.

When Lou came to bat that Tuesday, Walkup was already on the ropes, courtesy of an RBI single by Dickey that gave the Yankees a 2–0 lead. Lou delivered another hard blow, smashing a line drive that skidded past outfielder Sam West and bounced all the way to the flagpole four hundred sixty feet away, in the deepest part of Yankee Stadium's outfield. As West chased down the ball, Gehrig galloped around the bases; coming up on third, he got a green light from coach Art Fletcher and charged home. This time, his aggressive base running paid off. The Browns made an accurate relay to the plate but Lou beat it by a hair, slapping home plate with an outstretched left hand as he made a headfirst slide. It was more like Ty Cobb than Babe Ruth, but sixteen games into the 1938 season, Lou Gehrig had finally hit a home run.

The round-tripper seemed to loosen the hinges on Lou's swing and the hits began falling. He tallied four in the three games against the Browns, including a double that a St. Louis paper said "almost tore off George McQuinn's leg" at first base. The Tigers made a one-day stop at Yankee Stadium, and the home team beat them too, with Lou getting three hits and more importantly, taking part in three run-scoring rallies. The next day he hit his first real home run of the season against the White Sox, a two-run shot to the right-field stands that broke a tie and fueled a 7–3 victory. Lou's batting average finally crept over .200, and he proclaimed his slump to be over. "I was holding my right arm too stiff and high," he told one reporter. Better still, the Yankees won seven in a row, and a victory over the Indians on May 11th put the club atop the American League for the first time that season.

A threat to Lou's surge appeared on the 12th when the Yankees faced one of the few pitchers who could truly dominate him—the Indians' teenage fireballer, Bob Feller. Feller had arrived in the majors from the cornfields of Van Meter, Iowa less than two years earlier, armed with a lethal fastball and an almost unhittable curve. In his first major league start, he struck out fifteen in defeating the Browns. A few weeks later, he piled up seventeen strikeouts in beating the A's. He wasn't always so overpowering, and in his first one-inning stint against the Yankees that year he got hammered for five runs. But in 1937, Feller virtually owned Gehrig, allowing him only one hit in twelve official at-bats, and striking him out seven times. Lou could take solace in that the one hit had been a back-breaker, a two-out, two-run homer in the bottom of the ninth which tied the score at 5–5 and denied Feller a victory. The Yankees won the game off another pitcher in the tenth.

Although they faced off in only a few games, Gehrig and Feller made a deep impression on each other. Lou, not one to dole out praise for the opposition, lauded the eighteen-year-old Feller in the press, saying "He's as fast as any other pitcher in the game, and he's got guts." In his book, Feller said Lou had been one of his boyhood idols. The prospect of seeing Gehrig and Babe Ruth when they stopped in Des Moines during a 1928 barnstorming tour, he said, "was making me jump out of my skin." Nine years later, when he struck out Lou three times in one afternoon, it gave him immense pride and pleasure. "I'm not sure how often he struck out three times in one game, but it couldn't have been too many," he wrote. "And each time he was swinging. The great Lou Gehrig, one of the top hitters in baseball for more than ten years, couldn't hit my curveball. I didn't need any more encouragement than that."

The stars' first encounter of 1938 began with Feller setting down Lou on two straight strikeouts, once swinging on a full count, once looking. Lou dissected the first strikeout with admiration in a post-game interview. "I'm sure [catcher] Rollie Hemsley called for a fastball, Feller's specialty," Lou said. "But I saw Bob shake him off, give Hemsley the notice with his head. So I figured that Hemsley must have called for a curveball and Bob wanted to throw a fastball. I was set for a fast one. He threw me a quick curve. I missed it by a foot. When a pitcher has the moxie to throw something besides his Sunday ball in a pinch, watch out for him."

The Iron Horse said nothing about his third at-bat. Feller was working on a two-hit, 3–0 shutout when Lou came up in the sixth with Tommy Henrich on base. The fans greeted the Yankee captain with jeers. But Lou quashed the boos by pounding a Feller pitch into the lower right-field stands, cutting the Indians' lead to one run. A home movie taken by a fan that day shows him trotting around second base with his head down as if he wasn't sure how the fans would react to his success. He had nothing to worry about. "By the time he reached the plate the crowd was cheering, and he grinned and took his cap off to the crowd," wrote *New York Sun* columnist Frank Graham.

His final turn at bat didn't turn out as well. With the Indians still leading 3–2, he lined a single to right with nobody out. But he was thrown out at second base a minute later when he tried to advance on a dropped third strike by Hemsley— "a bonehead play," the AP called it. The ensuing loss pushed the Yankees back into second place, one game behind the Senators, and no doubt left Lou consuming a beer and cigarettes in the clubhouse, cursing his mistake.

He'd have plenty of time to review his shortcomings in the following week. The showers that had dampened opening day in Boston were following the Yankees around the league. A game against the A's on May 14th was halted in the fifth and would have to be replayed. Games in New York on the 15th and in St. Louis on the 18th and 20th were rained out entirely. "The weather gods are piling up a lot of doubleheaders for the Yankees," noted the *Times*. Even Joe McCarthy, normally not a complainer, griped about the weather during interviews with reporters. "How can they be the same old Yankees when they spend their time sitting around hotel lobbies waiting for it to stop raining?" he asked. "We've had so many postponements we don't know what we look like on a ball field."

Even an exhibition against a Yankee farm team in Butler, Pennsylvania was cut short, although that had nothing to do with rain. In that case, an estimated three thousand kids rushed the field in the seventh inning, seeking autographs from Gehrig, DiMaggio, and company. The Yankees, leading by fourteen runs, put down their gloves and picked up their pens for the giddy throng.

The appreciation was nice but idleness was not good for a guy in his mid-thirties who was used to playing every day and was unknowingly suffering from a motor neuron disease. The inactivity might throw him back into a batting slump. It might make his muscles tighten up. Conceivably, it could impact his treasured consecutive-games streak. If the rain ever stopped, Gehrig was scheduled to play in his two-thousandth straight game by the end of the month. Surely, nothing could stop him from reaching that milestone.

5

Two Thousand

The injury bug bit a few days later, May 22nd in Cleveland, and bit down hard. Lou had taken a mighty swing and blasted the ball, on the fly, all the way to the 435 marker on the right-field wall. The ball bounced off the fence and into the vast expanse that was the outfield of cavernous Municipal Stadium, with the Indians giving chase. Tommy Henrich was going to score from first, and anyone could see that Lou had a sure triple, maybe even an inside-the-park home run. He tore out of the batter's box, got his legs churning for a fast trip around the bases—only to be stabbed by a sharp pain in his lower back as he ran up the first-base line. His running turned into a fast hobble, then a near limp, forcing him to stop at second with an RBI double.

The game stopped for the next few minutes as Yankee trainer Doc Painter came out to massage Lou's back at second base, in the full view of teammates, umpires and a Sunday crowd of sixty-two thousand in the stands. His ministrations kept Lou in the game long enough to score on a single from second baseman Bill Knickerbocker. But when the Yankees took the field in the bottom of the sixth, Babe Dahlgren played first base and assumed Lou's number five slot in the batting order. It was the first time the youngster replaced Gehrig in the middle of a game.

The afternoon had begun promisingly for the Yankees. The team came into Cleveland hoping to erase the Indians' two-game lead in the American League race. They had squeaked out a 1–0 victory in Chicago the day before, only their second game that week because of all the rainouts. Pleased with Lou's recent resurgence, McCarthy promoted him to fifth in the batting order, moving Dickey down to sixth. But from the first pitch, everything had gone wrong. The Indians battered Monte Pearson and Bump Hadley for eight early runs while Yankee batters floundered. Even the challenge of facing Bob Feller was taken away when a back-muscle injury forced the Indians' ace to depart in the fourth inning after Lou faced him one time and struck out. Johnny Humphries and Mel Harder finished up the 8–3 win for the Indians.

The Associated Press reported Gehrig's injury as a "charley horse," while the *Cleveland Plain Dealer* described it as a mere "crick in the back." In reality, Lou was in agony. He had suffered this kind of pain before; sportswriters usually described it as lumbago, that catchall term for unexplained lower backaches. The most famous attack in July 1934 had forced him to leave a game against the Tigers in the fourth inning. The pain on that occasion was so bad that Gehrig found it hard to breathe, let alone swing a bat. The consecutive games streak survived only with the help of McCarthy, who put Gehrig in the leadoff spot the following day and removed him for a pinch-runner after he somehow slapped a single to right and limped to first base. Gehrig later said that before that game, the pain was so bad he needed help to get into uniform.

Doc Painter now hoped to head off a repeat of that incident and treated Gehrig with heat lamps and massage before putting his midsection in a plaster cast to immobilize his back. This was no time to risk the streak; Sunday's game put Gehrig just eight games shy of the two-thousand mark. Gehrig, despite his obvious pain, told reporters that he planned to play the following afternoon. That didn't stop a few New York papers from trumpeting the possibility the streak just might be snapped. "The consecutive playing record of Lou Gehrig, the Iron Horse, was in jeopardy today," wrote Bill McCullough in the *Daily Eagle*. James Dawson of the *Times* wrote "the club tonight faces the loss of Lou Gehrig," though he added the proviso that Gehrig could play parts of games if necessary.

The brewing drama became moot when an all-morning rain fell over Cleveland and washed out Monday's game, giving Gehrig a free day in which he refrained from working out, opting instead for a movie and a big dinner. When the teams returned to action on May 24th, Gehrig doubled to right his first time up and scored on a Dickey home run. He scored again after walking in the sixth. Joe McCarthy thereafter waved off any concern about his first baseman. "Oh, he pulled a muscle and his back is a little sore," the manager said. "But that doesn't bother him. He has started to hit and he'll be all right."

And in a general sense, McCarthy was correct. Gehrig was accustomed to playing through pain, and he was finally getting hits, enough to push his batting average into the .270s, the lower range of respectable by 1930s American League standards. In the last week of May, the manager restored Gehrig to his traditional cleanup spot, and Lou responded with several good days at bat, the best being a May 30th Memorial Day doubleheader against the Red Sox in New York. In game one, a sharp two-run single by Gehrig in the fourth knocked Lefty Grove out of the game as the Yankees cruised, 10–0. In the nightcap, his two-run homer in the sixth and a rally-fueling single in the eighth helped erase a four-run deficit as the Yanks came back to win 5–4.

Still, Lou wasn't quite his usual self, and the Yankees lost five of six at one point, dipping down to fourth place, their win-loss record hovering dangerously close to .500. As Gehrig approached his big milestone, rumors of his benching or eventual replacement continued to swirl. A note in an AP sports roundup on May 26th read: "Joe McCarthy is believed to have made up his mind on Tommy Henrich as Lou Gehrig's successor when and if the iron man [sic] cracks."

If he read the item, Gehrig had to be concerned. The source of that information could only be a Yankee coach or McCarthy himself. The team might be sticking with him at first base for the moment, but management was apparently making plans for a change in the not-too-distant future.

* * *

The May 30th twin bill against Boston had drawn over eighty-one thousand fans to Yankee Stadium, possibly the biggest crowd ever to attend a baseball game to that point in time. The next day emerged sunny and warm in New York and the Yankees were again playing the archrival Red Sox. The teams, which had almost identical records, were battling for control of second place, behind the surprising, surging Indians. And as all the newspapers announced, Lou Gehrig was about to play in his two-thousandth consecutive game, a feat the Associated Press trumpeted as "the greatest endurance record in sports" and *The New York Times* called "a record which probably never will be surpassed."

How odd then that May 31st, 1938 could have been mistaken for any other afternoon at Yankee Stadium. The Yankees made no special effort to promote the occasion and held only a small pre-game ceremony for Gehrig that was not broadcast over the public-address system. A crowd of just sixty-nine hundred was on hand to see the Iron Horse make baseball history. You could call it Lou Gehrig Under-Appreciation Day.

In a 1941 interview, Eleanor Gehrig said the night before the game, she tried to convince her husband to end the streak. She approached it from a business point of view, citing Gehrig's alleged lack of "color," as judged by the New York sportswriters looking for stories or snappy quotes to fill up their columns. Skipping the game, she argued, would obliterate that charge forever. "If you don't play," she said, "they'll write about you for days and everybody will say, 'That's some colorful ballplayer.' And if you do play, you know what you'll get out of it—a paragraph [in the papers] and a floral horseshoe."

Gehrig didn't buy his wife's logic. "You can't be serious," he said, reminding her about the ceremony the Yankees had planned. "I can't just walk out on them."

The morning of the 31st, Gehrig drove to the stadium, where he suited up and walked out to the infield for the celebration, such as it was. Someone had arranged baseballs on the grass to spell out "2,000" and Gehrig sat down behind them to pose for a few photographs. Then he gathered with about fifteen teammates near first base for the brief ceremony, captured for posterity by a Universal Studios newsreel camera. A smiling McCarthy, looking straight at his first baseman, gave Gehrig some typically low-key praise. "Lou, I want to congratulate you on a wonderful career and playing two thousand games without missing a game," he said. "And I hope I'm around here when you play your next two thousand. You've done a wonderful job, and you should be congratulated, and I'm sure that you're going to continue for a long time to come."

Gehrig shook McCarthy's hand and said, "Thanks, Joe." Then his teammates raised their caps to their captain for a photo that wound up in the next day's *New York Times*. That was it, the entire ceremony. Back to work, gentlemen.

The milestone touched off a new round of articles, commentary and sports-page cartoons about the Iron Horse and his streak. Most were laudatory, even reverent. "Here is a record which in itself may stand for all the history of baseball," wrote *The Morning Call* of Allentown, Pennsylvania, which noted that Gehrig planned to keep the streak going "to make things harder for the ballplayers of the present and the future." Columnist John Lardner joked that "The oldest inhabitant of the Bronx would not remember when the New York Yankees last played a game without Gehrig at first base." *The Sporting News* published an editorial that could have doubled as a retirement tribute, concluding with: "Lou Gehrig has already carved his name in heroic letters in the annals of the game, beneath which might fittingly be written: 'His like will never be seen again.'"

A few joined with Eleanor in calling for the streak to stop, however. Lester Rodney in the *Daily Worker* recommended that Gehrig take a vacation. "The darn thing's gotta end some time," he wrote. "How about now, when you plainly show that you could use a rest, Lulu? Go fishing for a week and I'll bet anyone in the office that you bat over .400 the first week you come back."

And a prescient fan of Gehrig's asked in a letter to the *Times*: "What has he to gain by stretching his consecutive play record to 2,500 games? . . . I think the club owners should have the foresight to stop him from injuring his health and his value as a ballplayer before the consequences spoil all the good Gehrig has done for himself and baseball." Under the letter, the *Times* said now that Gehrig had passed the two thousand game mark, he might listen to reason and take a day off when he needed one.

Talking to newspaper reporters before taking the field that day, Gehrig seemed intent on playing down his achievement. "No fuss please, it's just another ball game," he said. At the same time, he made it clear the streak was not going to stop anytime soon. "If I'm out of even an exhibition game, I'm nervous. I'd burn up more energy doing nothing, fishing or hunting, than playing ball," he said. He dismissed a question about lack of rest hurting his overall play: "If the strain was going to tell on me, it would have told on me the last two years, wouldn't it? Well, I hit ten and seven points higher than my lifetime averages [in] those years. I didn't hit early this season, but I'm hitting now."

As it turned out, Lou did very little hitting in that afternoon's game. The biggest noise he made came in the top of the fifth, when Boston's Jimmie Foxx, batting with the bases loaded, slammed a ball down the right-field line and into the stands. Umpire Cal Hubbard called it fair, giving Foxx a grand slam. Gehrig and Bill Dickey vehemently argued the call, and photographers caught Gehrig yelling and waving his arms at Hubbard, whose wide-open mouth suggested he was yelling right back. There wasn't much the Yankees could do about the call in those pre-instant replay days, except keep scoring. That they did despite Gehrig, who walked, grounded out, hit into a double play and popped out in his first four times at bat. In the eighth, with the Yankees leading 8–5, he finally knocked a single into center field, scoring Red Rolfe from third and helping the home team seal the win.

The game ended somewhere in the five o'clock hour, and Gehrig would normally head home soon afterward to get his usual extended sleep. Eleanor reported in her memoir that her husband came back that night carrying a giant horseshoe of flowers and an embarrassed grin, a sight that reduced her to uproarious laughter. And maybe he did, although the photos and film of the day do not show Gehrig receiving such a gift.

What Eleanor and Gehrig's other biographers neglected to mention is that on this evening the Yankee captain stayed out unusually late—not to celebrate his achievement, but to appear on nationwide network radio.

The radio industry of Gehrig's time bears scant resemblance to the one that exists today, where stations target listeners with narrowly-tailored slices of music, talk, sports or news. Nineteen thirty-eight was the height of radio's big-time era when the medium was the top source of in-home entertainment for most Americans and the three major networks—NBC, CBS, and Mutual—pumped out all manner of comedy, drama, news, and variety shows to tens of millions of listeners each day. The networks' prime time shows were big-budget productions that featured hosts, actors, singers, orchestras, announcers and sound effects men, all performing live on the air, often in front of a studio audience. If a program won any kind of popularity, companies like Ford, Firestone, Texaco, Kraft, or Campbell's Soup would step in and pay the bills to tout their products to a vast, unseen audience, unreachable only ten or fifteen years before.

The power of radio was demonstrated several times that year alone: when singer Kate Smith made an instant hit with her performance of Irving Berlin's "God Bless America"; when conductor Arturo Toscanini did the same with Samuel Barber's "Adagio for Strings"; when the nation came to a virtual halt to listen to the showdown between racehorses War Admiral and Seabiscuit. Perhaps the greatest demonstration of the medium's reach and influence came that Halloween night when actor Orson Welles starred in a play based on the science fiction novel *War of the Worlds*. The production, presented in a breaking news format, was so convincing that many listeners briefly believed an alien army from Mars had invaded Earth and was wiping out every police officer, soldier, and national guardsman in the state of New Jersey.

It was no wonder then that some would-be performers froze up in front of the microphone, a phenomenon known as "mike fright." Gehrig claimed after *Rawhide* that acting came easy to him, but his radio appearances tell a different story. During the 1936 World Series, he appeared on a broadcast of *Lux Radio Theater* with Carl Hubbell of the opposing New York Giants. He got through three minutes of scripted banter without mistakes but was stiff as a steel beam, even on silly lines like "Why don't you have dinner with me tomorrow night, Carl? We're having Yankee bean soup and Yankee pot roast." Listeners also likely noticed Gehrig's pronunciation of words like world, which came out *woild,* stamped hard by his New Yawk accent.

The nerves appeared again on July 30th, 1937, when Gehrig appeared on a broadcast of *Ripley's Believe it or Not.* He wasn't there to help present the show's trademark parade of the curious, gruesome and bizarre, but to do a commercial for the show's sponsor, a breakfast cereal known as Huskies. He wouldn't have to say much, just answer questions from the show's announcer, Ford Bond.

Bond asked Lou what he liked to eat for dinner. Lou stayed on script and said he liked a thick, juicy steak.

Bond continued: "And tell me, Lou, what do you like to eat for breakfast?"

Gehrig answered: "There is nothing I like better than a big bowl of Wheaties."

Listeners heard several moments of very painful silence.

Bond finally cut through the tension: "For breakfast, you have, er, Huskies?"

"Yes," said the embarrassed Gehrig, "I have Huskies."

Newspapers reported the mistake across the country, under headlines such as "Lou Gehrig Plugs Wrong Breakfast Food" and "Play Baseball Lou—Stay off Radio!" Huskies shouldn't have been that surprised by the blooper, as Gehrig had previously promoted Wheaties and was even the first athlete to appear on the iconic Wheaties box, in 1934. After the flub, Lou offered to void his eighteen-hundred-dollar Huskies contract and return the money. Instead, the company retained him, figuring the publicity he generated would only help sell the product.

Still, when Gehrig made another appearance on the Ripley program in October 1937, the sponsor took precautions. This time, Ford Bond started by chatting up Lou about his then-upcoming star role in *Rawhide*. Gehrig, reading his lines stiffly, said, "I'm going to have a pretty good role, I guess. But as for being a star, that's another thing. It's pretty tough to make the big leagues in Hollywood."

Bond jumped in: "Well Lou, if you play in as many movies as have you have baseball games, you'll be a star all right. And you can keep in shape out there too if you start the day by diving into a big bowl of . . . *Huskies*."

The audience got the joke and laughed. Gehrig, suddenly relaxing, got an even bigger laugh when he said, "That's a reaaaal load off my mind, Ford." He then nailed the topper like a pro, saying, "Because seriously, I do go for Huskies in a big way. They're the best tasting cereal I ever ate—and I guess I've tried them all!"

On the evening of his two-thousandth straight game, Gehrig went to the NBC studios at Rockefeller Plaza for another appearance on *Ripley's* broadcast at ten P.M. This time, he wasn't just a pitchman; he was the star attraction. A baseball player not missing a game for thirteen consecutive years qualified as a believe-it-or-not event in the minds of the producers. They had Gehrig don his acting hat and dramatize the event that originally put him in the Yankee lineup. No recording of the program is known to exist, but the surviving script shows Gehrig was willing to play along with a fanciful conception of his career.

Host Robert Ripley set the scene for listeners: June 1st, 1925 at Yankee Stadium.

> RIPLEY: "Our scene opens in the Yankee dugout, as the players are seated on the bench waiting for their turn at bat. At one end of the bench, an anxious rookie is seated. Miller Huggins, the pint-sized manager of the Yankees, looks over his players. He needs a pinch-hitter, for the bases are loaded and the Yanks are behind. With a sudden inspiration, he nods to the rookie and says:
>
> HUGGINS (played by an actor): Hey you, big boy. Come here.
>
> GEHRIG: Yes, sir! Want me to go in?
>
> HUGGINS: Yeah, you're going to go in as a pinch-hitter and you'll play first base the next time around.
>
> GEHRIG: Yes, sir! Anything else?
>
> HUGGINS: No, only this—it's up to you! This is your big chance. Go in there and see how long you can last.
>
> GEHRIG: Okay. But don't hold your breath because I feel like I'm going to last a long time!

After the "re-enactment," Ripley asked Gehrig a few questions about his consecutive-games streak. Lou's answers were likely scripted by the show's writers but they do reflect his own thinking. He said playing his two-thousandth consecutive game that day was a "great thrill." He said he consciously tried to build his streak after learning he was near one thousand games and could beat the previous record of thirteen hundred and seven. Asked whether he planned to end the streak, he said: "No days off for me . . . I'm going to stay in there every day as long as the boss thinks I am of value to the team." (Though one suspects Gehrig might change the word "boss" to "manager.")

Ripley couldn't resist milking Gehrig's famous flub one more time.

> RIPLEY: "The last time you were on my program you fumbled sponsors."
>
> GEHRIG: "Yeah, you've got to chalk me up with an error for that one . . . But lightning never strikes twice in the same place, Bob. And let me tell you it's been a pleasure to be on your Huskies program. "
>
> RIPLEY: "Lou, you didn't by any chance say Huskies, did you?
>
> GEHRIG: "Why certainly, Bob."
>
> RIPLEY: "Just in case you don't know it, Lou—we're on [the air] now for Post Bran Flakes."
>
> GEHRIG: "I give up Bob. I better stick to baseball."

In a sign of Gehrig's long-term popularity, a copy of the script for this show sold for four thousand seven hundred dollars at an auction in 1999. The front page of the script bears the ornate and recognizable signature of Ripley, used for years in his newspaper cartoons and TV shows, as well as the forward-leaning signature of Gehrig, with huge loops in the "L" and the "G." A handwriting analyst might look at Gehrig's autograph and conclude that the Iron Horse was confident and optimistic, maybe even a touch grandiose. But then, a little grandiosity might be expected given that a few hours before the broadcast, Gehrig had cemented a singular and lasting place in baseball history.

* * *

After May 31st, the excitement over Gehrig's streak died down. Unfortunately, his bat died down with it. After singling in a 5–2 Yankee win over the Tigers on June 2nd, he went twenty plate appearances without a hit. The slump ended only on June 7th when White Sox outfielder Mike Kreevich lost track of a high fly in the sun and let it fall for a double. When Lou finally showed life the following day, getting three hits and three walks in a double-header, the Yankees dropped both games. In the second game, Gehrig fell while making a throw to home plate and the ball sailed over catcher Arndt Jorgens' head, allowing a run to score.

Gehrig was thumping periodic home runs during this time but all were solo shots and none were the game-changers he had hit so frequently in the past. More often, he was falling short in the clutch. Against the Indians on June 12th, he came up against Bob Feller in the seventh with the bases loaded and the Yankees trailing by one run. Feller induced him to pop up for the third out. On the 18th, against the Browns, he batted in the eighth with two men on and the Yankees losing 1–0. Again, he popped out.

The following day, as the Yankees tried to overcome a six-run deficit in the ninth, Gehrig came to bat with two men on and the Browns' Bobo Newsom on the mound. Gehrig, who was celebrating his thirty-fifth birthday, was 0-for-3 on the day but could make up for it with a bases-clearing hit. Instead, Newsom struck him out, unleashing thunderous applause from the stands, according to the *St. Louis Star and Times*. The Yankees lost 10–9. At the end of the game, two full months into the season, Gehrig had only thirty runs batted in, an almost inconceivably low number for baseball's greatest hitter batting cleanup for the game's most powerful team.

Gehrig hit a homer in the series finale, an 8–4 Yankee win, before the Yanks traveled to Cleveland for a four-game showdown with the Indians. This series might have been the single most frustrating of Gehrig's entire career. Feller was on the mound again for the opener on June 21st, and he wasn't sharp, giving up seven hits and nine walks. But he kept the Indians in the game, in part by shutting down Lou Gehrig. In his initial at-bat, Lou struck out with a runner on first. Next time up, he grounded out with men on second and third.

In the seventh, Gehrig finally got on base, hitting a single to center and advancing to second on an error. When Henrich lined a single off the glove of shortstop Lyn Lary, Gehrig should have taken the easy advance to third. But he decided third base wasn't good enough and came charging around the bag, heading for home. Waiting for him at the plate was Indians catcher Rollie Hemsley, who was about thirty pounds lighter than the Iron Horse.

"Gehrig catapulted his two hundred five pounds of bone and muscle" into Hemsley, reported the *Cleveland Plain Dealer* the next day, under a photo that showed the catcher bracing for impact. "I thought a building fell on me when Gehrig charged into the plate," Hemsley told the newspaper. "I had the plate blocked and tagged him, but the collision almost jarred my teeth loose." It also aggravated a broken finger he was playing with, leaving the digit discolored, puffed and painful. But despite the bone-rattling crash, Hemsley held on to Lary's incoming throw, and umpire Harry Geisel called Gehrig out. The Yankees lost the game.

Hemsley, incidentally, wasn't the only American Leaguer to feel the wrath of a Gehrig slide. Later that year, White Sox third baseman Marv Owen disclosed there were three runners he never tried to block: Rudy York, Hank Greenberg, and Lou Gehrig. "All three of them are bum sliders," he said. "They slide late. They just jump up in the air and come down again without figuring beforehand just how they're going to descend. If you try to block them they'll come down on top of you or blow you over. It would be a wasted effort."

Gehrig was unscathed by the Hemsley collision but was even less effective on June 22nd as the Yanks and Indians played a doubleheader at Cleveland Municipal Stadium. Perhaps he was distracted. A crowd of nearly seventy thousand Indians rooters had swarmed the huge ballpark and filled it with what the *Plain Dealer* called a torrent of "yells, screams, whistles, hand-claps and other reverberating sounds." In game one, Gehrig flied out or popped up four times in a row, leaving several runners stranded and dooming the Yankees to a 3–1 loss. For game two, an unhappy McCarthy demoted him to sixth in the lineup. Gehrig responded with another 0-for-4 effort, grounding into a double play, popping up two more times, and striking out. The Yankees lost again, falling four and a half games out of first place. A photo published by several Ohio newspapers the next day showed Gehrig looking up helplessly as one of his pop flies floated above home plate, destined to plummet into catcher Hemsley's glove.

Gehrig's very un-larrupin' performance dragged his batting average down to .267 and sparked a new round of commentary about his struggles. "How the mighty are fallen!" wrote *Plain Dealer* columnist Gordon Cobbledick the next day in a piece that said "the collapse of Gehrig" was one of the factors short-circuiting the Yankee lineup. The *New York Post* called Gehrig the "big offender" in the Yankee offense and said he was swinging "a bat of straw." *The Sporting News* put Gehrig's struggles on the front page of its June 23rd issue. "Old Iron Horse Not What He Used Be," read the headline. Writer Dan Daniel said Gehrig was experiencing "the worst year of his life in baseball. He cannot get the old swing. He cannot put the old driving power on the ball."

Daniel's article raised the possibility that for the first time, Gehrig would not make the American League All-Star team. Baseball's annual All-Star Game had been played for five years to that point, and Gehrig had been the AL's starter at first base all five times. But Daniel wrote that based on their 1938 performances, Jimmie Foxx was the league's top first baseman, "and Hal Trosky and Hank Greenberg come ahead of Gehrig." There was no arguing the point. The four first basemen's Triple Crown stats, through games of June 22nd:

Foxx . . . . .343, 20 HR, 67 RBI
Trosky . . . . . . .351, 9 HR, 51 RBI
Greenberg . . .298, 17 HR, 36 RBI
Gehrig . . . . . . .267, 10 HR, 35 RBI

If one compares the four in terms of OPS—a stat not conceived in 1938—Foxx also came out on top at 1.152, ahead of Trosky (1.048), Greenberg (1.033) and Gehrig (.900). The Yankees trailed Foxx and Trosky's teams in the standings as well.

Gehrig's numbers ticked up over the next few days; he cracked a homer and two singles in the series finale against the Indians, and then unloaded against Tigers starter Harry Eisenstadt in

Detroit, bashing two doubles and a two-run homer. In the Detroit game, he had to overcome a bit of creative fan interference. “Umpire Bill Summers halted the game in the second inning to have ushers eject some boys from the front rows of the old centerfield bleachers. They were using a mirror to reflect the sunlight into Lou Gehrig’s eyes,” reported the *Detroit Free Press*. As soon as the flashing stopped, the Yankee captain smacked his first two-bagger of the afternoon.

But even on that fine day, his rivals outshone Gehrig. In the same game that Gehrig battered Eisenstadt, Greenberg smashed two home runs and piled up five RBI, powering the Tigers to a 12–8 win. In Cleveland, Trosky slashed out three hits including a game-winning, three-RBI double as the Indians beat the Red Sox 7–6. After the game, Trosky’s batting average stood at .363, second highest in the American League.

The American League was trying out a new All-Star selection process that year, partly in reaction to the alleged “packing” of the AL squad the year before by McCarthy. The Yankee skipper had put five of his own players in the ’37 starting lineup, including Gehrig, and played four of them the entire game, irritating the AL reserves who sat idle and the fans who came to see them play. Under the ’38 system, each of the league’s managers nominated a complete roster of twenty-three players for the All-Star team. The players who received the most “nominations,” or votes, were named to the team, with allowances being made to ensure there were enough players at every position and that each of the eight teams had at least one man on the roster.

So there was more than a little surprise in the baseball world on June 26th when the 1938 All-Star rosters were announced. The American League office never released the ballots of the individual managers or a tally of the overall vote. All people knew was that if the goal was to thwart Yankee domination of the All-Star team, it didn’t work. The Yankees had six players on the squad, more than any other team. No one could quibble with the selections of DiMaggio and Dickey and Ruffing, who were all having fine seasons. But Lefty Gomez? He had been *terrible* most of the first half; at the time of the announcement he had a 4–8 record and 4.77 ERA. And Red Rolfe, he of the four home runs and twenty-four runs batted in? There were at least three third basemen around the league who were producing more runs.

The greatest controversy surrounded the picks for first base. The league said it would take three first sackers to the All-Star Game in Cincinnati, which was a bit surprising itself. But the real surprise was the identity of those three men: Jimmie Foxx, Hank Greenberg and for the sixth year in a row, Henry Louis Gehrig.

Gehrig could not contain his joy at being selected, reported one of the New York dailies.

Some players and sportswriters in other cities could not contain their disgust.

6

All-Star

To understand the dust-up over Lou Gehrig's selection to the 1938 American League All-Star team, one must understand the displeasure, the frustration, the fuming indignation felt by other first basemen in the league who witnessed the All-Star Game every summer, saw Gehrig basking in the glow of huge crowds and national media attention and said, "That should've been me."

The All-Star Game then was no trivial matter. It had originated just a few years before, the brainchild of *Chicago Tribune* sports editor Arch Ward, who wanted to draw extra attention to the 1933 World's Fair in his city. In an era where tradition blocked the idea of inter-league play, the thought of the National and American Leagues' greatest stars going head to head electrified fans. Forty-seven thousand attended the initial contest in Chicago, followed by forty-eight thousand the next year in New York and nearly seventy thousand for the 1935 game in Cleveland. Millions more nationwide listened on the radio. Although it was conceived as a one-time affair, the game quickly turned into an annual event nicknamed the "midsummer classic," a chance for the baseball world to gather and gaze upon its finest players while celebrating baseball itself, then firmly ensconced as America's most popular sport and the national pastime.

Part of the game's appeal was that both leagues took it so seriously. The two "circuits," as they were called, were cooperative but legally separate entities then. They maintained a strong rivalry that stemmed from the American League's birth as a challenger to the established National in 1901. The sides had long made peace in the courts but the players, owners, and officials of each league still vied for on-field supremacy and bragging rights. The American League, in particular, approached the All-Star Game each year as a battle royale. Catcher Rick Ferrell recalled AL manager Connie Mack telling players before the initial '33 contest: "We're going to play to win and I don't want anyone to be disappointed if he doesn't get into the game. If we get ahead, I probably won't change the lineup." On several occasions, the AL's president, Will Harridge, explained his league's resolute attitude toward the game. "The American League has never regarded the All-Star Game as just a parade of stars," he said in 1935. "We have gone into it from the start with determination to win."

The players took the game seriously as well. Most considered it a significant honor just to be picked to represent their league, especially given the small size of the rosters—eighteen men per team in 1933, expanded to twenty in 1935, and twenty-three for the '38 contest. There were also dollars to be made. The players received no extra pay for being All-Stars but in a time before television or the internet, when many regular season games weren't even broadcast on radio, they knew the game could give them valuable national exposure. New York Giants pitcher Carl Hubbell was already a star by 1934, having won twenty-three games and the MVP award a year earlier as the Giants won the World Series. But Hubbell vaulted himself to the realm of celebrity in the '34 game when he struck out five future Hall of Famers in a row: Ruth, Gehrig, Jimmie Foxx, Al Simmons, and Joe Cronin. For the next few years, the Giants' ace enhanced his comfortable seventeen-thousand-dollar salary by endorsing everything from Dodge cars and Wheaties cereal to Pabst-ett cheese spread and Camel cigarettes. The last was a common product for athletes to promote in the 1930s before scientists recognized the link between smoking and lung cancer. Gehrig, a daily smoker, did ads for the same company.

Other players no doubt felt they could reap such rewards if given the chance to shine on the All-Star stage. But if that player was an American League first baseman and his name was not Lou Gehrig, he hadn't a prayer of cracking the starting lineup. In 1933, when fans voted for the starting nines, Lou outpolled his nearest rival, Foxx, more than two to one. In the next four seasons, when managers picked the teams, Lou was named the AL starter at first base each time. In all five years, in keeping with his iron man reputation, he played the full nine innings. He didn't contribute much at bat in the early games, but he made up for it with a home run at the 1936 contest at Braves Field in Boston and a four-RBI day at the 1937 game in Washington, including a two-run homer off future Hall of Famer Dizzy Dean. The runs provided most of the margin in the American League's 8–3 win.

These circumstances left other talented AL first basemen stewing on the sidelines every July. And the American League was packed almost top to bottom with good first basemen in this era. Take the 1936 season, for example:

- The St. Louis Browns had Jim Bottomley at first base. Bottomley enjoyed several Gehrig-like years for the Cardinals in the 1920s, especially 1928, when he led National League in homers and was named MVP. Even in 1936, when he was in his mid-thirties, he was still a solid player, batting .298 with ninety-five RBI. But there was no way Bottomley could make the All-Star team because . . .
- Joe Kuhel was better. Kuhel, who would spend 18 seasons in the majors, mostly with the Senators, enjoyed a career year in '36, batting .321 with one hundred eighteen RBI. His offense helped push Washington to a third-place finish, a strong showing for the often cash-strapped team. But there was no way Kuhel was going to be named an All-Star because . . .
- Zeke Bonura was better. Bonura simply had a monster year in '36, batting .330 with a dozen homers and one hundred thirty-eight RBI for the White Sox. He had a reputation as a weak fielder but led AL first basemen that season in putouts, assists, double plays, and fielding percentage. Still, there was no chance in hell of Bonura making the All-Star team because . . .
- Hal Trosky was better. Trosky played only ten seasons in the majors due to persistent migraine headaches but

looked like a potential Hall of Famer in his early years. In '36, he batted .343 while driving in a league-leading one hundred sixty-two RBI. And yet, he didn't make the All-Star team because . . .

- Jimmie Foxx was better. Foxx had already won two MVP awards with Philadelphia when the A's sold him to Boston ahead of the '36 season. Foxx rewarded his new employer with his usual greatness—.338 batting average, forty-one homers, one hundred forty-three RBI, even a career-high thirteen stolen bases. Foxx did make the All-Star team, but only as a reserve. He wasn't picked to start because . . .
- Lou Gehrig was the best first baseman in baseball that year. Gehrig put together one of his greatest seasons in 1936, bashing a league-topping forty-nine homers while leading the AL in runs, walks, on-base percentage, and slugging percentage. At year's end, he won his second MVP award as the Yankees romped to the pennant and crushed the Giants in the World Series.

But with all apologies to Trosky and company, the undisputed champ in the frustration department was another slugger with the given first name of Henry, also raised in New York. In fact, Henry Benjamin Greenberg, more commonly known as Hank, might have occupied the Yankees' cleanup spot for a generation had Gehrig not gotten there first. After graduating in 1929 from James Monroe High School in the Bronx, where he starred in both baseball and basketball, Greenberg was pursued by legendary Yankee scout Paul Krichell, the same man who signed Gehrig to the team and would later sign Phil Rizzuto and Whitey Ford. As part of his recruitment campaign, Krichell treated the young Greenberg to a game at Yankee Stadium. When Lou came up to bat, Greenberg recalled, Krichell leaned over and said, "He's all washed up. In a few years, you'll be the Yankee first baseman." Greenberg wisely didn't believe a word of it and signed with Detroit.

Four years later, he reached the majors and pummeled American League pitching. One year, he challenged the major league record for doubles in a season. In another, he fell just one

RBI short of Gehrig's AL record. When the Tigers made him their cleanup hitter in 1934, the team won its first pennant in a quarter century, and the next year Greenberg captured the home run title and Most Valuable Player award as Detroit won the World Series.

And yet, by 1938 Greenberg had yet to taste a single inning of All-Star baseball. In 1935, Hammerin' Hank drove in one hundred runs *before* the mid-season break, literally twice as many as Gehrig, who got off to a slow start. But the powers of the American League picked Gehrig to start at first base, and Greenberg didn't even make the roster. Upon being told he was left off the All-Star team, a *Detroit Free Press* reporter said Greenberg expressed "disappointment" and asked some pointed questions: "How many runs has Gehrig batted in? What's he hitting? How many home runs has he?"

AL president Harridge tried to put the best face on the decision. "What we want to do is put the ball club on the field that we believe has the best chance of winning . . . If we picked Greenberg for first base, along with Gehrig, then we'd be top-heavy at that position," he said. He neglected to explain how playing Greenberg at first might hurt the AL's fortunes.

In 1936, Greenberg missed most of the season with a broken wrist. In 1937, he finally made the AL All-Star roster along with Gehrig and Foxx—but manager McCarthy played favorites, keeping Lou at first for the entire game while Greenberg remained idle and Foxx made a lone pinch-hitting appearance. Both Foxx and Greenberg felt deeply slighted. A year later, ahead of the '38 contest, Foxx remarked, "I'll tell you one thing, if I don't play in this one, I'll never go to another." Greenberg, meanwhile, carried a grudge toward McCarthy for half a century. In his autobiography, published in 1987 after his death, Greenberg said, "I was picked for the All-Star team and went to Washington for the game, but I spent it sitting on the bench. All I did was sign autographs for a day and a half. I took the hot train ride from Detroit to Washington and back again . . . I was really annoyed."

Now it was the sportswriters who were annoyed, unable to square Gehrig's placement on the '38 All-Stars with the yawning gap between his run production and those of his peers. A columnist in the June 28th *Philadelphia Inquirer* was especially loud in his objections: "Gehrig? No, nein, non, nit. Whatever has the Iron Horse done this year to entitle him to selection? He is putting on the poorest batting front of his career, which is one of the principal reasons that the Yankees do not occupy the top place." A *Los Angeles Times* writer dismissed Gehrig and Lefty Gomez as "courtesy all-stars," chosen for past glories instead of their 1938 performance: "Gehrig is batting only .275, and how he rates the call over Hal Trosky, batting .355, is hard to understand."

"Columbia Lou has been the worst first sacker in the American League during 1938," wrote a columnist in the *Lafayette* (Indiana) *Journal*. "Lou is batting .275 and even New York writers admit he is playing his worst game in the field . . . We want to know could any other player on any team in baseball, except the Yankees, enter the all-star fracas with the above qualifications?"

Not surprisingly, some especially loud objections came from Trosky's stronghold, Cleveland. The editorial board of the Cleveland *Plain Dealer*—not the sports editor, the overall editorial board—took a direct shot at Gehrig, saying that if he was among the best the Yankees had, the team's failure in their recent series against the Indians was understandable. Trosky also got support from *Plain Dealer* columnist Gordon Cobbledick, who wrote, "Without having interviewed them on the subject, I fancy that Hal Trosky must be wondering what a guy has to do to make the all-star team and that Lou Gehrig must be wondering what a guy has to do to be left off it."

The heat grew intense enough that Harridge issued a statement defending McCarthy. "Mr. McCarthy should not be blamed for the fact that certain players were not named to the team," he said. The final roster was the result of votes by the league's eight managers, he reminded fans. "Only in the event of a tie was the [All-Star] manager permitted to make his choice between the players tying in votes."

Four days before the game, on July 2nd, McCarthy and Harridge were given a chance to make things right with the Troskyites. The Tigers asked the American League office if Greenberg could miss the game; the slugger's wrist was hurting and he needed X-rays, the team said. That wasn't really the case, as Greenberg later admitted in his autobiography. "When the 1938 All-Star Game came up and I was selected—even though I was having kind of a slow season—I refused to go and used those days of the All-Star break to work on my hitting," he wrote. The decision turned out to be a good one. In the first half of the season, Greenberg had hit twenty-two home runs. In the second half, he would slug thirty-six and make a run at breaking Babe Ruth's single-season record.

Harridge urged McCarthy to add Trosky to the roster. It made sense—just replace one first baseman with another and snuff out the controversy. But McCarthy instead chose to add one of his own pitchers, Johnny Murphy. Murphy, nicknamed Grandma, was known as the Yankees' top relief hurler. He was having a fine season, with a 4–0 record, seven saves, and a 2.27 ERA. But in an era when pitchers completed the bulk of their starts, he didn't get much use. On the day he was named to the squad, Murphy had pitched only thirty innings all season.

Trosky was livid. In another age, he might have unleashed his sentiments via Twitter, maybe something short and pointed along the lines of "Pinstripes get all the breaks" or "Numbers don't lie, Joe." Lacking that option, he bottled up his anger and trekked off to his hometown of Norway, Iowa to visit his mother, who had recently suffered a stroke. He would stay out of sight for a few days. His rage wasn't going away, though. Within a few days, the volcano inside him would erupt, blasting its fury in the direction of New York.

* * *

"We're going to, ah, let you hear the noise first, then imagine what's happened." With that, announcer Dick Bray fell silent for one, two, three seconds as a wave of clapping and cheering washed into his microphone. Bray then explained: "Louuuu Gehrig, one of the greatest of all time, is batting for Buddy Lewis, and what a hand he's receiving. Louuuu Gehrig." After Gehrig took an outside pitch for ball one, Bray laid out the scene for his listeners on the Mutual radio network: "You see the big smile on Larrupin' Lou as he walked up to the plate. Takes a stance in the batter's box, faces third base, toes his foot toward right field a little . . ." After another ball, the relatively lo-fi mike picked up a faint *thwack* as Gehrig knocked a grounder past first base. Second baseman Billy Herman scooted over, gloved the ball and threw to Frank McCormick for the out, on what Bray described as a very nice play.

Thus, the Iron Horse entered the 1938 All-Star Game, as a pinch hitter in the top of the fifth inning. It was an unaccustomed task for Lou, who remarkably had not entered *any* game as a substitute for thirteen years, since the earliest weeks of his consecutive games streak. He spent the first four innings of this one on the bench as McCarthy, yielding to popular demand, started Foxx at first base, batting fourth. But it was only a matter of time before the manager restored what he considered the natural order of things. Besides, the American League was trailing 2–0 and had landed only two hits thus far. The team needed a boost, he could argue. When the inning was over, he put Gehrig at first base and moved Foxx over to third.

In truth, Lou really could have used the off-day recommended by some observers. The previous week had been something of a trial. Not only did he have to contend with the harsh press, but after a surge at the end of June—he finished the month with a solid nine home runs, twenty-one RBI—he had fallen back into a mini-slump, hitting mostly singles and striking out unusually often. In an interview published July 3rd, he insisted his streak was not hurting his performance. "Being in there day in and day out hasn't had any bad physical effect at all that I've been able to notice," he said. "I'll be all right. I'm feeling better up at the plate now—looser and easier. It's just one of those things."

However, the last day before the all-star break, July 4th in Washington, made those assurances sound hollow. The Yankees had arrived in town the night before, after a five-hour train trip from New York. Then, the team played a daytime doubleheader against the Senators in humid eighty-degree weather. They won the first game in two hours, but the nightcap stretched on for three, a long game by 1930s standards. The length was partly due to a bang-bang play in the third when Joe Gordon fielded a sharply-hit grounder and threw to Gehrig to nip the Senators' Sammy West at first. West and his teammates ferociously argued the call with umpire Joe Rue, and the crowd showed its solidarity by hurling food and pop bottles at the arbiter, a few of which nearly hit Lou, standing only a few feet away. These bottles were glass, not the plastic variety introduced a few decades later.

No one was hurt, but it took the ground crew fifteen minutes to clear the field. The delay came back to haunt both teams, as the game settled into a 4–4 tie and the umps had to call a halt after thirteen innings because of darkness. Gehrig played all twenty-two innings on the day and managed only a single hit, an RBI single, in ten at-bats. His game two performance must have galled him: no hits in five at-bats, with four men left on base.

Afterward, most of the players could look forward to a few days of rest. But Gehrig and his fellow all-stars had to take another train, a ten-hour ride westward to Cincinnati. At least there was a novelty aspect to the trip; Cincy was one of the few cities in the majors that didn't have both National and American League teams. So this may have been Lou's first visit to Crosley Field, home of the National League Reds.

He arrived in Cincinnati to find a city going gaga at the prospect of seeing him and the other luminaries. The Reds had received over one hundred forty thousand ticket requests for the twenty-eight thousand seats in their little ballpark. With demand far outstripping supply, scalpers had a field day, selling two-dollar tickets for as much as twenty bucks. Meanwhile, hundreds of autograph hounds and picture takers stalked the lobby and sidewalks of the Netherlands Plaza Hotel where the visiting players were lodged. Some players obliged, and "a female candid camera addict had the National League eating out of her hand," noted *The Cincinnati Post.* On game day, the *Post* published its own two-page photo spread of the all-stars in its sports section. Lou's picture loomed larger than any other player's.

Gehrig no doubt found Crosley Field to be small and quirky as Yankee Stadium was vast and majestic. The stadium's seating capacity was one-third of the Yankees' edifice, and a renovation the previous winter had reduced the distance between home plate and the center field fence to three hundred and eighty-seven feet, the shortest in the majors. The field itself sat several feet below street level, a feature that allowed the Mill Creek River to inundate the stadium during a 1937 flood. (For a laugh, Reds pitcher

Lee Grissom and groundskeeper Matty Schwab rowed a boat out to the pitcher's mound.) The stadium's most famous idiosyncrasy was in the outfield; the ground sloped upward a few feet in front of the walls as a kind of warning track. Locals referred to the slope as the incline, the embankment, or the terrace. Visiting outfielders who sometimes tripped on it called it a hazard, or names unprintable in a family newspaper. Only the Reds' outfielders were familiar enough with the hill to play it well—a fact that would impact Gehrig's day before it was through.

Crosley was ahead of other stadiums in just one significant way: electric lights. The Reds became the first major league team to install lights during the 1935 season, and the increased attendance from night games saved the club from bankruptcy. Lou was undoubtedly glad the All-Star Game was to be played in the daytime. He didn't like night baseball, as he stated in a 1939 interview. "You can't see what you call the spin on the ball," he said. "You see, it looks faster than it really is, and your timing's slightly off."

If his struggles and the recent criticism were bothering him, Lou showed no signs of it after arriving in Cincinnati. He uttered no complaints about not starting. He confidently predicted the Yankees would capture the American League pennant. ("We'll catch the Indians and hold them off all right.") He admitted to being thrilled when Hubbell mowed down the AL's best in the '34 game. ("That exhibition of pitching by Hubbell was amazing.") During batting practice, he slammed three balls in a row into the right-field bleachers. And upon taking the field in the sixth, he prevented the NL from extending its lead, scooping a low throw from shortstop Cronin out of the dirt to retire Ernie Lombardi for the last out and prevent a runner from scoring from third.

Bob Elson from Chicago station WGN had assumed the announcing duties by the time Gehrig came to bat again in the top of the seventh with two outs. "Here's Lou Gehrig coming up, swinging a couple of bats," he said as the Yankee captain approached the plate. Gehrig's opponent was Mace Brown of the Pirates, a righty relief specialist who was having a career year, notching eleven victories during the first half of the season. The American League was still down 2–0 but DiMaggio stood on second, with

Cronin occupying first. A double could tie the game; a home run would give the AL the lead.

However, "Columbia Lou," as Elson called him, could not strike the killing blow. After taking a ball inside and a strike at the knees, he slapped a grounder to the right of shortstop Leo Durocher. The AL caught a break when Durocher fumbled the ball, allowing Gehrig to reach first and the other runners to advance. But the rally fizzled when Brown struck out Detroit slugger Rudy York on a three-two count.

The National League had extended its lead to 4–0 by the time Lou came up again in the ninth. The two additional runs came in the eighth on a freak play, an "infield homer" by Durocher. With the Reds' Frank McCormick on first, the Cards' shortstop bunted, prompting first baseman Gehrig and third baseman Foxx to charge the plate. The ball went straight to Foxx, who picked up cleanly and fired to first, but in the words of Elson, "ooops—he threw it away!" Second baseman Charlie Gehringer had failed to cover the bag. A bad bounce into right field and a bad throw by DiMaggio into the dugout allowed both McCormick and Durocher to come around and score.

At the start of the ninth, Elson opined that "American League chances are remote, to say the least." But DiMaggio led off the inning with a single, and after Dickey flied out deep to left, Cronin slashed a double, driving in Joe D. That brought Lou to the plate again to face a tiring Mace Brown. A home run would cut the NL lead to one. Lou laid off Brown's first three pitches, working the count to two balls, one strike. On the fourth, he saw something he liked and summoned some of the old power, smashing a line drive toward the right-field wall, three hundred sixty-five feet away. The only thing standing between ball and fence was Ival Goodman, a first-time all-star who also happened to be the Reds' regular right fielder.

"He hits a long fly ball, Goodman the right fielder goes back . . . he caught it!" Elson exclaimed as the crowd roared. "Gehrig slammed a long fly ball way back into right field, and Goodman ran up the embankment, leaped up and caught it for the second out. The ball was hit *very* hard." The *Cincinnati Post* suggested the next day that only Goodman, with his "super-knowledge" of how to play the right-field incline, could have caught the ball.

The Reds' outfielder undoubtedly had an advantage, being familiar with the slope. Would the ball have fallen in if Goodman wasn't in the game? Would it have soared over his head and into the stands if ALS wasn't sapping the strength from Lou's mighty frame? There's no way to know.

Cronin scampered to third on the play but the game ended minutes later as Brown struck out Philadelphia A's outfielder Bob Johnson. With that, fans poured onto the field, as they often did in those innocent days, to congratulate the all-stars or get their autograph, Gehrig no doubt being a target. Afterward, the players retreated to a clubhouse that *Cincinnati Enquirer* writer Lou Smith reported as quiet. "There wasn't much noise in the dressing room, but Larrupin' Lou Gehrig, who's been in all of them, said there never is much after the All-Star games, win or lose," Smith wrote. "They [the players] don't know each other too well, being enemies five months out of the year and allies only the one day," Smith wrote.

Asked why the National League triumphed, Lou offered sports' most ancient cliché: "They had the better club today."

* * *

By the next morning, Lou and his fellow Yankee all-stars were on their third long train ride in five days, heading north and east to Boston, where the Yankees began a three-game set that Friday. The Bronx Bombers would tag Red Sox pitching for twenty-three runs that weekend but get only one RBI from Gehrig, on a sacrifice fly. The Iron Horse drew six walks in the series, including four in one game, an indication perhaps that Boston was pitching around him—or that he was saving his swings and his strength.

After the Boston series, the *New York Post* ran an article speculating on Lou's future. "Many fans wondering if club's Iron Horse Is definitely fading," read the subhead. Gehrig tried to put those thoughts to rest the next day, slamming a line-drive home run and pulling off a rare bunt RBI single as the Yankees swept a doubleheader from the Browns. The *Post* effectively retracted its criticism with a new article, entitled "Gehrig Smacks Critics in Eye With Stellar Performance."

The Yankees had been heading to Boston when Hal Trosky finally blew his top. After visiting his mother in eastern Iowa, Trosky was traveling back to Cleveland when a reporter caught up with him at an Iowa City airport and asked about the All-Star Game snub. Trosky pulled no punches. "I'm glad they got beat," he said, referring to the AL squad. "It served them right. The American League's lineup was composed of a bunch of old cronies—washed up ballplayers who have seen their best days, especially with the bat."

In case there was any doubt who he was talking about, Trosky named names. "Look at Gehrig," he said. "He hasn't been hitting a lick all season and they name him to the lineup just because he's played in two thousand five hundred ball games and the other five All-Star contests. They think they owe it to him. Well, if that's the way they feel about it ok. But if they want an all-star game why don't they make it an all-star game?"

With those impolitic comments, Trosky effectively killed his chances of ever making the AL all-star team, even during his fine 1939 and 1940 seasons. But the fact is that regarding Lou, his remarks were largely on-target. The Iron Horse *was* getting older, he wasn't really hitting, and a lot of observers were saying he was over the hill. There was still no sign that McCarthy was seriously listening to any of this, or that he was thinking about removing Gehrig from the lineup. But Lou had to see the overall trend. For the first time since he began playing every day thirteen years before, there were people who wanted him off the field.

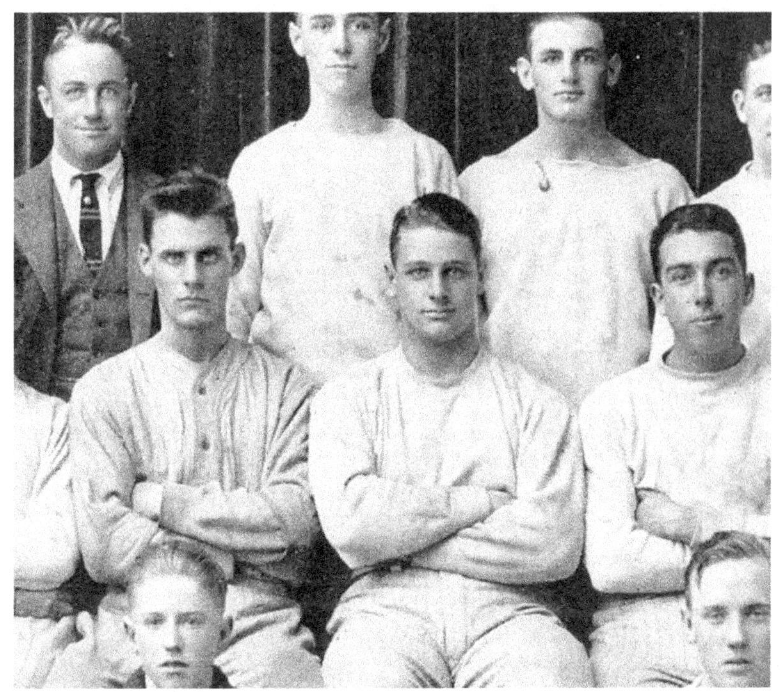

Gehrig on his High School of Commerce baseball team. By age sixteen, he was getting a reputation as "another Babe Ruth." (1920 High School of Commerce yearbook.)

As pictured in his high school yearbook. The "H" is for Henry, Gehrig's real first name. (1921 High School of Commerce yearbook.)

Playing for Columbia University, 1923. Gehrig had to sit out the '22 season after playing professionally under an assumed name. (Columbia University.)

In his lone season with Columbia, Gehrig crushed seven home runs in nineteen games. The Yankees signed him for a $1,500 bonus as soon as the season ended. (Columbia University.)

Gehrig played the offensive line for the Columbia Lions football squad in the fall of '22, and made the yearbook, although he left school before graduating. (The 1923 Columbian.)

Gehrig dons the Yankee pinstripes, 1923. (Brooklyn Daily Eagle.)

Blink and you'll miss it: Gehrig peers through a car window (right) during Babe Ruth's scene in the 1928 silent movie classic Speedy, *starring Harold Lloyd. (Screenshot,* Speedy.*)*

The heart of Murderer's Row, circa 1930: Gehrig, Ruth, and Yankee second baseman Tony Lazzeri. (New York Public Library.)

Lou donned caveman gear in October 1936 in hopes of landing the lead role in the next Tarzan movie. Producer Sol Lesser didn't picture him swinging from trees but was impressed enough to invite him to Hollywood. (Publicity photo.)

Topping his dark suit with a cowboy hat, Lou chats with newsmen in the opening scene of Rawhide, *his 1938 Western. (Screenshot,* Rawhide.*)*

Babe Ruth, in retirement, watching a game from the stands. (Universal Newsreel Library, National Archives.)

Joe DiMaggio, 1939 World Series. (Universal Newsreel Library, National Archives.)

Lou in his prime, at the 1937 All-Star Game in Washington. Left to right: Gehrig, Joe Cronin, Bill Dickey, Joe DiMaggio, Charlie Gehringer, Jimmie Foxx and Hank Greenberg. All seven are in the Hall of Fame. (Harris & Ewing Collection, Library of Congress.)

A sweaty Lou puts on a smile for the newsreel cameras during spring training, March 1939. Behind the scenes, Lou and the Yankees were growing alarmed at his weak hitting and even weaker fielding. He would remove himself from the lineup on May 2. (Universal Newsreel Library, National Archives.)

Yankee general manager Ed Barrow steadies Lou as they listen to the tributes on Gehrig Appreciation Day, July 4, 1939. (Universal Newsreel Library, National Archives.)

Gehrig delivers the speech he is best remembered for: "Today, I consider myself the luckiest man on the face of the Earth." (Universal Newsreel Library, National Archives.)

Gehrig made multiple appearances at the 1939–40 World's Fair in New York. Here he signs cards from the fair's "sports school" for admiring kids. (New York Public Library.)

Playing umpire with Yankee catcher Bill Dickey and the president of the World's Fair, Grover Whalen, 1939. (New York Public Library.)

Lou tests out a fishing rod as a concerned Eleanor Gehrig and Whalen look on, 1939. (New York Public Library.)

Gehrig looks wistfully at the field from the Yankee Stadium dugout during the 1939 World Series. A year earlier, he was still in the lineup despite the creeping effects of ALS. Now he could no longer play, but traveled with the Yankees all year as the team won its fourth straight championship. (Universal Newsreel Library, National Archives.)

7

Reversal

On July 17th, as the Yankees played the finale of a three-game series against Detroit, Lou was thrown at and knocked down by one of the surliest pitchers in the American League. Oddly enough, it was a member of his own team.

The incident happened in the bottom of the fourth inning, as Tiger outfielder Chet Morgan dropped a bunt in front of home plate. The Yankee pitcher was Spud Chandler, a former University of Georgia football player known for brushback pitches, hard slides and stomping on the mound. A magazine profile once called him the team's "angry ace." Chandler wasn't angry at Lou—but seeing the bunt, he picked up the ball and fired it hard to first base. The throw bounced off Lou's glove, putting Morgan on base with what the official scorer termed a single, and leaving the Yankee first sacker in severe pain around his right thumb. He toughed it out for another two innings and even batted in the fifth, flying out to center. But come the seventh inning, with the Yankees sailing to a 16–3 victory, Lou was replaced by backup Babe Dahlgren. The mere fact that the Iron Man had departed early was news, noted in accounts of the game the next day. "Gehrig Hurts Finger" was a common headline.

Most papers carried a wrap-up provided by the wire services, but at least two gave readers more details. The *Brooklyn Daily Eagle* reported that Gehrig lost the throw from Chandler because of a "white background"—presumably the shirts of people in the crowd—and jammed the thumb on his gloved hand, giving him a painful bruise. The *Detroit Free Press* gave a more extensive account that hinted at Lou's deteriorating condition: "When Morgan dropped a single in front of the plate in the fourth, Chandler threw the ball to first so hard that it went through Lou's hands and struck him in the stomach, scoring a clean knock-down." Even the best fielders drop a throw now and then. Yet it's hard to imagine a healthy Gehrig letting a throw whack in the stomach, let alone put him on the ground.

That night, Lou Gehrig was X-rayed at New York's St. Vincent Hospital, and doctors found a fracture in the thumb. He was outfitted with a cast, but as usual, he shrugged off any suggestion that he might miss a game. It helped that Monday the 18th was an open day on the schedule, giving Lou's powers of recuperation a chance to work. When the afternoon of the 19th arrived, he reported to Yankee Stadium as always, ready to play. *New York Sun* columnist Frank Graham caught up with him before the game and in his column the next day, sketched the portrait of a man quietly soldiering through his troubles.

> Under the stand, at the foot of the steps leading down from the Yankee dugout, Lou Gehrig was sitting on the concrete base of a girder, smoking a cigarette.
>
> "Is the thumb broken, Lou?" a newspaperman asked.
>
> "Yep," Lou said, smiling. "She's broken."
>
> "What are they going to do—put it in a splint?"
>
> "It was in a splint," Lou said. "They took it out."
>
> "You're not going to play today, are you?"
>
> "Sure," Lou said. "Why not?"
>
> On the bench, the Yankees watched the Indians in the last few minutes of their fielding practice, and coach Arthur Fletcher was yelling at the Indian players. Nobody paid any attention to him, but he kept right on yelling. Gehrig, having finished his smoke, came up and sat down on the end of the bench near the water cooler.
>
> [When the Indians finished] the Yankees trooped up out of the dugout to take their fielding practice, leaving Gehrig sitting alone in his corner.
>
> "What are you going to do, Lou—play one inning to preserve your record?" a newspaperman asked.

"One inning?" Lou said. "I should say not."

"What—the whole game?"

"Sure," Lou said. "If I didn't feel like playing more than one inning I would go home now and go fishing."

[Former Yankee turned Indian] Johnny Allen, who had been shagging flies in the outfield, stopped at the end of the dugout on his way to the clubhouse . . . Allen looked down the bench to where Gehrig sat alone, huge bare arms folded.

"What's the matter, Lou? Not getting tired, are you?"

Lou, staring out at the field, grinned but didn't say anything.

"Can you imagine that?" Allen said. "He's only been playing every day for twenty years, and he's getting tired. A sissy, I guess. The real old guys in the league like [Goose] Goslin are just getting warmed up and having fun and this guy is sitting there taking it easy while all the other ballplayers are out there running around. What's the matter, Lou? No guts?"

Gehrig, still staring across the field, grinned but remained silent.

"Come on Lou," one of the newspaper men said. "Say something in your defense."

Gehrig laughed. "I can't think of anything to say," he said.

Lou, true to his word, played the entire contest that day. It was not one of his best games. Three times he came to bat with men on base, and all three times he made an out sans RBI. Mel Harder pitched the Indians to a 5–3 victory, inching them to just a half-game behind the first-place Yankees. After the game, Gehrig was given a new cast, no doubt as he puffed on another cigarette.

The thumb injury and his determination to play through it sparked one of the most direct and vicious attacks on Lou in his entire career. Henry McLemore was a well-known newspaper columnist who in 1938 worked for the United Press wire service. He covered both sports and news events, coupling lively, descriptive writing with a biting wit and an almost cynical tone. Sometimes his writing crossed the line into plain meanness. A few years hence, after the Japanese attack on Pearl Harbor, he would support a successful campaign to send Japanese-Americans to internment camps. "I am for immediate removal of every Japanese on the West Coast to a point deep in the interior," he wrote in January 1942. "I don't mean a nice part of the interior, either. Herd 'em up, pack 'em off and give 'em the inside room in the badlands. Let 'em be pinched, hurt, hungry and dead up against it."

In his July 20th, 1938 column, McLemore called for the removal of Lou Gehrig too. He acknowledged in the top paragraph that his opinion would get him labeled as a "heretic" in many quarters, but pressed on and laid out his disdain for Lou's consecutive-game streak.

> "To come right out and say so, I consider Gehrig's insistence on playing even when he has fractured bones (such as he now has), concussions, fever and the all-around miseries as abnormal and none too flattering. Usually, it is the dumb or the desperate who continue to carry on while in pain. The human thing to do when you're hurt is to take it easy, not pull out all the stops marked "heroic."
>
> Granting that Gehrig's refusal to give in and miss a game when he is injured is good for his scrapbook and ego, I wonder if it is good for his team? There have been times, when Lou was younger and better, when he was a better first baseman injured than anyone who could have been put in to replace him. But I doubt that is true today. He knocked but one ball out of the [in]field against the Indians in a crucial game Monday and it was plain that he was favoring his badly swollen thumb.

He concluded:

> I think Gehrig would do the game a great favor if he would just up and go fishing one afternoon a week. If he hasn't any tackle I would be glad to lend him some, and I might even throw in a can of worms to boot.

Softer but similar commentary came from Lester Rodney of the *Daily Worker*, who wrote that "Manager McCarthy should be criticized for not saying 'OK Tarzan, take a few days off while

Dahlgren plays first base." Edward Murphy of the *Sun* also chimed in: "If he continues to go through hitless games, the Yankees, of course, will suffer."

Gehrig got ample opportunity to peruse the papers and read all the criticism, because starting on July 20th the weather gods cursed Yankee Stadium with four straight days of rain, wiping out the remainder of the Cleveland series and the start of the team's next series against the White Sox. Of course, Lou may have found the respite a blessing. The time off allowed his thumb to partially heal and gave the rest of his body a chance to recover from the rigors of the long season as well.

The only downside is that the cancellations, combined with the many rainouts from earlier in the season, would give the Yankees a long string of doubleheaders in the coming weeks. Two on July 24th and 26th. Another on July 31st. And then, starting in mid-August, ten twin bills in sixteen days, all of them to be played under the sun at the hottest time of the year. It may be the single most grueling stretch of doubleheaders the Yankees or any other team ever faced. Lou, if he wanted to maintain his streak, would have to play both games in all of them. It was a tall order for a ballplayer of any age. It would be harder still for a thirty-five-year-old who unknowingly was starting to feel the effects of ALS.

* * *

The first day back, the July 24th doubleheader against the White Sox, was another rough afternoon for Lou. In game one, he came up with no score and DiMaggio on second. He hit a tapper back to pitcher Thornton Lee, a made-to-order easy out—but Lee, a poor fielder, threw it past the first baseman, allowing DiMaggio to score and for Lou to replace him on second. Bill Dickey then followed with a double, and Lou came around to score as well. The two runs were all the Yankees needed as Gomez tossed a six-hit shutout. The Yankees dropped the nightcap, however, and Lou got no hits in either game.

The following day the Yankees began a two-week road trip, and upon reaching St. Louis, Gehrig launched a modest ten-game hitting streak, helped no doubt by batter-friendly Sportsman's

Park and the Browns' pitiful pitching. In the second game of the series, he doubled and enjoyed his first four-RBI day of the season. In the third game, he blasted his first homer in two weeks, lofting the ball onto the right-field pavilion roof. In the series finale, he homered again. "Even with a broken thumb he is dangerous," opined J. Roy Stockton in the *St. Louis Post-Dispatch.* The Yankees took three of four from the Browns, and Lou must have boarded the train out of St. Louis a little hopeful his slump was finally over.

But it wasn't—not really. All of his hits in the next six games were singles and produced only three RBI. The Yankees kept winning and stayed ahead of Cleveland, but had an ongoing power shortage in the middle of their batting order. "Unless Lou Gehrig perks up he is unlikely to bat in his customary one hundred runs this season," Associated Press reporter Sid Feder wrote in a late July column. It was true. At the end of that month, Lou had sixty RBI—a fine total for most ballplayers, but not the Yankee captain. At the same point the previous year, he had eighty-three RBI. At the end of July 1936, he had ninety-seven.

Another Gehrig-successor story popped up the same week. Several newspapers reported the Yankees were grooming Ed Levy, a twenty-one-year-old playing Class A ball, to replace the Iron Horse. "The latter is still in there, but this season he showed definite signs of faltering as his hitting fell off and his play afield slowed," read one report. Levy, a six-foot-five Florida native, was indeed having a fine season for the Yankees' Binghamton, New York farm club, clubbing a dozen homers to go along with a .318 batting average. But the success may have gone to his head. The following spring, Levy would tell reporters, "I'm going to be the greatest right-handed first baseman that ever lived." He also had the nerve to hold out for a higher salary before reaching the majors. It would be another three years before Levy made the Yankees, and when he finally did he batted a lowly .215 over parts of two seasons.

Only a couple of developments might have distracted Lou from his struggles as August began. One was his undiminished popularity. In mid-July, the Kellogg's cereal company ran a promotion asking baseball fans to pick their favorite player at each position, for an "All-America Baseball Team." Fans could submit their votes at grocery stories. Lou won the first base position in a landslide, getting nearly twice as many votes as his closest competitors, Jimmie Foxx and Hank Greenberg, according to the company. Unlike many popularity polls, this one came with a real gift, a new Buick sedan, presented to Gehrig before a mid-August game at Yankee Stadium.

AP reported the story this way: "Henry Louis Gehrig may be in the worst slump of his fourteen-year major league career but he is still the People's Choice for first base."

Lou was shocked to get picked and made his feelings known in a letter sent to and published by *The Sporting News*. The letter stands out as one of the most emotional statements he ever wrote or said. It was written for public consumption, and its elegant phrasing suggests Eleanor helped to compose it. But the sentiments unquestionably came straight from Lou, and they hinted at the toll his subpar hitting was taking on his psyche:

> "I hope it does not sound untruthful to say the award came as a complete surprise. Wallowing in the worst slump of my career, it did not occur to me that the fans would think of me as a prospect for the honor. When the news came, the encouragement it gave me cannot be described by a mere phrasing of words. The feeling was so deep and profound that long after my career is ended, there will always be that warming remembrance of a great tribute paid me by the fans when psychologically I needed it most.
>
> "In the future, I shall do everything possible, both on and off the ball field, to justify their faith, and I want them to know that whatever success I may yet achieve will be due to their encouragement at this time."

Then there was the Jake Powell affair. Powell was an outfielder from Maryland who the Yankees acquired from the Senators in a June 1936 trade. In two-plus years as a Yankee, Powell had shown himself to be a good fielder and capable hitter, though he gradually lost playing time to Tommy Henrich, who had more of a power stroke. In terms of his accomplishments, he was best known as a surprise hero of the 1936 World Series, when he lashed out ten hits in six games, including a go-ahead home run in the Yankees' clinching victory.

But what Powell was really known for was his hot temper and aggressive, sometimes dirty play. In April 1936, while still with the Senators, he crashed into Hank Greenberg's outstretched arm on a close play at first base, breaking Greenberg's wrist and knocking the Tigers' first baseman out for the entire season. On July 3rd, 1937 in Washington, he ran into his former teammate Joe Kuhel on another play at first, prompting Senators faithful to hurl expletives and objects from the stands. Despite the fans' protests, Powell stayed in the game and scored the winning run. That outcome only angered the Senators, and when the teams met again a week later, Kuhel and Powell got into a mid-game fistfight. Powell got the better of the exchange, judging from a wire photo that showed the Yankee landing a solid right to Kuhel's jaw. Tolerance for hostilities in baseball was much higher then, and while both players were thrown out of the game, the only subsequent punishment they got was a twenty-five-dollar fine.

The American League was less lenient with Powell in May 1938 when he turned his fists on Red Sox manager and shortstop Joe Cronin in an on-field altercation. The two had bad blood going back several years when Cronin managed the Senators. Perhaps because Cronin was a manager, or because league powers were getting tired of his antics, AL president Will Harridge handed Powell a three-game suspension in addition to fining him another twenty-five dollars.

All this was in the background when the Yankees went to Chicago for a four-game series at the end of July. Before the first game on the 29th, Powell gave a live interview to WGN radio's Bob Elson, the same announcer who called the All-Star Game. Everything went fine until Elson asked how Powell stayed in shape during the off-season. Powell responded: "I'm a policeman in Dayton, Ohio and I keep in shape by cracking niggers on the head with my nightstick."

WGN quickly cut off the interview but was barraged by outraged callers, prompting several on-air apologies that emphasized the live, uncontrollable nature of the broadcast. The next day, three local black civic groups filed a protest with baseball commissioner Judge Kenesaw Mountain Landis, saying Powell had "insulted twelve million Negro citizens" and should be barred from playing professional ball ever again.

Landis—a tacit supporter of baseball's longstanding ban on black players—refused to go that far but suspended Powell for ten days. In a statement, he said Powell had made "unethical and disparaging remarks" but added that he believed the comments were made more out of carelessness than intent. Yankee general manager Ed Barrow echoed that comment, saying Powell's remark was a slip of the tongue that caused him "to say something that he did not mean at all." And Yankee manager Joe McCarthy sidestepped the central issue, saying that radio stations should stop doing live interviews of ballplayers unless the interview followed a script, and managers got to see the script in advance.

Such was the stance of baseball toward racism in 1938.

Lou, incidentally, appeared to bear no animus against black people. In his younger years, he often took the field in post-season exhibition games against Negro League teams. In October 1927, he and Babe Ruth played a game in Trenton, New Jersey against the Royal Giants, a team in the Eastern Colored League. The Babe hit three home runs in the game; Lou managed a single and double. In October 1929, a Gehrig-led team of big leaguers played a doubleheader at a field in the Bronx against the Lincoln Giants, another team from the ECL, this one managed by future Hall of Famer John Henry Lloyd. Playing in front of eight thousand fans, the teams split the games, with Lou hitting what *The New York Age* reported as the "longest home run ever made at this park" in game one. Lou, who had done some pitching in college, then started and won game two.

Without making a point of it, Lou also voiced support for ending the ban on black players. *Daily News* columnist Jimmy Powers polled major leaguers about the subject at a February 1933 awards banquet. "The only important man present vetoing it was the guest of honor, John J. McGraw," he wrote. "The others—Branch Rickey of the Cardinals, John Heydler president of the National League, Jacob Ruppert of the Yankees, Frankie Frisch, Herb Pennock, Lou Gehrig—all displayed a refreshing open-mindedness."

In any case, Powell's suspension made no difference to the Yankees, who swept the White Sox four straight, then went to Detroit and took two of three from the Tigers. The Yankee lead was two and a half games as the team went into Cleveland for a crucial three-game set. Some sportswriters cast the series as a showdown for the pennant. The Indians were expecting gigantic crowds, the biggest in team history. The Yankees saw the series as an opportunity to show the league they were still the best. The Yankees' first baseman? He just wanted his bat to wake up.

* * *

In the 1930s and for many decades afterward, newspapers often published a complete index of major league players and their statistics every Sunday, with the players listed top to bottom according to their batting average. If Lou opened a sports section on the morning of August 7th and ran his finger down the list, he would have found himself in the middle of the pack, among the fair-to-decent hitters—guys good enough to stay in the lineup but vulnerable to a benching if their performance slipped much further. An 0-for-4 performance the previous day deflated his batting average to .274. He had remained stuck on seventeen home runs since the St. Louis series and had sixty-three RBI. Not since 1926, the year before his big breakthrough, had Gehrig's stats been so ordinary.

More advanced statistics that virtually no one tracked back then would have given him a slightly rosier picture. His on-base percentage was a very respectable .398, and his OPS (on-base plus slugging percentage) stood at a solid .884. Still, there was no question he was playing below his usual standard and being outclassed by his top rivals, Jimmie Foxx and Hank Greenberg. Greenberg was on a home run tear, having crushed fifteen round-trippers since July 1st alone. Foxx had driven in two more runs the day before, increasing his RBI total to one hundred seven, the best in either league.

The Yankees had won the first two games of the Cleveland series, 6–1 and 7–3, maintaining their hold on first place and edging away from the Indians. But the bats of DiMaggio, Dickey, and Gordon were doing most of the work. A more productive Gehrig was needed to keep the Yankee train running at high speed.

Over fifty-six thousand fans poured into Cleveland Municipal Stadium that afternoon to see if the Indians could regain some momentum. Mel Harder, an ace curveballer and two-time twenty-game winner, was back on the mound for the Indians. Harder had already beaten the Yankees twice that season, including the game three weeks earlier that Lou played with a fractured thumb. Lou had struggled against the veteran Cleveland righty all year, scratching out a lone single in eleven at-bats. But his thumb was better now, and suddenly he looked more comfortable at the plate. In his first at-bat, he blasted one of Harder's offerings to deep right-center, where it fell in just beyond the outstretched glove of center fielder Earl Averill. Lou rumbled around the bases for a triple, his third of the season.

The Yankees could not push him across, so the game was still scoreless when Lou came up again in the fourth. DiMaggio had just reached base on a pop fly that dropped into short center field, only the second Yankee hit of the day. Harder went to his bread and butter, an inside curve. But Lou wasn't fooled and belted the ball into the right-field stands to give the Yankees a lead they never relinquished. "To all intents, Gehrig won the ball game with his smash into the seats," wrote Gordon Cobbledick of the Cleveland *Plain Dealer* in his report the next day. Final score: Yankees 7, Indians 0.

The two long hits set off one of the most extraordinary stretches of Lou's extraordinary career. For the next three weeks, he again was the fearsome hitter who wowed his teammates and terrorized American League pitchers. It was as though the clock had been turned back two years, to his last MVP season, or even a decade, to the awesome peak years of the Ruth-Gehrig Murderer's Row. You could call it the Indian summer of a great Yankee's career.

On August 10th in Washington, the Senators jumped out to an early 2–0 lead, and pitcher Chief Hogsett retired Lou on a groundout in the first, stranding two Yankee runners. But he had no such luck in the second when Lou singled in Red Rolfe with two outs, or in the fifth, when Lou doubled and came around to score. Reliever Pete Appleton didn't do much better, giving up an RBI single to the resurgent Iron Horse in the sixth. The lead seesawed between the teams before the Yankees pushed across the winning run in the tenth on a rally aided by a Gehrig walk.

The Philadelphia A's were the next team to feel the wrath of Lou's revived bat. The A's came to New York on August 12th for the first of the ten doubleheaders the Yankees would play in the next two and a half weeks. Lou went hitless in game one, a Philadelphia 5–4 victory, but battered the poor A's pitching staff in the nightcap. In the second, he crushed a home run off starter Buck Ross. In the fourth, he singled off first baseman Lou Finney's glove to drive in DiMaggio and scored on a Selkirk home run. In the fifth, he singled again. In the sixth, batting with the bases loaded, he hit what the *Philadelphia Inquirer* called a "looping left field double" that drove in Henrich and DiMaggio. He had potential to do still more damage in the seventh, coming up with no outs and two men on but lined out to first. The final numbers on the day: four hits, four RBI, easily Lou's best performance of 1938 to date. The Yankees won 16–3.

Two days later, Lou helped carry the Yankees to a doubleheader sweep. In game one, he homered off one of the A's more respectable pitchers, Bud Thomas, and tied the score in the eighth inning with a triple that drove in Henrich. In game two, he connected for a single, double and another homer, this one a two-run shot. The Yanks breezed 9–2, increasing their lead over Cleveland to seven and a half games.

"He is the menace of old," wrote Rud Rennie of the *New York Herald Tribune* in a story published the next day. "The fans sense it. They greeted him yesterday with those burst of hurrahs which they reserve for strong men whom they expect to do big things. Lou has not had many such receptions this year. But he is getting them now."

All this was just the warmup for the afternoon of August 16th. The Yankees were now in Washington for another doubleheader. Game one was scoreless in the second when Lou batted and was promptly hit by a pitch from rookie starter Ken Chase. The beaning caused no injury to the Iron Horse. Judging from subsequent events, however, getting hit may have gotten him fired up:

- After taking first on the hit-by-pitch, Lou advanced to second on a passed ball and came around to score on a Gordon double. *Score: Yankees 1, Senators 0.*
- When he batted in the fourth, Lou lashed his own double to left off Chase, driving in DiMaggio from first. He scored again minutes later on another hit from Gordon. *Yankees 3, Senators 0.*
- The Yankees batted around in that inning, ousting Chase. His replacement, Chief Hogsett, intentionally walked DiMaggio to pitch to Lou. The Yankee captain made Hogsett pay, blasting a two-out homer to right that scored DiMaggio, Rolfe and himself. *Yankees 10, Senators 0.*
- In the sixth, Lou singled off Pete Appleton, pushing DiMaggio to third. Both men subsequently scored, with Lou galloping in from first on a Joe Glenn triple. *Yankees 14, Senators 0.*
- In the seventh, Lou singled off Appleton again, this time driving in Myril Hoag. *Yankees 15, Senators 0.*

And after seven innings, Gehrig rested. Babe Dahlgren played the last two innings at first in the 16–1 Yankee rout. Lou's final stats for the game: four hits, four runs scored and five RBI, all but one of them coming with two out.

The daily papers would have certainly showered Lou with praise, except that his career-long tendency to get overshadowed reared up yet again. In game two, Joe McCarthy decided to start Jake Powell for the first time since the end of his suspension. Senators fans—some enraged by Powell's racist remark, others angered by his punching of Joe Kuhel or their team's humiliation in the opening game—showered the Yankee outfielder with boos and thrown objects all afternoon. The situation nearly boiled over in the bottom of the sixth, after the Yankees seized a 3–1 lead when Powell had to dodge a torrent of pop bottles and endure chants of "Take him out!" as he tried to go to his spot in left field. According to

The New York Times, the game was "halted several minutes while five Negro ground attendants gathered the glassware in baskets." The paper said another bottle whizzed behind Powell's shoulders, missing him by inches after he reached first base in the seventh.

When *Times* editors wrote headlines that night, they had a choice who to emphasize—Gehrig, one of the most accomplished and beloved players in baseball, or Powell, one of the most hated. The result: "Powell Survives Bottle Barrages as Yankees Rout Senators 16–1, 6–2." Lou merited a third-line subhead.

Still, Lou's resurgence didn't totally escape press attention. In the days that followed, several sportswriters tried to explain how Gehrig had suddenly turned around his season. A few reported that he had switched to a lighter bat, to enable a faster swing and not get blown away on fastballs. This was nothing new for Lou. As early as 1930, he asked his bat maker of the time, the Hanna Manufacturing Company, to gradually reduce the weight of his bats as the season wore on. His spring training models that year weighed a touch over thirty-eight ounces; the ones delivered in August weighed about thirty-six and a half. But in 1938, perhaps in concession to his waning strength, Gehrig ordered the lightest bats of his career from his current bat maker, Hillerich and Bradsby. Early in the year, he was using bats that weighed a hair over thirty-five ounces. His explosion in August followed the delivery of some new thirty-four-ounce models.

Another popular explanation was a change in batting stance. Early in the year, while struggling to get hits, Lou had adopted a stance in which his right foot pointed toward the outfield; announcer Dick Bray noted it when Lou first came to bat at the All-Star Game. But on August 7th, he went back to his traditional stance, with both feet pointed toward home plate. Rud Rennie of the *Herald-Tribune* said it was a conscious decision. "He returned the style of hitting that made him famous," Rennie wrote, and suddenly regained the power stroke that had eluded him all season.

"I don't know what did it, except going back to my old stance," Lou told another reporter. "I couldn't figure out how the other one was wrong but I guess it was. I won't monkey with it again."

There's one other possible reason for Lou's mid-summer resurgence—a temporary reversal of his ALS symptoms. ALS is a progressive disease, one that gradually, inexorably paralyzes and kills its victims. But occasionally, patients get a small, short reprieve. In the mid-2010s, researchers led by Dr. Richard Bedlack at Duke University analyzed seventeen ALS clinical studies where participants' symptoms had been tracked using the ALS Functional Rating Score, the same system which other researchers used to assess Gehrig's condition in *Rawhide*. Under the system, doctors evaluate ALS patients' ability to speak, walk, breathe and perform other basic motor functions. Then they assign a score of zero to four points for each function; the higher the score, the more normal the functioning. The study found that fourteen percent of patients, nearly one in seven, showed brief improvements in their scores, indicating an upturn in their condition.

Bedlack says scientists aren't sure why that happens. He says one possibility is that patients are making mental and/or physical adjustments of the kind Gehrig did. But there could also be a medical phenomenon at play. "It's possible this disease is a dance between whatever is killing the motor neurons and the body's attempt to have the surviving motor neurons send out branches to reconnect with the muscles and try to make you stronger again," he says. "There's a constant push and pull between those two things. And it's possible the body's ability to re-enervate outraces de-enervation for a while." There's no way to tell if that's what Gehrig experienced. "But clearly there was an improvement in his power," Bedlack says.

On August 18th, the Yankees played another doubleheader against the Senators. Lou was a comparatively tame 2-for-6 in game one but came through when it counted. With the game tied 5–5 in the top of the eleventh, he batted against Washington's best pitcher, knuckleball specialist Dutch Leonard. Leonard had struck out Gehrig with the bases loaded in the sixth. This time, though, Lou found a pitch he liked and doubled off the right-field wall, driving in DiMaggio with what turned out to be the winning run.

The game marked the Yankee debut of pitcher Wes Ferrell, a former Indian, Red Sock and Senator who the Yanks had just picked up for the pennant drive. In an interview years later, Ferrell said he had strong memories of this game, in part because the Senators had just released him and the team's owner, Clark

Griffith, still owed him a mandatory ten days' severance pay. "I beat them in eleven innings—and Griffith is still paying me out," he recalled, with obvious glee.

But that wasn't the only thing Ferrell recalled:

> "You know, something happened in that game which I thought curious at the time, though now, with hindsight, I can understand it. We should've won the game in nine innings, but Gehrig made a bad play on a fielder's choice and let the tying run in. Instead of going to the plate and throwing the man out, he went the easy way, to first base. It was the kind of play you'd never expect him to make. Nobody knew at the time, of course, that Gehrig was dying. All we knew was that he wasn't swinging the bat the way he could, nor running the way he could."

In actuality, the play Ferrell remembered made the score 5–4, but the Senators tied up the game moments later, sending it into extra innings, where Lou's hit made up for his lapse in the field.

The schedule ground on, taking the Yankees up to Philadelphia for a four-game weekend series. Friday and Saturday were single games for a change, and a less-tired Lou destroyed the A's in both. On Friday, he slugged a second-inning home run which sailed out of Shibe Park and "bounced on the front porch of a house on 20th Street," according to the *Daily News*. The Yankees won the game 5–2. On Saturday, he came to bat in the first with the bases loaded. A's fans must have known what was coming. Starter Buck Ross tried to sneak a fastball by Lou and failed. The ball sailed into the right-field stands, giving Lou his only grand slam of the season and the twenty-third of his career. The career mark would stand as a major-league record for over seventy-five years until broken by Alex Rodriguez.

For good measure, Lou drove in two more runs in the sixth with a double, finishing off an 11–3 win. The victory just about finished the AL pennant race. Three weeks earlier, the Yankees led the Indians by a half-game. Now they were in front by ten.

If the American League had given player of the week honors in 1938, Gehrig would have been the runaway winner in each of the previous two. Overall, he bashed American League pitching at a .419 clip over the period. In fifteen games, he clouted seven homers, seven doubles, two triples, and drove in twenty-seven runs. His on-base percentage was .486; his OPS, a ridiculous 1.421. And he made not a single error at first base during the stretch.

In comparison, Hank Greenberg hit .255 over the same period and drove in fifteen runs. Jimmie Foxx hit .279 and knocked in eleven.

Lou's hitting that week forced the sportswriters to break out their superlatives. The *Brooklyn Daily Eagle* declared him a "batting madman," and Grantland Rice said he was coming on like a prairie fire. Rice, in fact, devoted much of his August 18th column to Gehrig. Early in the year, he recalled, Gehrig looked slow as the Yankees struggled. "Weeks went by and then two or three months. He was not covering much ground at first base and he couldn't hit. What had appeared to be a mere batting slump at the outset of the season looked like the breaking up of a great ball player." But now, Rice said, "Gehrig is hitting the ball again—hitting home runs and timely singles and driving runs over the plate. The Iron Horse is snorting again and the pitchers don't like to see him looming up at the plate in a pinch."

How good was Lou feeling? The day after the Philadelphia series, rather than stay home and rest, he went fishing off the coast of Brielle, New Jersey with Eleanor and Fred Fletcher, the outdoors columnist for the *Daily News*. The fish weren't biting that day, and Gehrig made only one catch, a bluefish weighing four pounds. "Just why Gehrig, on his one fishing day in seven months, should be deprived of the lusty pull of tuna on a light rod, I do not know," Fletcher wrote. But the day wasn't a total waste, as the boaters got the thrill of seeing whales leap out of the Atlantic waters. "One of them was seventy feet long," said Fletcher. "It is the first time the Gehrigs had ever seen one of these mammals."

It's tempting to think Lou could have stayed red hot under the right circumstances. But August 21st marked the start of doubleheader week, the product of the rainouts that had plagued the Yankees all year long. The team played six twin bills in seven days, including five in a row starting on the 23rd. Superman himself would have wilted under the strain, and Lou suffered a couple of 0-for-5 games during the stretch. Yet he carried on as always, playing twelve complete games, going the distance even when the Yankees won laughers by scores like 11–1 and 15–3. The Yankees won nine of the twelve, cementing their hold on first.

Lou wasn't an offensive hurricane during the week but his bat contributed to several fresh Yankee wins. One was a 15–9 slugfest against Cleveland, notable for being the last time Lou faced off against Bob Feller. The Indians' young fireballer won seventeen games that season and led the American League in strikeouts for the first of seven times. On this day, though, he struggled mightily to subdue anybody's bat. The Yankees were already up 10–4 in the fifth when Gehrig came up with two outs and DiMaggio on second. History does not record what kind of pitch Feller threw, only that Lou deposited it somewhere over the outfield walls for his twenty-sixth homer of the season.

Lou's most dramatic hit of the week came in the second game of the August 23rd doubleheader against the White Sox. The Sox were going for a sweep after winning game one 11–3. Sox righty Johnny Rigney had limited the Yankees to one run and three hits through seven innings, and the Yankee crowd—perhaps excited by a close game amid a skein of lopsided wins—began rooting him on, "giving him the kind of a hand usually reserved for a home town performer," according to *The Chicago Tribune.* Then came the bottom of the eighth. DiMaggio worked a one-out walk. Gehrig came to bat. Rigney had held him in check thus far—groundout, fly out, groundout. This time, there was no out. Lou banged the ball into his favorite part of the ballpark, the right-field stands, for what became the game-winning hit in a 3–1 Yankee victory.

There were a little over seventeen thousand fans in Yankee Stadium that afternoon to see DiMaggio and Gehrig trot around the bases with the winning runs. They had no idea they were watching history. The blow off Rigney was not the final home run of Lou's career. But it was the last time one of his four-baggers produced a Yankee win.

8

Singles Hitter

The idea almost certainly came from the Browns, who were desperate to boost their usual, pitiful attendance of eleven or twelve hundred fans per game. Let's do a home run contest, the team said—you know, to see who can hit it the farthest. Three sluggers from the Yankees against three from St. Louis. We'll do it before a Sunday doubleheader, churn up some publicity, attract a bigger crowd and both teams can make good money. For fun, we'll get U.S. Army engineers to measure the shots. And to make this even more interesting, the winner will get a hundred bucks. Runner-up gets fifty. Whaddaya say, New Yorkers? Are you in?

They hardly needed the money, but Gehrig, Joe DiMaggio, and George Selkirk all agreed to take part in the contest before the September 18th doubleheader at Sportsman's Park. They probably did it just for a lark, a little fun to be had while the Yankees finished their cakewalk to the American League championship. The Yanks led Boston by fourteen games entering the day's action and would clinch the pennant that afternoon when a rainout left the Red Sox without enough games to catch up before the official end of the season. Or, it could be the Yankees simply asked Gehrig and friends to help the ever-downtrodden Browns. The twin bill drew about eight thousand five hundred fans—a fair-to-middling crowd for most other teams, but a big day for the Brownies, in fact, their third-biggest attendance of the year. The following day's game between the same teams would attract a paid crowd of seven hundred fifty-one.

Many of the fans were already in their seats when the hitting contest began at 12:30 before Sunday's first game. It was good hitting weather—sunny, a little breezy, the temperature in the low fifties. If he chose to bear down, Gehrig had a reasonable expectation of winning the contest or at least making the top three. Selkirk couldn't match the power of Gehrig or DiMaggio; he hit just ten homers that season. The Browns' side had one big bopper in Harlond Clift, an all-star third baseman who slugged thirty-four round-trippers that year. But Beau Bell was more of a doubles and triples guy and the last contestant, a backup outfielder named Mel Mazzera, didn't hit much of anything. Even taking his ongoing off-year into account, Gehrig was unquestionably the premier home run hitter of this bunch. And he had swatted a ball onto the roof of the Browns' park as recently as July. Given the right grooved fastball, he could win this competition with one mighty swing of the bat.

The fans watching got their money's worth, as all six players hit at least one home-run-length ball. But the order of the finish must have surprised a few folks. The winner was Selkirk, whose biggest blast, as measured by artillery experts from the U.S. Army's Jefferson Barracks, traveled four hundred and forty-four feet. Bell came in a close second, followed by DiMaggio, Mazzera, Clift, and bringing up the rear, Lou Gehrig. In fact, Gehrig's longest shot, four hundred and six feet, was fifteen feet shorter than the longest hit by Mazzera, a guy who clubbed fewer than a dozen home runs in his major-league career.

The last-place finish may have stung Gehrig, who went out and banged a first-inning home run off Bobo Newsom in game one of the doubleheader. But really, neither he nor the fans should have been too astonished by the results. In the weeks preceding the contest, Gehrig had undergone a remarkable transformation. For over a decade, Larrupin' Lou had been the hair-trigger bazooka of the Yankee lineup, raining doubles and triples on the opposing team's fielders and feeding home run balls to fans in the bleachers. But starting in the last week of August, after the skein of doubleheaders that must have drained more strength and vitality from his limbs, the slugger that Yankee fans had come to know and love disappeared. In his place was Lou Gehrig, singles hitter.

In a 1945 interview with Joe Williams, Joe McCarthy recalled an unusual conversation he had with Gehrig during the '38 season. "We were playing a midseason series with Washington," McCarthy remembered. "For some time, I had noticed that Gehrig wasn't getting his body into his swing, wasn't taking his full cut. I called this to his attention and his answer startled me somewhat. He said, 'You know, Joe, I think it's best for me to make sure I get a piece of the ball. If I get enough little hits I can lead the league in hitting.'"

McCarthy added: "Well, I knew that wasn't the real Gehrig talking because he'd rather hit a home run than twenty singles. I had begun to suspect something was happening to him, but this was the tipoff . . . that he knew something was happening to him too."

In fairness, Gehrig may have cut down his swing to push his batting average above .300, which most players and sportswriters of the time considered the benchmark of a successful year. All season long, journalists harped on the fact that Gehrig's average was below this magic line. Even the communist *Daily Worker*, amid its daily meat of union news and Stalinist propaganda, published a one-panel cartoon of Gehrig in late August with the banner, "Can He Reach .300?"

But the altered swing also had to be a reflection of Gehrig's creeping ALS. As the disease robbed him of the strength to pound homers and run out extra-base hits, he apparently decided this was the best way to help the team. He was now using patience instead of power, slapping his hits or waiting for a base on balls, instead of trying to crush the ball into the stands.

McCarthy said his talk with Gehrig took place at midseason, but evidence suggests it came later, for as the Yankees entered the home stretch, Lou effectively became a leadoff hitter batting in the middle of the lineup. The second game of a doubleheader against the Indians on August 27th marked the new Lou's debut. The game was a classic example of Yankee power and domination, with the home team bulldozing their way to a 13–0 victory. Tommy Henrich and Joe Gordon walloped two home runs apiece, and Monte Pearson pitched a no-hitter, the only one thrown in the heavy-hitting American League that season. Gehrig? He singled twice and drew a walk. All three times he came around to score. He had no runs batted in.

"Somewhere in the creeping mystery of that summer," Eleanor later wrote, "Lou lost the power." In terms of her husband's stats, "somewhere" can be pinpointed to the last week of August 1938.

* * *

That same week, AP sportswriter Eddie Brietz passed along a note to readers: "If Lou Gehrig can belt nine more homers this season he'll be the second player in major league history to whang five hundred four-basers." Gehrig was ten shy of five hundred but never mind; Brietz was stoking interest in the countdown to the milestone. Such an achievement would be cause for a major celebration in 1938. To that point, only Ruth had clubbed so many homers in a career, and no other active players except for Jimmie Foxx and Mel Ott were even remotely close. Given the number of games left on the schedule, and the home run pace Gehrig maintained through most of August, it seemed possible he could smack his five hundredth homer by the final day of the season.

But batters who don't take big swings don't whang anything, and from August 27th onward Gehrig seemed locked in one-base-at-a-time mode. On the 28th, he walked twice against the Browns. The next day, he accepted three free passes. In a three-game series against the Tigers, he walked in five out of twelve plate appearances. Three other times, he singled.

The contrast between this new Gehrig and his Tigers counterpart Hank Greenberg could not be greater. In the August 31st game, both men got on base three times. Gehrig hit a single and drew a pair of walks. Greenberg doubled twice, crushed his 46th homer of the year and drove in three runs. The Yankees lost, 12–6, in part because Gehrig came up small in the clutch; batting in the eighth with the bases loaded, he popped out to second.

That failure aside, Gehrig wasn't slumping per se; he was just suddenly playing a type of baseball that would have been more appreciated twenty years earlier, in the Deadball Era, or seventy years in the future, when high on-base percentages were all the rage. In fact, in the two weeks beginning on the day of Pearson's no-hitter, the new Gehrig was, in some ways, sensational. In sixty-one plate appearances, he lashed out nineteen hits and drew sixteen walks, giving him an on-base percentage of .574. He even stole three bases. The Yankees won eleven of fifteen games, expanding their league lead.

This was not the first time the Yankees had seen Gehrig on the basepaths so much. He had put together several medium-sized hitting streaks during his career, and just a year earlier he compiled three separate runs of getting on base in at least twenty games in a row. But this latest on-base streak stood out for its lack of power. Of his nineteen hits, all but three were singles. His RBI total was six. He hit no triples and no home runs. It was as though Albert Pujols had morphed into Ichiro Suzuki.

The newspaper scribes made only glancing mention of Gehrig's new hitting style. They remained fixed on Gehrig's achievements with what a later generation of baseball fanatics would call the counting stats. Lou made headlines on September 5th when he had two RBI during a doubleheader sweep of the A's. That gave him one hundred and one for the year and marked the thirteenth straight season he had knocked in at least a hundred runs, a new major league record. He also scored twice, giving him a hundred runs for the thirteenth straight time, another record. Harold Burr of the *New York Post* wrote: "Gehrig may not be smashing home runs over the right-field barriers of the American League the way he used to do but he's still breaking records held by his boyhood hero, Babe Ruth." He also noted Gehrig drew fresh boos from the Yankee faithful, once when he misplayed a ground ball and again when a grounder bounced over his head.

Gehrig focused on the positive in his postgame comments, revealing a mix of humility and pride. "Sure, it makes me feel good to know that I'm busting records as I go along," he told reporters. "But the real satisfaction is that my individual accomplishments aren't interfering with the club's progress. I intend to keep swinging away and as long as we win I am happy. Of course, it's not going to make me angry when you fellows tell me I broke this or that record."

The writers hadn't forgotten about his consecutive-games streak either, and Gehrig made headlines again on September 9th when the streak reached twenty-one hundred. The afternoon contest before a Ladies' Day crowd of sixteen thousand at Griffith Stadium in Washington was the last great game of Lou Gehrig's career.

Gehrig may have been looking forward to this day, as the Senators started Dutch Leonard, the knuckleballer who he had torched for a game-winning-RBI double three weeks earlier. Leonard was in good form this day, limiting most of the Yankee lineup to only one hit, a single by Henrich. But he couldn't shut down the Iron Horse—"the only Yank who could fathom Dutch," reported *The Sporting News*. His first time up, Gehrig singled and was advanced over to third, only to get tagged out on a pickoff play. In the fourth, he singled again but was stranded at first. In the seventh, his efforts finally bore fruit, as a single past second baseman Ossie Bluege fueled a rally that resulted in scores by DiMaggio and Gehrig himself. Lou added one more single in the ninth for good measure as the Yankees came out on top 2–0.

In its wrap-up, the Associated Press said Gehrig "staged a one-man celebration" of his consecutive games streak. It also noted that with the four hits, Gehrig had finally hoisted his batting average above .300. This time, it was the *Post* that ran a cartoon highlighting people's obsession with the number. The drawing by artist Gus Uhlmann showed New Yorkers citywide discussing and cheering Gehrig's batting average—among them the Statue of Liberty, who said, "Psst!! Did you hear? Lou's batting .300."

A few days later, Lefty Gomez offered a quip about Gehrig that found its way into papers nationwide: "He has a better constitution than the United States."

But had he looked more closely, Gomez would have seen the constitution was fraying at the edges. After September 9th, Gehrig's torrent of singles and walks slowed to a stream, and ones he did have seemed less timely, less consequential. The Yankees tailed off along with their first baseman and posted a losing record for the month, although they still won the pennant by nine and a half games. There were moments when the team missed Gehrig's old power and reliability. On September 15th against the Tigers, the Yanks were trailing 6–4 in the bottom of the ninth. Tommy Henrich kept hopes alive with a two-out single off Detroit pitcher Harry Eisenstadt. DiMaggio then followed with another single. Gehrig could now win the game with a home run. "Ruin stared Eisenstadt in the face when Gehrig stepped up," the *Detroit Free Press* reported. "But Harry maintained his poise and succeeded in fanning Lou for the final out."

Gehrig was also being less insistent about playing the entire game every day. On September 19th against the Browns, he played one inning at first base and then departed for Dahlgren. On the 29th in Philadelphia, he did the same thing. In the final game of the season in Boston, Dahlgren replaced him in the ninth. The shortened appearances allowed him to maintain the consecutive-games streak, which stood at two thousand, one hundred twenty-two by the end of the season. But together, they indicated that the legs of the Iron Horse were getting weaker.

Speaking in hindsight, fellow players said they noticed a difference in Gehrig as the season wound down. For most of his career, Gehrig was renowned for the ferocity with which the ball leaped off his bat. "Ruth, when he hit a hard ball, it was always in the air, but Gehrig, you almost took your life in your hands, he hit such vicious shots," recalled Tigers Hall of Fame second baseman Charlie Gehringer. But Gehringer's teammate, pitcher Elden Auker, told ALS researchers that "about the middle of the 1938 season, I felt, as did other pitchers on the staff, that Lou seemed to be losing his power. His walking and running appeared to be slower. His swing was not as strong as it had been in the past years." Auker dated the change to July first—an assessment contradicted by Gehrig's power surge in August—but the overall impression holds up to scrutiny.

Cecil Travis was a hard-hitting, all-star shortstop for the Senators. He had been a regular in Washington's lineup since 1934, and played over a hundred games against Gehrig, watching him bash away at a long line of overmatched Senator pitchers. The destruction had continued as always on Gehrig's four-hit, five RBI day a few weeks earlier. But Travis later told Richard Lally, author of the Yankee oral history *Bombers*, that toward the end of the '38 season "you could see something was off with Lou."

Travis felt Gehrig's reflexes had slowed and that more ground balls were getting by him at first base. As for Gehrig's hitting: "At the plate, the ball didn't sound the same coming off his bat, even when he hit it good. Just didn't have that same loud crack like a pistol shot. His timing was off by a fraction." The result was more lazy fly balls, Travis recalled—along with more swings and misses.

"The thing that shocked me was how it all happened so quickly," Travis said. "Most of that season, when we played him, he looked the same as always. Strong as an ox, nothing wrong with him at all. Then, within weeks, he started to look tired out there."

The weariness showed up in photos as well. In pictures taken during 1936 and 1937, Gehrig still looks like a vital young man. In 1938, he suddenly seemed to age five years, with more gray in his hair and deeper lines around his eyes and mouth. His posture is slouchier too, and in a couple of dugout photos with teammates, he looks noticeably less energetic than those around him. In one, he seems to be leaning on his bat to hold him up. One contemporary writer who noted the changes said he was "commencing to resemble a distinguished executive." ALS does not cause wrinkles or gray hair, but the stress about his performance and general health could have contributed to Gehrig's older appearance.

The last week of the season brought yet another of the Gehrig-replacement rumors that had dogged him all year. This one emanated from Detroit, where Hank Greenberg was crushing homer after homer, making a push to surpass Babe Ruth's record of sixty round-trippers in a season. His final total of fifty-eight would fall short of the Babe but doubled Gehrig's 1938 output. Amid the excitement, the *Detroit Free Press* dropped a bomb that said the Yankees and Tigers were discussing a trade that would send Joe DiMaggio to Detroit in exchange for Hammerin' Hank—and leave Larrupin' Lou sitting on the bench.

"Several reasons have been advanced as to why the Yankees might consent to a trade," wrote *Free Press* sports editor Charles P. Ward. "One is that Gehrig has begun to slip. The years and his consecutive games streak have got him down . . . Another is that Greenberg, being Jewish, would prove an attraction to a great part of New York's population." Other motives put forth included Greenberg's family roots in the Bronx and the notion the Yankees wanted to get rid of DiMaggio after his holdout of the previous spring.

As the article noted, Greenberg and DiMaggio were both thumbs-down on the proposed trade, and it never came to pass, if it was seriously discussed at all. Gehrig's reaction to the story went unrecorded but he was no doubt against it too, given it would mean the end of his streak and the loss of his job at first base. Just reading about the rumor in the press must have given him another jolt; it suggested the Yankees had growing doubts about his ability to continue, and demonstrated how callous the front office could be, even to the team's biggest and most popular stars. The Yankees had dumped Ruth after fifteen wondrous years, after all. The same thing could happen to him.

Tired as he was, Gehrig still had another big blow left in his bat. It came on September 27th as the Yankees played out the schedule. The Tuesday afternoon game at Yankee Stadium had no impact on the standings and held little interest for the public, as evidenced by a paid attendance of fewer than three thousand fans. It would have no bearing on baseball history either except that in the fifth inning, Gehrig stepped to the plate to again face his recent favorite whipping boy, Dutch Leonard. Leonard had retired Gehrig on a grounder in the first and a flyout in the third. Maybe he could escape without damage today? No such luck, as Gehrig sent a Leonard pitch sailing into the stands. It was no cheap shot, either. *The Washington Post* described it as "home run far into the Washington bullpen in right-center," a drive of about three hundred sixty feet.

It was Gehrig's final homer of the season, and the last time he hit one in a game that counted.

The season wound down a few days later, with the Yankees limping to the finish, dropping ten of their last fifteen games. Gehrig didn't stop singling and walking entirely but a lack of multi-hit days allowed his batting average to drift down to a final .295, a fact that merited a "Gehrig Falls Below .300" headline in *The Sporting News*. He still ranked among the American League leaders in several categories. His twenty-nine homers and one hundred fourteen runs batted in were both seventh best in the league, his one hundred fifteen runs scored was tenth, and his one hundred seven walks was fifth. He was one of only seven AL players to amass over three hundred total bases. In terms of the advanced stats favored by today's baseball obsessives, Gehrig didn't fare too badly either, ranking twelfth in OPS at .932, and among the top ten in runs created, at-bats per home run, and win probability added.

For almost any other player, 1938 would have been an outstanding season. Only for Gehrig did it count as a disappointment. His batting average had fallen over fifty points from the year before. It was the first time in a decade he failed to hit thirty homers. He struck out seventy-five times—a low total for many sluggers, but for Gehrig, the second-highest mark of his career.

Perhaps with these stats in mind, the nation's preeminent sportswriter, Grantland Rice, made the Yankee captain the focus of his column on September 29th, six days before the World Series began. "The world series [sic] offers to Lou Gehrig—among other things—an opportunity to put a smashing climax to a long uphill fight that began with the opening of the season. Starting from away back, the iron horse has come pounding up the line in his old fashion, or something closely akin to it," Rice wrote. For much of the season, he said, Gehrig had been "weary of mind and body" and fretful about his inability to start hitting. But now, he said, "Lou is himself again—grinning, laughing, bouncing around, getting the old joy out of playing ball. His troubles are all behind him, and with the world series just ahead, he is as pleased as a kid with a little red wagon."

There are no quotes from Gehrig in the story, and no real evidence he was truly feeling so giddy. What Rice really seemed to be saying, without using loaded words like "aging" or "reputation," was that Gehrig, after a year of subpar play and persistent criticism, finally had a chance to show the naysayers that he was not washed up.

* * *

For much of the season, fans assumed the Yankees' World Series opponent would be the Pittsburgh Pirates. The Pirates, a scrappy team with just slightly above-average hitting and pitching, somehow pushed their way to a seven-game lead in the National League standings at the start of September. Pirate management prepared for postseason play, installing extra seats at their ballpark, Forbes Field, and dispatching their top scout, Joe Schultz, to watch the Yankees and take notes. But the lead melted away as the Pirates played .500 ball and the second-place Chicago Cubs reeled off seventeen wins in twenty games. At month's end, the teams met for a climactic three-game series at Wrigley Field.

In game one, the Cubs rode the damaged but skilled arm of Dizzy Dean to a 2–1 victory, cutting the Bucs' lead to a half-game. The next day, September 28th, the score was tied in the bottom of the ninth with darkness falling over the unlit park. If Pirates relief ace Mace Brown could get three outs, umpires would declare the game a tie, to be replayed in its entirety the next day. But with two men down, on a count of no balls and two strikes, Brown threw a curveball that hung over the plate. Cubs catcher/manager Gabby Hartnett whipped his bat around and blasted the ball into the left-field bleachers, giving the Cubs a dramatic 6–5 victory. Joyous Cubs fans rushed the field to escort Hartnett around the bases, while Brown retreated to the clubhouse, where he got so despondent that teammate Paul Waner worried he might commit suicide. The "Homer in the Gloamin'"—named by a sportswriter after a popular 1911 song—put the Cubs in first place and destroyed the last ounce of fight in the Pirates. The Cubs went on to win the pennant with just eighty-nine wins, still one of the lowest totals for a champion in National League history.

The developments set up a rematch of the World Series from 1932 when the Yankees swept the Cubs in four lopsided games. In that series, Gehrig had burned the Cubbies' pitching staff for nine hits in seventeen times at bat, piling up three homers and eight RBI. As usual, Ruth got the headlines, for his famous (and as noted, mythical) "called shot" homer to center field. But the memory of Gehrig's onslaught had not faded from the Cub players' minds. "I'll tell you, that Gehrig, he was awesome," said Cubs second baseman Billy Herman, recalling the '32 Series. "He was so big and strong and hit that ball so hard, unbelievable."

In those days before television, inter-league play and online video, Herman and his teammates had no way of knowing that

Gehrig's vaunted strength had declined in the intervening years—and in fact was slipping away a little bit more each day, even as he tried to power the Yankees to another world championship.

9

World Series

To say the Yankees were favored to beat the Cubs in the 1938 World Series is to say Mount Vesuvius was favored to defeat Pompeii. The Yankees had outscored the Cubs by over two hundred fifty runs during the regular season and walloped three times as many home runs. The Yanks at one point led their league by sixteen games; the Cubs, never more than two. The Chicagoans had suffered Series losses in 1929, 1932 and 1935, while the New Yorkers were gunning for their third straight world championship, a feat that had never been accomplished in the World Series' thirty-five year history.

On the eve of the series, betting experts installed the Yankees as three-to-one favorites. With those odds, reported the AP's Gayle Talbot from Chicago, "There isn't much betting. The locals think their club, on the crest of a great winning streak, has a good chance to jolt the formidable Yanks, but they aren't letting their enthusiasm run away with their financial judgment."

Baseball experts were in near-universal agreement the Yankees would defeat, perhaps steamroller their opponents with little or no trouble. Of the eighteen baseball writers polled by *The Sporting News*, sixteen favored the Yanks. Joe Williams of the *World-Telegram* wrote that if the Yankees didn't win, Commissioner Landis should investigate. The Yankees themselves seemed to have no worries about the outcome. Joe McCarthy told a reporter the team hadn't even bothered to scout the Cubs. Even the Cubs' second baseman, Billy Herman, later admitted he had little hope. "We were overmatched," he said.

Lou made no public predictions but behind the scenes was confident, even cocky, as Eleanor made clear when a reporter asked what she and her husband would do with their share of the World Series money.

> "The winnings? Right into the bank," she says. "Against that rainy day when Lou won't be able to see the fast ones anymore."
>
> But he's good for seven more years anyway, says the missus. "After that—well, he may have to take up moving pictures in earnest."
>
> Mrs. Gehrig is just as excited about the series starting Wednesday as she was over her first [as Gehrig's girlfriend] in 1932.
>
> "I came down with a severe case of goose pimples then," she recalls. "Darned if I haven't got them again. Of course, the Yankees are going to win in four straight."
>
> How does she know?
>
> "Lou told me so!"

One of the few positions where experts thought the Cubs stacked up well against the Yankees was, ironically, first base. The Cubbies' first sacker was James "Rip" Collins, a smallish (5'9") switch-hitter who was just nine months younger than Lou but didn't make the major leagues until 1931, Lou's ninth season with the Yankees. Collins once possessed a good power stroke and led the National League with thirty-five homers in 1934, as his Cardinals captured the NL flag and beat the Tigers in the World Series. Since then, however, his power had waned and he was now below average at the plate compared to hard-hitting NL first basemen like the Dodgers' Dolph Camilli and the Reds' Frank McCormick, not to mention American League behemoths like Gehrig, Foxx, and Greenberg.

A year earlier, when Lou was still in his prime, sportswriters wouldn't have rated Collins on the same planet as him. This time, though, they only gave the Yankee first sacker a minor edge, or no edge at all:

> "The only place on the infield where the Cubs might have an advantage is at first base, where Rip Collins has been fielding beautifully. His series rival, Lou Gehrig, isn't as agile as in his earlier days."—Irving Vaughn, *Chicago Tribune.*
>
> "Lou Gehrig at first base is past his prime. It isn't likely that the Cubs would take him in an even swap for their first sacker, Collins."—William J. Madden, *The Record* (Hackensack, N.J.)
>
> "'Iron Hoss' Lou Gehrig has slowed up that important 'step' afield around first base and has been fighting his way out of the batting doldrums but he still rates the call over . . . 'Jim the Ripper' Collins of the Cubs. Gehrig is shading .300 at the plate, but Collins is down around .260."—AP.

Lou may have been reading the critiques about his fielding, for at some point late in the '38 season or early in '39, he switched to a larger first baseman's glove. He acknowledged the change in March 1941, just three months before his death, when *New York Times* sports editor James Kiernan visited his home and picked up the mitt from a shelf in the living room. "Jimmie Foxx gave it to me," Lou said. "For years I used the smallest glove of any first baseman I know. But toward the last, when I couldn't bend over so well, I was having trouble getting in the low throws and short hops. Jimmie suggested I try a little bigger glove. He gave me one. That's it."

Lou didn't say when he made the switch, but it's worth noting that the Yankees' final 1938 regular season games took place in Boston; Foxx could have given him the glove then. And if it seems odd that the Red Sox' first baseman would assist a Yankee, remember the fierce rivalry that existed then between the National and American Leagues. Foxx may have wanted to give his league-mate an edge in the World Series.

* * *

Wrigley Field, where the series was to open on October 5th, held some nice memories for Lou. It was there in June 1920 that he first came to national attention, while starring for his championship High School of Commerce team. The boys traveled from New York to Chicago to play another baseball powerhouse, Lane Tech, in what was billed as the "High School World Series." Lou, who had just turned seventeen years old, was hitless his first four times at bat. But in the top of the ninth, batting with the bases loaded, the Iron Horse-to-be stepped into a fastball and sent it for a ride, slugging it well over four hundred feet, completely out of the stadium. *The Chicago Tribune* described the moment: "The ball sailed out high and far and cleared the right wall screen by many feet, finally landing in Sheffield Avenue and bouncing on to a front porch across the street. It was a blow of which any big leaguer would be proud and was walloped by a boy who hasn't yet started to shave."

Wrigley again proved much to Lou's liking during the '32 World Series. The Yankees played only two games at the park during their four-game sweep. In the first, Lou blasted two solo home runs, the margin of difference in the Yanks' 7–5 win. In the second, his two hits and three RBI helped power a 13–6 victory that clinched the series.

Maybe those memories were why Lou was in good spirits when the Yankees boarded a Chicago-bound train on the afternoon of October 3rd. He was one of several Yankees seen shaking hands and signing autographs for a crowd of several hundred well-wishers who had gathered at Penn Station for the team's send-off. Shortly before departure, a photographer caught Lou and Eleanor sporting wide smiles as they stood in a train door with Joe McCarthy and his wife Elizabeth. Wives didn't normally come on road trips, but this was the World Series, and a Yankee party of over eighty was on board as the train pulled out at five P.M. for the overnight journey.

Lou once told an interviewer he got "tight as a drum" before every World Series game. However, no anxiety was in evidence as the Yankees conducted their last pre-series workout the following day. "They were relaxed and arrived at Wrigley Field with a jaunty, carefree air as though this was just another series during the regular season. Bill Dickey was talking about hunting and Lou Gehrig about fishing," wrote one reporter. Both men and a few of their teammates cracked home runs over Wrigley's ivy-covered walls during batting practice. Perhaps stung by the recent criticism, Gehrig also put in some work on his fielding. "Team followers were surprised to see even Lou Gehrig take long infield drill," reported the *Detroit Free Press*, adding, "Lou has been dodging infield practice as much as possible the past few years."

Despite the gloomy predictions for their team, the Cubs had no trouble selling out Wrigley Field—overselling it, in fact, packing over forty-four thousand fans into a stadium that officially seated six thousand less. Then as now, owners of the tall houses on Sheffield and Waveland Avenues behind the park reaped rewards too, with one lady, a Mrs. Rosa Rupp, selling seats on her rooftop for five dollars apiece, and offering sandwiches to her guests for an additional fee.

Wherever they sat, the fans got a pretty good show. In game one and beyond, the Cubs put up a good fight, keeping the scores close and mostly avoiding the offensive barrages that buried them in 1932. Occasionally, the Cubs even took the lead, although the Yanks' triumph was never in doubt. Astute fans could also enjoy the level of talent on display. By series' end, ten future Hall of Famers would take the field, three of whom remain well-known figures nearly a century later—Dizzy Dean, Joe DiMaggio, and Gehrig.

Gehrig biographers paint him during this World Series as a horse on his last legs, a flame flickering out, a virtual bystander to the Yankees' romp. "Gehrig, the most productive hitter to that point in World Series history, was almost invisible throughout the competition," wrote Jonathan Eig in *Luckiest Man.* In *The Iron Horse*, Ray Robinson called Gehrig's batting stats "a hollow imitation of his halcyon years." There's some truth in those characterizations; contemporaries thought he was slow and the power was missing from his swing. Lou's hits in the series "had no oomph," said Cubs outfielder Phil Cavarretta. He said that when he stood on first base in game three, Gehrig paid him a nice compliment—"the way you hustle, young man, don't change." But, Cavarretta added, "looking back, I could tell from his voice that he was starting to get sick then, young as he was. His voice was very weak. It wasn't a good strong voice."

At the same time, a close analysis of the games shows Lou was hardly a ghost in pinstripes. The '38 World Series is one of the few stretches of his career from which there are surviving game films, radio broadcasts and detailed inning-by-inning accounts that allow a modern observer to make independent judgments about his performance. Those records show that the Iron Man was growing slower and weaker but still contributed to the Yankees' wins through timely hits, fine baserunning, and solid fielding. In no way was he a drag on the team as it drove for its third straight championship.

Game One: Lou's first at-bat came in the second inning with the game scoreless and the bases empty. Cubs starter Bill Lee walked him on four pitches. Trotting down to first, Lou slipped into an odd skipping motion, as though he had pulled a leg muscle. However, when Bill Dickey lined a single to right, he got a good jump and scrambled safely to third, executing a smooth, feet-first slide. The game film suggests the throw from right fielder Cavarretta arrived at about the same time, just slightly off-target, and that third baseman Stan Hack could have tagged Lou out. Instead Hack rifled the ball to second, in an unsuccessful effort to stop Dickey from taking an extra base. Lou ran home with the game's first run a minute later when Selkirk hit a grounder that was fumbled by second baseman Herman.

Lou batted next in the third with the Yankees leading 2–1. Facing Lee again, he lined a clean single down the right-field line. As always, he was aggressive on the base paths and decided to go for a double. But this time, the throw from the outfield—Cavarretta to Herman to shortstop Billy Jurges—beat him by several steps. Observers denigrated both Lou's decision-making and foot speed. "The tip-off on Gehrig came in the opening game when he tried to stretch a single to right into a two-base hit," wrote Charles Ward of the *Detroit Free Press*. "To those watching the game, Lou seemed to spend a great deal of time running in one place."

On his third at-bat, Lou struck out, but not before slamming three hard fouls into the stands, one of which struck the wrist of a Dixon, Illinois man, Sterling Shrock. Shrock had to go to a hospital for X-rays and was wearing a metal splint to protect the wrist the next day.

In his last time up, Lou worked Lee to a count of three balls, two strikes. The next pitch came in low and outside; Lou thought about swinging but pulled his bat back for what he assumed was ball four, and began jogging down to first base. But catcher Gabby Hartnett whirled around and told the umpire, Charley Moran, that Lou had tipped the ball into his glove. After a moment's hesitation, Moran agreed and called out "Strike three!" This triggered an outburst from Lou that was not caught on film but sounds like George Brett's crazed rush at umpires in the famous "Pine Tar Game." "Lou yelled bloody murder and for a time it looked as though the usually peaceful Iron Horse wanted to commit mayhem on the Kentuckian," said *The Sporting News*.

Famed newspaper columnist Damon Runyon devoted ink to the rhubarb the next day:

> The classy customers were edified by the spectacle of Lou Gehrig of the Yankees getting downright vexed at an umpire, and waving his arms and shouting like a common, tobacco-chewing second baseman instead of the highest-salaried fellow in baseball and a movie star . . . There was a terrific to-do at the home plate as Lou gurgled in his throat and gave Charley Moran mean looks and Charley gave Lou mean looks right back, and the other Yankees held Lou and nobody held Charley. Millionaire Jake Ruppert's manager, Joe McCarthy, finally came out on the field and told Lou to pipe down and told Charley whatever it is a manager tells an umpire, which is generally plenty.

After the game, Lou apologized to Moran for his display of anger but insisted the umpire should have allowed him the base on balls. "It was the worst decision called on me in my entire baseball career. No wonder I was burned up," he told newspapermen.

The Yankees won the game 3–1.

Game Two: On a cool, windy day in Chicago the Yankees faced the former Cardinal ace, Dizzy Dean. Ol' 'Diz, as he liked to call himself, was a shadow of the thirty-game winner he had been a few years before. Minutes after Gehrig tagged him for a home run in the 1937 All-Star Game, Earl Averill hit a line shot off

Dean's left foot, breaking his toe. Dean foolishly tried to pitch just a week later and altered his throwing motion to ease pressure on the foot. The change damaged his shoulder muscles, leaving him with a chronically sore right arm. The Cubs still thought he had value, and paid the Cardinals one hundred eighty-five thousand dollars for his services a few days before the '38 season began. He couldn't pitch very often, but when he did, he kept batters off-balance with slow curves, good control, and a very occasional fastball. His final record for the regular season: seven wins, one loss, and a 1.81 ERA.

In Lou's first at-bat, Dean walked him on five pitches, with Mutual radio announcer John Harrington taking note that Dean was throwing mostly "slowballs." Two outs later, Lou was still on first when Joe Gordon hit a grounder toward the shortstop position. It had all the makings of the third out, but Hack and Jurges both charged the ball, collided and tumbled, allowing the hit to dribble into shallow left field. DiMaggio scored from second on the play, and an alert Gehrig, running smoothly and with decent speed, came in all the way from first, giving the Yankees a 2–1 lead.

The Cubs were up again 3–2 by the time Lou came to bat again in the fourth. Dean decided to work him extra-quickly this time, and delivered his first four pitches in about thirty seconds, judging from the radio broadcast. The pace didn't seem to help Dean, who ran up a three-ball, one-strike count. But Lou thought his opponent needed to be slowed down and decided to use a little gamesmanship. Harrington described the action:

> Ready for the next ball to be pitched—Gehrig says something to Hartnett. Hartnett nods. Just as Dean gets ready to pitch, Gehrig steps out of the batsman's box. He's grinning about something, and again he steps out as Diz starts to wind up. (Loud catcalls from the crowd.) Diz just looks at him. He's working very fast and [Gehrig] steps out a third time. And he steps out a fourth time as Diz gets ready. (More catcalls.) Dizzy yells at the umpire. The trick [by Gehrig] is to try to get his man. And apparently, it's worked.

Finally, Lou stepped in the batter's box and hit a sharp grounder between first and second. First baseman Rip Collins made a grab for it but slipped and the ball bounced off his shoulder, going into right field. Lou was given credit for a single. He was erased a minute later when Dickey grounded into a double play. Even on this play, Lou was aggressive on the base paths, as Harrington noted: "Gehrig went in kind of hard and bumped Jurges, but he immediately got up and spoke to Billy, as if to say he was sorry he bumped him, he was not charging Jurges to hurt him . . . Jurges grinned and said ok."

Lou's last two at-bats were uneventful, resulting in a fly out against Dean and a strikeout against Larry French. But the Chicago crowd hadn't forgotten his antics in the fourth. When he came to bat in the seventh, he was greeted by an avalanche of boos.

On the backs of home runs by Frankie Crosetti and Joe DiMaggio, the Yankees won the game, 6–3.

Game Three: If Lou still harbored resentment against umpire Moran, he might have enjoyed a bit of *schadenfreude*—pleasure in another person's pain—during the fifth inning of game three. With runners on first and third, Joe Marty of the Cubs slapped a ground ball to Rolfe at third base, who threw to second for one out. Joe Gordon whipped the ball toward first, trying for the double play. But the throw went grossly off-line and struck Moran flush in the face, opening a deep cut under his left eye. The Cubs' trainer ran out to the infield and treated the bleeding umpire while players and the other umpires gathered around. Lou milled around on the edge of the group, chewing gum and not looking especially concerned.

Lou delivered his only hit of the game an inning later, a single to center that advanced DiMaggio to third. He moved to second on a walk, then scored on a single by Gordon on the left side. Again, the game film shows him running smoothly and with adequate speed. Also, *The Sporting News* praised his fielding skills: "He refuted reports that he had slowed up to a walk in the field. He reached out with his gloved hand and grabbed Cavarretta's rifle shot in the eighth and tossed the ball over to [pitcher Monte] Pearson for the put-out. It saved a run, as [Joe] Marty followed a moment later with a four-bagger."

Before sixty-five thousand at Yankee Stadium, the home team triumphed 5–2.

Game Four: By now, what little drama the series held at the start had been drained away, replaced with resigned admiration for the Yankee juggernaut. This day, the Yankees jumped out to an early lead and never relinquished it, as Ruffing shut down small Cub rallies inning after inning. The Cubs meanwhile shuffled through six pitchers—a very high number for the era—in a futile effort to avoid their fate. Late in the afternoon, after Cavarretta doubled, the New York crowd began rooting for the Cubs, so starved were they for some doubt and tension in the outcome. “Somebody started the rhythmic clapping that a crowd usually starts when a rally by the home team seems in the offing,” reported *The Daily Worker.* “It seems as though everybody picked it up. For a few moments, the Stadium rocked with the sound which suddenly seemed to give expression to the unspoken hope, even among Yankee fans, that the Cubs might make a fight of it.”

Lou spent most of the afternoon fighting for a hit, being held to a groundout and two pop flies in his first three times at bat. Finally, in the bottom of the eighth, he came through, lining a single past Collins at first. He moved to second on a wild pitch, then came around on a Myril Hoag double over third base. The score was part of a four-run rally that sealed the game for the Yankees, 8–3.

In the ninth, Lou made the final putout on a throw from Ruffing. The end of the game stirred only a brief cheer from the crowd of sixty thousand, who treated the result as a foregone conclusion. Not even Mel Allen in the CBS radio booth got excited, saying simply, “And so, the world champions for 1938 are the New York Yankees, champions for the third straight time.”

The Yankees were more celebratory in the clubhouse, shouting and spraying champagne, while an impromptu chorus that included Tommy Henrich and Joe Gordon belted out songs such as “For He’s a Jolly Good Fellow” and “The Sidewalks of New York.” The usually undemonstrative Dickey gave Ruffing a big kiss on the cheek. Lou stayed out of range of the newsreel cameras and was reported to be in a sedate if happy mood, smoking a cigarette. Only later, at the now-annual championship party at the Commodore Hotel, did he let loose, downing hard liquor and riding a chair like a bucking bronco. "Old Rawhide really went to the corral Saturday night," wrote Cy Peterman in the *Philadelphia Inquirer*. "Those of us who saw that movie debut voted his bow-legged progress at the party more realistic than any cowboy's strut." It may have been the only time in his career that Gehrig was publicly drunk.

Later, when the hangovers dissipated, writers couldn't help but note that Lou, who had banged out ten homers, eleven extra-base hits, and thirty-five RBI in his six previous World Series appearances, failed to produce any of the above in this year's contest. McCarthy, who as noted had begun to suspect something was wrong with Gehrig, protected his star. "But did you see him hustle?" he told a reporter who raised the subject. "He was like a sophomore out there. As long as we win Lou is happy. He is over the stage of seeking individual laurels."

Lou defended his performance to Grantland Rice, notably choosing to focus on his fielding. "So they say my legs are gone. Did you see me go from first to the plate on an infield tap? Did Cobb ever do that? Gone? My legs are just getting good," he said.

The days after the clincher, most of the Yankees left New York for the winter. DiMaggio headed back to his native San Francisco, McCarthy to his hometown of Buffalo, and the rest of the Yanks to other points south and west. The exception was Lou, who stayed at his home north of the city. He did not sit idle. Fred Fletcher, the outdoors columnist for the *New York Daily News*, was lying in bed the early morning of Monday, October 10th when a persistent ring awakened him. "Half asleep, I answered the phone and it was Capt. Lou Gehrig of the Yanks," Fletcher reported a day later. "Lou insisted that I accompany him immediately on a fishing trip . . . He [had] attended the Victory Dinner at the Commodore Sunday night and did not arrive home until early morning. He probably had only two or three hours of sleep when he phoned." Fletcher already had plans for the day, but the two men, accompanied by Eleanor, rented a boat and went fishing in Great South Bay on Tuesday morning, catching several flounders.

For a man suffering from ALS, it was a remarkable burst of energy, no doubt brought on by a post-championship high and a pent-up desire to go fishing, always his favorite non-baseball activity. Still, something that Fletcher wrote suggested that Lou was continuing to lose strength. During their phone call, Lou asked Fletcher to send him some custom-made rods and tackle. "He ordered two of the lightest possible rods that can be made. The butts are aluminum and the tips of bamboo, weighing less than three ounces," the columnist wrote. As with his baseball bats, Lou now favored less weighty tools for his hobby.

Fun as fishing could be, Lou hadn't necessarily planned to spend his off-season around New York. When the season ended, he still had a movie contract, and there was still the chance that Sol Lesser would invite him back to Hollywood to make a follow-up to *Rawhide*. However, his movie career came to an abrupt end one day after the World Series, when the producer announced he had dropped his option to put Gehrig in another film. In fact, Lesser said he was eliminating all his contracts with adult actors to concentrate on movies starring children. "I feel there is a greater market today for pictures with youthful appeal than at any time in this business. Anyway, I'm going to stake everything I own on that belief," he said. Lesser would reverse that decision within a year, producing the first screen adaptation of the Thornton Wilder play *Our Town*, a movie that would earn an Oscar nomination for best picture. Perhaps the noise about kids' movies was a polite way of saying he didn't want to make cowboy flicks with baseball stars anymore.

Lesser's decision was likely one of the smaller shocks of Lou's life. It may have even come as a relief, given the endless heckling about Hollywood and klieg lights he endured during the '38 season. He certainly didn't need more movie money; the World Series winnings which Eleanor had forecast materialized in a check for five thousand seven hundred dollars and change, his share of the series attendance receipts. And if he wanted the spotlight, he could get that in New York. Christy Walsh was working to give him a role at the coming 1939 World's Fair in Flushing Meadows. He continued making local radio and charity appearances. He also accepted a pair of unusual invitations, both with political overtones. One was to speak at the annual public forum sponsored by the *New York Herald Tribune*, where prominent speakers from the political, business and entertainment worlds pontificated on the United States' current problems. The other was to appear at Madison Square Garden in a show to benefit Jewish refugees fleeing Nazi Germany.

These activities were a noted departure from Lou's previous off-seasons, which mostly revolved around fishing, exhibition games, and various banquets. Maybe Lou was looking beyond sports and thinking about the role he wanted to play in society. The movie biz was fun but not really his speed; he needed to do something with a little more depth. With his good looks, good reputation, college learning, and recognizable name, he might carve out a career in politics or business. If he wanted to stay in baseball, he definitely had the makings of a manager or executive. Team owners had turned away the ever-undisciplined Ruth when he campaigned for those roles. But Lou, with his reserved, frugal nature and Columbia pedigree, might have fit well into a team's front office, maybe as a vice president or assistant to the general manager.

Alternately, it could be that Lou was trying to distract himself. For as 1938 wound down, he and Eleanor couldn't help but notice that his body was not operating as it should. He dropped small objects like silverware for no reason. When they went ice skating, he kept falling. He seemed to get tired for no reason. And he was losing weight—not a huge amount, but enough to show up in photos, where he now looked less muscular in the torso and shoulders, and bonier in his face. For a man who prided himself on his toughness and invincibility, the changes in his physical condition had to be upsetting, and a cause for alarm.

10

Citizen Lou

He got through the *Herald-Tribune* forum on October 25th without any stumbles, either mental or physical. If he hadn't . . . well, people would have chalked it up to nerves. The forum, sponsored by the *Tribune*, a fierce rival of the *Times*, was an annual high-level summit of the intellectual and influential. Each year, speakers gathered at the Waldorf-Astoria, New York's biggest and swankiest hotel, to voice their thoughts about America's problems in speeches aired live over the big radio networks. The fact that Gehrig was invited spoke volumes about the esteem in which he was held. Other speakers that day included first lady Eleanor Roosevelt, Hollywood censorship chief Will Hays, and New York City's longtime planning czar, Robert Moses. That was just day one; day two featured labor leader John L. Lewis, future Republican presidential nominee Wendell Willkie and President Franklin Roosevelt himself, speaking in a remote hookup from Washington about the need for the United States to be well-armed in case of another world war.

These were real heavyweights—not in the Ruthian sense, but in society and the world of ideas. No one thought Gehrig could solve the nation's labor issues, the Depression or the crisis brewing in Europe, where Germany had just seized a large chunk of Czechoslovakia with the acquiescence of Britain and France. Still, the forum organizers wanted to hear from him. The opening session of the event was entitled "Keeping the Mind of the Nation Young" and included a section on the importance of sports. This was a topic the Yankee captain was well qualified to discuss.

The NBC microphones were on when Helen Reid, wife of *Herald-Tribune* publisher Ogden Reid, strolled to the podium and gave her guest a nice introduction. “No program on sports could be complete without a representative of our national game,” she said in her crisp, patrician accent, “and I was enchanted to find that the first baseman of Colonel Ruppert’s team of Yankees was known to many as a successful speaker as well as popular hero on the diamond.” She listed some of his accomplishments, including the consecutive games streak and his role in “Rawhide.” Despite the movie’s success, she said, “this star is sure to continue his fame in the baseball world . . . I am delighted to have the pleasure of presenting to you Mr. Lou Gehrig.” After brief applause, Gehrig took the podium and delivered what might be called the second-best speech of his life.

Baseball, he asserted, was important to keeping Americans’ spirits high and channeling their energy in a positive way. He used himself as an example, recalling how he grew up poor in a poor New York neighborhood but steered clear of trouble by focusing on athletics. He said as he got older, he drifted away from some of his childhood pals and lost track of them when he enrolled at Columbia.

Then . . .

> “A few years ago, the Yankees went up to Sing Sing Prison to play an exhibition game with the convicts’ team. And when we went out on the field, it sounded like old home week to me. A lot of the convicts in the stand were yelling “Hey, Lou.” “How’re you, Lou? “Remember me, Lou?” And I looked around and there were several of the fellows I had known and run around with when I was a kid.
>
> And it made me think for a minute. Maybe if they had gone in for sports they would be able to walk out of that gate when the ball game was over. And maybe if I hadn’t gone in for sports, I wouldn’t have been able to.

Gehrig would repeat this story on several future occasions. While he never identified the convicts he recognized, at least part of the story can be verified: The Yankees played an exhibition game at Sing Sing Prison on September 5th, 1929. Ruth was the center of attention that day, signing dozens of baseballs and smashing three home runs off inmate pitching.

Not everyone saw sports as useful or meaningful, Gehrig acknowledged—a point of view his parents once held, and one that still held sway for some during the Depression, when many people had to forgo athletics, school or simple leisure to scratch out a living. One time, he recalled, the Yankees had just arrived at a St. Louis train station when he was accosted by an old lady who could not understand why people were excited by the team's presence, or why the players bothered with baseball at all. "They ought to be ashamed of themselves—big, strong men like that playing games. They ought to go to work,'" he recalled the woman saying.

But the world would be a much less pleasant place if everyone just worked, Gehrig said.

> What I mean is, that there is work to be done and it is important work in keeping the people amused, interested, possibly raising their excitement. It would be very dull without the theater, the movies, the swing bands, even the funny papers. Didn't somebody say something about the evils of all work and no play? I think he did, and I think he was right.

Only once during the speech did Gehrig connect baseball to the greater upheaval in the world of 1938—the trends toward totalitarianism and war abroad, the strength of radical, racist, and anti-Semitic movements in America, and the growing fear that a new world war might be right around the corner. Baseball, he insisted, could help keep it all at bay.

> I think that baseball is playing a very important part in keeping this country out of a lot of trouble it might otherwise be in. When the public goes out to the ballpark in the afternoon, it isn't gathering in dusty cellars holding meetings. When the public is discussing the pennant races and speculating on who's going to win the World Series, it doesn't have to work off its natural instincts for excitement in starting a war.

Those were the comments that got picked up by wire services and published by newspapers around the country the next day. Some papers played the speech as straight news, coupling it with comments from other celebrity speakers like actress Katherine Hepburn and tennis superstar Helen Wills Moody. A few mocked the Yankee captain's political pretensions, running his picture under a headline that read, "Gehrig in Unfamiliar Role" and belittling his speech as an off-season diversion. The photo showed Lou with his hand on his forehead, glancing down at his notes with a concerned look on his face. The caption read: "Gehrig does look scared, doesn't he?" Perhaps he was—or he might have just lost his place on the page.

But his most enlightening comments were ones that didn't get published, except in a book containing all the forum's speeches. These remarks had nothing to do with the world's problems. Rather, he talked about his own, like the criticism he received in the press, the heckling he got from the stands and the whispers among baseball insiders that the Iron Horse was losing both strength and speed. "I know they're beginning to refer to me as an old man," Gehrig told the forum. Sometimes, he said, he would read about himself in the newspapers and unconsciously reach for his whiskers, a reference to the idea he was a greybeard. "But they're not there—yet," he added.

Then came words that all but leap off the page, given the tragedy Gehrig would soon have to face. "At thirty-five I don't feel it necessary to start walking around with a cane, or being pushed in a wheelchair," he said. "Maybe I'm just an optimist. Or maybe the game has kept my mind young, and I'm kidding myself into thinking that I'm still a long way from being the old man that the papers call me."

It was the first time Gehrig publicly acknowledged his skills might be fading. It also may have been the first time he hinted, ever so obliquely, that he sensed there was something wrong with his body, something that Father Time and the rigors of over two thousand major league baseball games could not adequately explain.

* * *

Gehrig's next public appearance came about three weeks later, at the Madison Square Garden benefit for European Jewish refugees. Jews had been fleeing Germany since 1933 when the Nazis rose to power and stripped away their rights and property in a prelude to the Holocaust. With America and most European countries closed to large-scale immigration, tens of thousands of German Jews flowed to one of the only safe havens available, the British-controlled territory of Palestine. Activists were hoping to build a Jewish state there. But at that moment, the arriving refugees were impoverished, stateless and desperate. Sympathy for them ran high in New York, in part because of the city's population of one and a half million Jews, in part because of growing hatred for Hitler and his notions of Aryan superiority. New Yorkers and Americans nationwide had cheered wildly the night of June 22nd when heavyweight boxing champ Joe Louis needed a mere two minutes to knock out challenger Max Schmeling, who Nazi propagandists had built up as a supposed example of German greatness. It was one of the first times that white Americans embraced a black athlete.

Until 1938, Gehrig took no public stance on the movement that had gripped his parents' native land. To be fair, no one asked him to. Sportswriters of the time rarely sought athletes' opinions about political or social issues. In the winter of 1934–35, after Gehrig and Ruth headlined an all-star baseball tour of Japan, Lou and Eleanor had traveled around the world, visiting Singapore, India, Egypt, Italy, France . . . and Adolf Hitler's Germany. Eleanor recalled in her memoir that Lou talked with people at a Munich beer hall and learned that "*die Juden* and other minority groups were on the brink of a disastrous time." Upon returning to New York, Lou told reporters he had stopped in Munich, and his mother said he had also visited relatives in the town of Baden Baden. But no reporter asked about his impressions of life under the Nazis. All of their questions had to do with the games in Japan and his salary demands for the coming season.

Still, because of his heritage, at least a few people vaguely associated Gehrig with the newly aggressive Germany. A May 1938 cartoon published in the *Detroit News* and reprinted in other papers showed Hitler and Italian dictator Benito Mussolini sitting by a huge globe, discussing how to divide up the world. Mussolini's suggestion to Der Fuhrer? "You get Lou Gehrig and I get DiMaggio!" It didn't help matters that Lou's childhood neighborhood, Yorkville, was the headquarters of the pro-Nazi German-American Bund. The Bund also had a unit in his adult hometown of New Rochelle.

In reality, Gehrig had no ties to the Bund or any other pro-Nazi group. He did pick Schmeling to defeat Louis ahead of their famous bout, but so did nine other Yankees in a poll taken by the *New York Sun.*

Gehrig may have taken his cue on the refugee crisis from his boss, Yankee owner Jacob Ruppert. Like his first baseman, Ruppert had deep German roots. But not long after Hitler took power, the Yankee owner signaled his sympathy for Germany's Jews, donating the use of Yankee Stadium for the first big fundraising event of the United Palestine Appeal, later known as the United Jewish Appeal, on September 20th, 1934. "No catastrophe in modern times compares in its tragic effects with the blow that has been struck at the Jewish people in Germany," Ruppert declared, according to the UPA. The Yankee owner called on "Jew and Christian alike" make a success of the show. Lou didn't attend that event—the Yankees were in Detroit at the time, playing the Tigers—but some thirty-five thousand others did and were treated to a "Night of Stars" starring Jack Benny, George Gershwin, George Burns, Gracie Allen and dozens of other big names from the worlds of music, acting, and comedy. The fundraiser became an annual event.

Four years later, Nazi Germany was starting to gobble up nearby countries while driving an ever-increasing number of Jews to flee for their lives. The situation got worse one week before the '38 Night of Stars when the Nazis orchestrated an orgy of violence against Jews across Germany and Austria. On the night of November 9th and 10th—thereafter remembered as *Kristallnacht,* the Night of Broken Glass—Nazi mobs destroyed hundreds of synagogues, thousands of Jewish-owned businesses, and killed at least ninety-one people. The savagery sparked protests and calls for action across the U.S. and in Britain. President Roosevelt chimed in, saying he could "scarcely believe that such things could occur in a twentieth-century civilization." But neither the U.S. nor the other countries of Europe flung open their doors to assist the Jews trapped under Hitler's thumb.

In New York, the UPA focused on helping the refugees, setting a fundraising goal of one hundred thousand dollars. To that end, they enlisted celebrities who would donate their services for a show. Among those who signed on were songwriter Irving Berlin, comedians Eddie Cantor and George Jessel, bandleader Cab Calloway, dancer Bill "Bojangles" Robinson, boxer Jack Dempsey, actors Orson Welles, Raymond Massey, and Walter Huston, and the choruses of several Broadway musicals. Someone—perhaps an increasingly frail Ruppert, who was listed as a boxholder for the event, or perhaps Robinson or Dempsey, both of whom were friends of Gehrig—convinced the Yankee captain to appear as well.

If anyone thought Gehrig might be a Nazi sympathizer, his mere attendance at the November 16th event was enough to kill that notion. The program opened with the playing of the "Star-Spangled Banner" followed by the future Israeli national anthem, "Hatikvah." Both the American and future Israeli flags were raised. Between the songs, dancing and excerpts from Broadway plays, speakers like Mayor Fiorello La Guardia and his predecessor Jimmy Walker denounced Nazi brutality. "Never before have Nazism and anti-Semitism reached such bestial heights in Central and Eastern Europe," said La Guardia. "For millions of Jews in these regions, the only salvation is flight and the so-called civilized world, which has permitted these atrocities to continue unabated, should at least provide some measure of sanctuary."

Lou also took the microphone, addressing the crowd of twenty thousand. His complete remarks appear to be lost to history. But the gist came across in a single line reported by the *Daily Worker*: "I'm glad to be in a country where I can wear the World's Fair emblem on my sleeve and play baseball, and not in a country where I'd have to wear the swastika."

He also may have mentioned his heritage, as the show business newspaper *Variety* reported that Gehrig, "speaking as an American of German descent, particularly wowed the attendance."

It's possible that Gehrig's appearance was a favor to Ruppert. At least one other Yankee, Lefty Gomez, attended the event. However, organizers no doubt saw the potent symbolism of a German-American athlete, one who spoke fluent German and whose mother had immigrated to America less than forty years before, showing public support for Jews. Gehrig, no dummy, must have seen it too.

He likely *felt* something as well, because in November 1939, even as ALS was making it hard for him to walk, he attended the UPA show at Madison Square Garden for a second time, appearing briefly on stage and receiving a huge round of applause from the crowd. "It's a pleasure to be here where no bombs are falling," he said, a reference to the fact that World War II had begun in Europe less than three months before.

* * *

Between fishing dates on Long Island Sound, Gehrig remained visible as fall turned into winter. On December 9th, he appeared with Ruth on WNEW radio to publicize a community center for poor children. On the 23rd he served as a Santa Claus at a Christmas toy giveaway sponsored by the Salvation Army. Occasionally, his photo or name popped up in the society or gossip pages. Walter Winchell, whose column was published in hundreds of newspapers nationwide, reported with a whiff of disdain in early December that the "Lou Gehrigs of the N.Y. Yankees have engaged a but-lah for their New Rochelle manse!" Winchell retracted the report after Eleanor called his office and said they hadn't.

More often, though, his name was brought up in relation to other ballplayers who, in the imaginations of various scouts and scribes, might replace him as the Yankees' first baseman soon. During the World Series, former major leaguer Lefty O'Doul, the manager of the San Francisco Seals in the Pacific Coast League, predicted his first baseman Len Gabrielson was destined to be Gehrig's successor. Gabrielson would play all of five major league games. Later in the month, a sportswriter touted Frank

Milani of the Yankee farm team in Wenatchee, Washington as the next Yankee first baseman. Milani would never advance past class-A ball.

The AP's Drew Middleton tossed several names into the pot in December. One was the aforementioned Eddie Levy; the others were Fred Collins and Johnny Sturm, the first sackers of the Yankee affiliates in Binghamton, New York and Louisville, Kentucky, respectively. Collins, like Milani, would top out in Class-A ball. Sturm would at least reach the majors and spend 1941 as the Yanks' regular first baseman. But his anemic batting numbers—a .239 average with three home runs—ensured it would be his only major league season.

In fact, the Yankees would never find a true replacement for Gehrig. After his retirement, the team would run through a long string of light-hitting, glove-challenged or aging first basemen—Sturm, Buddy Hassett, Nick Etten, George McQuinn, Johnny Hopp, Johnny Mize, Joe Collins, others—that didn't end until the arrival of Bill Skowron in the mid-1950s. The team wouldn't have another MVP at the position until Don Mattingly turned in a very Gehrig-like year in 1985.

One name that didn't pop up in the reports, oddly enough, was the Yankees' current backup at first, Babe Dahlgren. Few seemed to have a high opinion of his abilities, even his hometown *San Francisco Chronicle,* which said during that off-season Dahlgren had "no bat power" and had lucked into a soft job with the world champion Yankees: "He is carried to replace the mighty Lou Gehrig when needed, but the Old Iron Horse goes on year after year, playing a part of every game . . . so Dahlgren sits in the shade and watches him." This younger Babe would emerge from the shadows sooner than anyone suspected.

Amid all the speculation, Lou put on a brave face for the public, insisting he would come roaring back in 1939 and regain his former glory. "Jimmie Foxx made a strong comeback [in 1938] after a poor season and I am sure I can do the same thing. I haven't lost any of my enthusiasm," he told one reporter. To another, he said, "There'll be a different Gehrig out there next year. I'm far from through. Gehrig knows what Gehrig can do." Asked what happened in '38, he blamed his struggles on poor training habits. “The reason I was a flop last year was because I was not in condition,” he said. “I thought I would be able to get by, so I sneaked off on some of the exercises. Of course, I passed up the ones most grinding and they are the ones most essential. For one thing, I was not running enough. And running is paramount for the benefit to legs and wind.”

Fellow Yankees expressed confidence in their first baseman. “Lou had what some call a bad season last year, but it was only a bad season for Gehrig,” said McCarthy. “Plenty of first basemen would like to have a few bad seasons like that. He drove in over a hundred runs, didn’t he?” Joe DiMaggio said Gehrig was sure to have a better year, as did George Selkirk, who said, “This talk about Lou being on the downgrade is bunk. He’s as strong and powerful as ever and always keeps himself in marvelous condition.”

Bill Dickey acknowledged his road trip roomie had played about twenty-five years’ worth of baseball in the span of fifteen. “No one can go on forever. But Gehrig isn’t through yet. No man takes better care of himself,” he said.

However, no amount of care and exercise could counteract what was happening inside Gehrig’s body. The motor neurons that linked his muscles to his brain and spinal cord were continuing to wither and die, robbing him of a little more strength, coordination and control over his body with each passing week. Comments he made later to his doctors or reporters make clear that as 1938 turned into 1939, he was experiencing the classic early symptoms of ALS: muscle twitches, or fibrillation in his lower back and legs; unusual fatigue after doing anything physical; gradual and unexplained weight loss; and clumsiness in simple tasks like holding a teacup. Eleanor noticed during that off-season he had trouble raising his feet when he walked. “Lou would miss a curb and he would turn and look at me quizzically as if to say, ‘Now why did I do that?” she recalled.

At Eleanor’s urging, Lou consulted a physician in New Rochelle and underwent several examinations. The doctor, his name never revealed by the couple, diagnosed his patient with a gall bladder ailment. This conclusion seems odd on multiple levels. The gall bladder is a small, pear-shaped organ which stores bile produced by the liver and releases it into the digestive system to help break down fatty foods. A disorder can trigger health problems such as fever, nausea and stomach pain, and make the sufferer feel sluggish. But Gehrig reported none of these during the '38 season. Also, a gall bladder condition would not explain the loss of coordination remarked upon by so many observers.

The problem was that Gehrig's doctor wasn't a neurologist. Neurology—the branch of medicine dealing with the nervous system—was still in its infancy in 1938. The American Board of Psychiatry and Neurology had been founded only four years before and had granted credentials to fewer than one hundred specialists in the field. Researchers of the time had figured out motor neurons' role in transmitting signals between the brain and body. But a more detailed understanding of how the nervous system functioned, or why it sometimes ceased to function, was still decades away.

ALS presented an even greater mystery. A renowned French doctor, Jean-Martin Charcot, performed pioneering research into the disease in the 1860s. Charcot conducted autopsies of people who died after experiencing increasing paralysis without suffering significant pain or cognitive deterioration. In all the bodies, the doctor found hardening in certain portions of the spinal cord. Recognizing that all the victims had died of the same condition, he defined the disease and gave it its unwieldy but descriptive name. Amyotrophic is a Greek-derived word meaning muscle atrophy. Lateral indicates the location of the dying nerves, in the lateral spinal cord. Sclerosis refers to the abnormal hardening of body tissue. In much of Europe, ALS is still widely known as Charcot's disease.

The disease has always been rare. Today, about six thousand people in the U.S. are diagnosed with ALS each year. In Gehrig's time, with a smaller population and less awareness of the disease, the number was just twenty-five hundred. Unfortunately, that rarity meant there had been little study of the ALS by the time Lou experienced the symptoms. Trained doctors of the era could spot ALS in a patient by studying his or her musculature, but it remained unknown to the average general practitioner, let alone the public.

Based on his later comments, Lou accepted the New Rochelle doctor's diagnosis and adopted a new diet heavy in fruits and vegetables to treat it. "He was completely sold on the gall bladder deal," Eleanor recalled. She, however, was not. "I was beginning to think it might be a brain tumor. But neither of us wanted to bring it up because it might frighten the other," she said.

Unaware of Eleanor's growing alarm, some sportswriters recommended that Gehrig cut short his off-season and head to Florida for early workouts, to ensure he was in top shape before the '39 season got underway. One suggested, without presenting corroborating evidence, that the Yankee captain had enjoyed better seasons in the years he began his training earlier. Lou batted away the idea. "You hit or you don't," he said. "If my better seasons followed early departures for Florida, it was just a coincidence. I've never been handicapped by lack of training. If I have a bad spring, such as I had last year, it's just because things turned out that way."

Behind the scenes, though, Lou was having other thoughts. The first to get wind of them was the renowned baseball writer Fred Lieb and his wife Mary. Lieb, who would spend an incredible seventy years covering baseball, was probably Lou's best friend in the sports writing fraternity. The two had met soon after Gehrig joined the Yankees and by 1926 had become close, in part because both Fred and Mary had developed a nice rapport with Christina Gehrig on her visits to Yankee Stadium. "As far as Lou was concerned, anyone who did something nice for Mom Gehrig did something nice for him," Lieb wrote in his memoirs. The friendship strengthened when Fred took Lou and other ballplayers to Japan for exhibition games after the 1931 season. It grew even stronger on the boat ride across the Pacific when Mary counseled Gehrig not to give his mother veto power over girlfriends and possible wives.

Later, the couple managed the trick of supporting Lou and Eleanor's marriage while staying close to Lou's mother. Christina would give Fred tidbits about the friction with her daughter-in-law, like the fact that Eleanor got offended when Lou talked to his parents in German, a language that Lieb could speak and Eleanor could not.

The Liebs lived in St. Petersburg, the site of the Yankees' spring training camp. Fred said that in early 1939, he and Mary received a letter from Eleanor, asking them to find a small house and rent it for the Gehrigs' use. "Lou hadn't been too well, she wrote, didn't have the old starch," Lieb recalled. "They wanted to come down a month before the club started training so Lou could fish or just sit in the sun." While fishing was Lou's favorite pastime, the second part of the request was out of character; he was not known for parking himself by the pool. He and Eleanor may have hoped the Florida heat would bake the stiffness out of his legs. The Liebs found a place two blocks away from their house and waited for the Gehrigs' arrival.

In the meantime, Lou and Eleanor had to venture out from time to time into New York's cold winter winds. After eight months of struggling with phlebitis and other ailments, Jacob Ruppert died the morning of January 13th. The baseball and brewing worlds stopped to honor the Yankee owner, whose money and executive management were prime factors in transforming the Yankees from a perennial also-ran into the most successful franchise in all of sports. One of the last people to see Ruppert alive was Ruth, who came to visit "the Colonel" at his Fifth Avenue mansion for the night before his death. "Hello, Babe," Ruppert whispered as Ruth came to the side of his sickbed. The Babe admitted to the press that he couldn't help but cry when he left the room. It was the first and only time the owner, who usually addressed players with a formal "Mr.," had called Ruth by his famous nickname. "When all's said and done, the Colonel was a second father to me," he said.

Gehrig displayed no such emotion; he and Ruppert had enjoyed a cordial but businesslike relationship. His statement sounded like a press release: "I have been an admirer of the Colonel since I joined the club and always appreciated his ability in business, as well as his manner of dealing with myself and the other players." Despite the lukewarm words, Lou was named an honorary pallbearer for Ruppert's funeral, held two days later at St. Patrick's Cathedral in New York. Ruppert was a popular man, and over four thousand mourners crammed themselves into the giant edifice for the service. Lou and Eleanor were among them, their presence recorded in a newspaper photo that showed them and Joe McCarthy all wearing appropriately dark overcoats and somber expressions.

Ruppert's passing meant that Lou would negotiate his 1939 contract with the Yankees' longtime front office czar, Ed Barrow. Two days after Ruppert's funeral, the executors of the late owner's will named Barrow president of the Yankees, with undivided authority over player contracts, trades, and other baseball matters. Barrow took the appointment as his due. "There won't be any real change. I always made the decisions, and it was only very seldom that Colonel Ruppert questioned my judgment. I think we'll rock along about as usual," he said, adding that he thought the Yankees could win another world championship.

The thought of discussing salary with Barrow instead of Ruppert had to give Lou pause. Not only was the bushy-browed, straight-laced Barrow a tough negotiator, but Lou entered contract talks in a weakened position. The downturn in his '38 stats, the abundance of power hitters in the Yankee lineup and the continued reign of the reserve clause gave him little leverage. And the Yankees had never hesitated to force wage cuts on star players coming off poor seasons. Over Ruth's final three seasons with the Yankees, the team slashed his salary from eighty to thirty-six thousand dollars per year. During the same period, aging shortstop Joe Sewell saw his peak salary of fourteen thousand shrink by half. More recently, the Yankees had tried to cut Lefty Gomez' salary from twenty thousand to a paltry seventy-five hundred. Gomez dismissed the offer as a "bat boy's salary" and negotiated with the Yankees well into spring training. But in the end, he had to accept losing one-third of his previous paycheck.

Barrow mailed out 1939 contracts to Yankee players on January 21st and refused to disclose the club's offer to any individual player, though he acknowledged a handful of players were being offered lower salaries. One writer reported the Yankees wanted to slash Gehrig's salary by nine thousand dollars—a cut of over twenty percent from his '38 wages. Sportswriters got ready to fill their columns with juicy holdout stories of the kind that Gehrig (and DiMaggio) had provided a year earlier. But Lou threw the newsmen a knuckleball. On the evening of January 24th, he drove over to Barrow's home in Larchmont, a short distance from his own, for impromptu salary negotiations. The Yankee president and his first baseman talked for less than an hour before agreeing to terms. The press bandied about different figures but in fact, Gehrig would play the 1939 season for thirty-six thousand dollars, a relatively small reduction. He was the first Yankee to sign his contract that year. The fact that he would remain the best-paid player in baseball for the third year in a row made the cut easier to digest.

To reporters, Lou proclaimed himself fully satisfied and predicted a good season. "I'll play one hundred fifty-four games, bat over .300 and hit a new wage peak in '40," he said. He also revealed what Eleanor had hinted to Fred Lieb, that he'd be going down to Florida early to get extra conditioning before the start of spring training.

He had one charity commitment to fulfill before heading south. In mid-January, Lou had agreed to help promote a fundraising campaign for the National Foundation for Infantile Paralysis, the disease better known as polio. There's no record of his reasoning, though in hindsight, it's hard not to see his decision as another signal of distress over his own weakening body. Lou publicized the campaign with one of his periodic national radio appearances, this time on the crime-fighting drama "Gang Busters." He was introduced by program narrator Norman Schwarzkopf Sr., father of the Persian Gulf War general known as "Stormin' Norman." Lou urged listeners to help fight "a type of public enemy in our great country, an enemy that destroys health and destroys lives . . . especially the health and happiness of our children." The one-minute speech is fairly unremarkable except for one moment when Lou's New Yawk accent kicks up and he reminds the audience that the campaign coincides with President Franklin Roosevelt's *boith*day.

Lou also attended a fundraising party hosted by Jack Dempsey at his restaurant on Eighth Avenue. A photo taken that afternoon shows Gehrig shaking hands with the former boxing champ, surrounded by dozens of boys ages ten to fifteen, all of whom look very, very excited to be in the presence of such sports legends. Lou is sporting a wide smile and looks as though he doesn't have a care in the world—a rebuke to the adage that the camera doesn't lie.

Lou and Eleanor headed south to Florida on February 16th, eleven days before the Yankees opened camp. When they arrived in St. Petersburg, Fred Lieb didn't notice anything wrong with his guest right away. "Lou looked well and still had his distinctive hearty laugh," he wrote. In fact, for the next week, Gehrig did nothing but relax, eschewing any training regimen in favor of the great outdoors. First, he was reported hunting in the Everglades with Yankee coach Art Fletcher, an unusual occurrence only in that Lou rarely stalked wildlife. Next, he spent several days fishing in the Miami area with *Daily News* outdoors columnist Fred Fletcher, who was wrapping up a twelve-week winter sojourn along the Atlantic coast. Fletcher told his readers that he, Lou and Eleanor went trolling for tarpon and blue marlin in the Government Cut, a man-made shipping channel off Miami Beach. Basking in warm weather, sailing on a private boat with a captain, the three enjoyed idyllic conditions.

Even here though, possible signs of Gehrig's increasing weakness came through. Fletcher wrote that on February 22nd, Lou got a nibble on his line. The catch turned out to be mahi-mahi weighing about twelve pounds. Gehrig would normally have zero trouble reeling in a fish of that size. But on this day, according to Fletcher, Lou "magnanimously" turned the rod over to Eleanor, who pulled in the gold and green fish.

Fletcher may have detected something was wrong with his fishing buddy, for when he devoted a column to the highlights of his winter in the south, he characterized his time with the Yankee captain as an act of kindness and service. His "best deed" of the trip, he said, was helping Gehrig get ready for spring training. "Lou told me that in the few days he spent with me, his mind was at rest. He is brown as a berry and in perfect shape. Watch Der Gehrig 'go to town' this coming baseball season," Fletcher wrote.

Lou hoped his friend's prediction was right. At the end of the week, he and Eleanor left the fish behind, checking into St. Petersburg's Suwanee Hotel, the local Yankee headquarters. As promised, he was reporting to camp one week early. When team drills started on Monday, February 27th, he was there, running and batting and fielding with the other early arrivals, doing sit-ups to take off the winter flab. It was a hot day, and Lou told reporters he sweated off seven pounds. He also noted that his leg muscles were sore, a telltale sign of the cramping that affects many ALS patients.

From there, it was all downhill.

11

ALS

The rest of the story is well known. From day one of spring training, observers noticed a sharp decline in Gehrig's power, reflexes, and speed. No amount of practice and exercise could seem to shake the rust off his limbs. In the field, he was suddenly prone to letting easy grounders slip by his glove. At bat, he swung at and missed fastballs he used to pound over the outfield fence. At times, Lou looked disturbingly clumsy. In one of the few existing pieces of film from that sad spring, he loses his balance and falls backward while attempting to step away from an inside pitch. On the next pitch, he hits the ball but his body language betrays the exhaustion he's feeling. His swing, once among the smoothest and most powerful in baseball, now takes a monumental effort—and produces only a short fly to right.

The failures were not for lack of trying. "He responded the way you'd expect: by driving himself harder as if he could rebuild the tension in all those muscles," Eleanor wrote in her memoir. "In our hotel, he did exercises; at Huggins Field, he circled the track extra times like a hungry rookie." Joe McCarthy noticed the effort and tried to cast it as a positive. "He stayed out there so long and worked so hard yesterday he was almost too tired to get his uniform off," the manager said on March 8th. But at the same time, McCarthy ordered Tommy Henrich to work on his first base skills and played Henrich at first the next day when the team played its initial intra-squad game.

When the exhibition games started, Lou was back in his normal position but looked awful both at bat and in the field. In a

March 17th game against the Red Sox, he made two errors in the seventh, helping the Sox mount a four-run rally. Two days later, he made the third out with men on base three times. The next day, he let in another run with a fourth-inning error. Newspapermen began writing that that something was radically wrong with the Yankee captain. "Lou Gehrig's spring form is the worst he's ever demonstrated in the sixteen years he's been with the Yankees," wrote George Kirksey of United Press on March 20th. "He can't get off a dime around first base and he's been looking feeble at the plate. When he looks bad or misses one he indicates by gestures that with just a little more effort he could have made the play. It's the same defense mechanism Babe Ruth acquired in the last stages of his career."

The sight of the mighty Gehrig struggling to hit or field stunned his teammates and the memory of it would stay with them for decades. "In the batting cage, he would miss the first eight or nine pitches before connecting—not foul them off, miss them," remembered Joe DiMaggio forty years after the fact. "And when he did start to connect, he'd hit a weak dribbler or a soft line drive on one hop to the second baseman."

"I have a vivid memory of a spring training game in Clearwater," Tommy Henrich recalled at age eighty-two. "Gehrig was on first base, and somebody hit a ball to the right-center wall. That would naturally be good for two bases, but I remember watching Gehrig run from second to third and it looked like he was running uphill. He was getting no place. It was that apparent. It was a very obvious sign."

"It was really tough," remembered Frankie Crosetti soon before his eighty-fifth birthday. "You could never imagine this big, strong fellow . . . would come up with something like this. It was only spring training though, and you just figured he'd get going."

But when Lou didn't get going, McCarthy began to issue warnings. First, he benched Lou for a day in favor of Henrich. When that produced no results, he threatened to unilaterally end The Streak. "I will not play Gehrig unless he improves considerably in the next two weeks," the manager told reporters as the Yankees left St. Petersburg for their annual preseason exhibition tour. A distressed Lou lifted his game somewhat as the Yanks crisscrossed the South. But his hitting remained sporadic, his running and fielding shaky. For every good day, like a three-hit, five-RBI game he enjoyed in New Orleans, there were several disheartening ones where he could only muster a walk or a pop fly single. Even his triumphs came with qualifiers. When he scored from first on a double in Fort Worth, the *Daily News* celebrated with a photo of his slide into home and the caption "Gehrig CAN Run." But the local *Fort Worth Star-Telegram* told the real story: "His legs were wobbling like their owner had been chipped on the chin. He couldn't have made it another ten feet."

On April 13th, Lou enjoyed one last taste of athletic glory, stroking four hits, including a pair of home runs, in a game against the Dodgers in Norfolk, Virginia. Knowledgeable observers weren't fooled, however; Lou popped the homers over a short right field fence, approximately two hundred fifty feet from home plate. A columnist for the local *Virginian-Pilot* newspaper wrote, "He hit two homers and two singles, but Lou has lost the glow of youth. One can notice that from the top row in the stands."

McCarthy kept Lou in the lineup as the 1939 season began, hoping for the best. Instead, he found himself saddled with the worst first baseman in the league. On opening day against the Red Sox, Lou hit into a pair of double plays and dropped a throw in the ninth inning as the Yankees tried to protect a 2–0 lead. Over a three-game series in Washington, he managed only one hit, a meaningless infield single. Against Philadelphia, he finally got a clean hit to left field but was thrown out by a mile as he tried to take second base. On several occasions, he let grounders or line drives bounce off his glove. Most worryingly of all, Gehrig—one of the greatest RBI men in baseball history—kept failing to drive in runners in scoring position. In eight games he knocked in only one run, and that came on a groundout.

Senators catcher Rick Ferrell, one of Lou's better friends around the league, saw him during the Washington series. Before one game, the Yankees and Senators visited Arlington Cemetery in Virginia to honor Civil War General Abner Doubleday, who baseball's powers had recently declared—wrongly, as it turned out—to be the primary inventor of the sport. "It was a special occasion," Ferrell said. "We were going to play the Yankees later in the day, and this was about ten o'clock in the morning. We stood there at Doubleday's grave and I looked across the marker at some of the Yankees and there was Lou. He looked awful. I moved over to Dickey. I knew Bill was Lou's roommate. And I asked Bill what was wrong with Lou. 'He's just having trouble getting into shape this spring,' Bill said. 'He'll be all right.'"

The teams proceeded to Griffith Stadium in Washington for that afternoon's game. "The first time [Gehrig] came to bat that day," Ferrell said, "Lou'd swing and miss balls by six inches. And he'd take pitches right down the middle of the plate. Lou never did that before. And I sat back there catching and watching him and I said to myself, 'There's something bad wrong with Lou.'"

For the first week of the season, the proud Iron Horse remained in denial. In interviews, he acknowledged he wasn't hitting and conceded that he was not in tip-top shape, but predicted an imminent return to form. "I am improving every day," he insisted on a day the Yankees and Red Sox were rained out in Boston. His said his teammates had pointed out defects in his batting stance and declared that he was now swinging more naturally. He said the next step was to build up his legs, which he said had gone "soft" during the off-season due to lack of jogging. As for ending the consecutive games streak, Lou wouldn't hear of it. "Snapping my streak would do me only harm," he said. "I am not tired. Taking a day off would be silly."

To James Kahn of the *Sun*, he said he was glad his teammates and the fans continued to root him on, even though in fact that support was rapidly eroding. "When you're down on yourself, it means everything to have the fans and the fellows on your own team to slap you on the back and say you're going to be okay," he said. "And I will be, just as soon as I can shake myself out of this frame of mind this bad spring has put me in. I can feel the difference in myself. Things are getting easier. I'll be all right."

Lou also gave an interview to Henry McLemore, a surprise given the way the syndicated columnist had ripped his consecutive games streak the previous summer. McLemore wrote that he found Gehrig in a corner of the Yankee dressing room after a game, smoking a cigarette, drinking a glass of beer and fretting about his poor play. The columnist approached Lou and asked:

if you could do your career over again, would you push yourself to play in every single game, even when you were sick or had broken bones? Lou thought for a few seconds, then answered: "Yeah, I would. Yeah, I'd do it just the way I have. Maybe it wouldn't be smart, but it's all I know. Work, I mean. I never have known anything but work since I was six years old." After a pause, he added: "I know what you're thinking, that I had nursed myself along I wouldn't be worrying too much today. My legs would be faster, my eyes sharper, everything would be better. But you're wrong. Wrong about me, anyhow. I never could help giving all I had."

He was still giving maximum effort, only now it didn't seem to make a difference. At Yankee Stadium on April 29th, he let his team down twice—once in the fifth, when he flied out with two out and two men on base, and again in the seventh, when he grounded out with a runner on second. The Yanks lost to the Senators 3–1.

Things reached a tipping point, for both Lou and the fans, on April 30th. Four times that afternoon Lou came to bat with at least one teammate on base. Four times, he was set down without even advancing the runners. A hit would have been especially welcome in the sixth, when Lou batted with two outs, Red Rolfe on third and the teams locked in a scoreless tie. But all he could manage was an infield grounder for the third out. The Yankees lost again, 3–2.

According to Eleanor's memoir, after the game, Lou was walking toward the Yankee clubhouse when he overheard someone say, "Why doesn't he quit? He's through. We can't win with him in there." The unidentified player or coach wasn't the only one thinking that way. The next day, Bill McCullough wrote in the *Daily Eagle*:

> Three times yesterday Gehrig was in a position to knock over what would have been the winning run and three times Gehrig looked feeble. His eyesight seems to have failed him and the tip is out that he can no longer pull a ball to right field with any force behind it. . . . When he fizzled during the first week of the season, Yankee fans kept encouraging

> him but as the race gallops along and Lou continues to slap weakly at the ball and staggers around first base, the fans no longer are showing sympathy. Yesterday . . . Gehrig was booed in no uncertain terms as the three [Senators] pitchers curbed him.

That night, Lou went home and talked with Eleanor about removing himself from the lineup. She gently suggested the time had come. A few hours before the Yankees' next game in Detroit on May 2nd, Lou met with McCarthy and said he was benching himself for the good of the team. The manager inserted Babe Dahlgren to take his place. When the crowd of eleven thousand was informed Gehrig had chosen to end his streak, it gave him a long, hearty ovation. In the dugout, Lou found it impossible to hold back tears. It eased the pain only slightly when the Yankees erupted for seventeen hits that afternoon and routed the Tigers 22–2. Dahlgren, who homered in the third inning, asked Lou in the seventh if he wanted to "get in there." Lou said no.

They didn't say it out loud, but Lou's teammates were relieved at his decision. They were perplexed by his fall-off, they were sympathetic, but saw no way he could continue as the Yankees' regular first baseman. "You couldn't figure out what the heck happened to him since the end of the ['38] World Series," said Henrich. "The truth of the thing was, he didn't show one sign of getting better."

* * *

For a few weeks after leaving the lineup, Lou continued to take batting and fielding practice, hoping his athletic gifts would magically return. The Iron Horse insisted he was not ready to be put out to pasture. "I just can't understand. I am not sick," he said the day of his self-benching. His attitude had not changed when *World-Telegram* columnist Joe Williams caught up with him two weeks later. Williams had noted that Lou was spending every game at the side of McCarthy in the dugout, studying the action on the field. Did that mean he was interested in becoming a manager? Gehrig all but swatted away the question. "Don't try to get me thinking along that line. One problem at a time is all I can handle, and right now my main problem is to get back into the lineup," he said.

As late as the end of June, Dahlgren recalled, Lou was making noise about returning. When a photographer asked Lou to pose as though he was cheering for Dahlgren behind first base, he got a firm no. "I'm not cheering for him, because I'm going to be playing first base again myself," Gehrig said.

But the workouts only confirmed that Lou's strength and coordination were getting worse. Eleanor began urging him to see doctors at the Mayo Clinic in Rochester, Minnesota, considered then and now to be one of the nation's most advanced medical facilities. Lou hesitated at first and even dismissed a report of his impending visit as just a rumor. He may have changed his mind on June 6th, during the Yankees' second trip of the year to Detroit. Several former Tigers were at Briggs Stadium preparing for an old-timers' game, among them Sam Crawford, an outfield star of the early 1900s who was now approaching his sixtieth birthday. Gehrig watched as Crawford smacked several line drives in batting practice, smashing one ball off the right-field fence. Then Lou stepped in to face the same easy tosses and hit nothing but grounders and pop flies. "When I barely knocked the ball out of the infield, I resolved on the spot to hurry to a hospital," he later said.

Lou arrived at the Mayo Clinic on June 12th, and doctors put him through a week of questions, exams, and tests, hoping to identify his mystery illness and find a cure. However, the first doctor to meet with Gehrig, Harold Habein, had a strong hunch of what was wrong. "When he took off his clothes for the examination, the diagnosis was not difficult," Habein wrote in unpublished memoirs unearthed by Eig for *Luckiest Man.* The doctor saw wasting of the muscles in both hands, and what he called the "telltale twitching" of numerous muscle groups. "I was shocked because I knew what these signs meant—amyotrophic lateral sclerosis," he wrote.

ALS, then as now, was both incurable and fatal. Habein's mother had died of the disease just a few years before.

The Mayo Clinic has never released Lou's medical records, citing patient privacy, but the tests evidently confirmed Habein's hunch. On June 20th Lou returned to Yankee Stadium with a letter outlining the official diagnosis. Before that afternoon's game, Ed Barrow called reporters into Joe McCarthy's office inside the Yankee clubhouse. "Gentlemen, we have bad news," he said, and read the contents of the letter.

> TO WHOM IT MAY CONCERN:
>
> This is to certify that Mr. Lou Gehrig has been under examination at the Mayo Clinic from June 13 to June 19, 1939, inclusive. After a careful and complete examination, it was found that he is suffering from amyotrophic lateral sclerosis. This type of illness involves the motor pathways and cells of the central nervous system and in lay terms is known as a form of chronic poliomyelitis (infantile paralysis.)
>
> The nature of this trouble makes it as such that Mr. Gehrig will be unable to continue his active participation as a baseball player inasmuch as it is advisable that he conserve his muscular energy. He could, however, continue in some executive capacity."
>
> Signed,
>
> Harold C. Habein, M.D.

Habein's choice of words, apparently aimed at helping the Yankees and the public better understand an unfamiliar illness, ultimately sowed confusion. Did Lou have polio? No, he did not, but that didn't stop *Daily News* columnist Jimmy Powers from writing a story in August 1940 that said several Yankees may have acquired the dreaded disease from their former teammate. Gehrig was incensed. "This story is beyond belief," he told Grantland Rice. "There is no money in the world that would make me take a chance with my teammates, my other friends and the public in general." Within weeks, he filed a libel suit against the *Daily News*, seeking one million dollars in damages. The newspaper paid him a small amount to settle the case after Powers retracted the story and the paper apologized in print.

Habein also failed to explain that Lou's prognosis was terminal. Eleanor later said she had secured a promise from the Mayo Clinic doctors never to tell Lou he was dying. Gehrig's main contact at the clinic, Dr. Paul O'Leary, maintained the façade for almost two years, repeatedly telling his famous patient that with rest, luck and a proper course of treatment, he might arrest the progress of the disease. In one April 1940 letter, O'Leary assured Gehrig that he had at least a forty-five percent chance of recovery. "Accordingly, I urge that you keep pushing ahead and that you realize there will be days when you do not seem so good, but I am sure that such days will become of shorter duration and further apart," he wrote.

Today, such dishonesty would be condemned as unethical. But then, doctors often conspired with families to withhold bad or upsetting news from a patient facing a grim prognosis. Eleanor said her goal was to keep her husband from sliding into hopelessness and depression. "I thought I had him fooled all the way down to the end," she told a reporter three months after Lou passed away. "I kept pitching and he kept in there all the time with his head up, and I was sure he didn't know that he was going to die."

But Gehrig confidantes said he was aware the end was drawing near. Bill Dickey recalled that one day in the latter part of the 1939 season when Lou was still traveling with the Yankees, he and Lou got off the team train in Washington's Union Station to find a bunch of boys seeking the players' signatures. "And I guess we signed autographs for twenty or thirty minutes," Dickey said. "And finally, we went out, took the last cab to the old Wardman-Park hotel, and Lou looked at me and said, 'Look at all those kids, having all that fun, and here I am dying.' So I knew that Lou knew he was gonna die."

Eleanor came to the same realization as well. "He wasn't really being fooled by anybody," she said. Every morning, a doctor would come to examine Lou at the couple's home. According to the doctor, Eleanor said, "Lou would say after the examination was over, 'Well doc, how am I doing today? And then would wink at him, and would say, 'I'm doing better, isn't that right, Doc?' And he would wink at him again."

The Yankees and the sportswriting fraternity did understand that Lou's career was over, and within days of the diagnosis, the team declared it would honor him between the games of a July 4th doubleheader at Yankee Stadium. Lou Gehrig Appreciation Day, as the Yankees dubbed it, still stands as one of the most famous events in baseball history. Nearly sixty-two thousand fans—more than the Yankees drew for most World Series games at the time—packed the stands to pay tribute to the man who had brought them so many victories and so much joy. Ed Barrow made the occasion even more special by bringing in over a dozen of Gehrig's former teammates, mostly from the legendary 1927 team, including Hall of Famers Tony Lazzeri, Waite Hoyt, Herb Pennock and of course, Babe Ruth. Also present were Everett Scott, the shortstop whose consecutive-games streak Lou had broken, and Wally Pipp, the first baseman who Lou replaced in 1925.

Gehrig, wearing his Yankee pinstripes, his cap tucked under his right arm, stood in the sun and listened as a parade of speakers applauded his character and contributions to the game. Mayor LaGuardia praised him as a "prototype of the best sportsmanship and citizenship." Postmaster General James Farley, a rabid baseball fan, told Lou, "You will live long in baseball. For generations to come, while boys in America play baseball, they will point to your record with pride and satisfaction."

Joe McCarthy all but sputtered when he presented Lou with a trophy from his teammates: "Lou, when you came to my room in Detroit some time ago and told me you thought you were hindering the chances of the ballclub by staying in the ballgame, that was a day I never wanted to see, cause I never thought . . . that I would . . . uh, that is the time would come when you and I would . . . well, we're not gonna part, but . . ." McCarthy just shrugged his shoulders, acknowledging that he was at a loss for words.

Only Ruth, characteristically, chose to lighten up the mood. "In 1927, Lou was with us, and I say that was the best ball club the Yankees ever had," he said, a remark that drew a cheer from the crowd, though no reaction from Gehrig. He also recommended his old teammate get some rest and relaxation: "I don't know if the club is gonna let him do it, but my idea is to let Lou go up into the mountains—I saw a fishing rod here a minute ago—let him go up there and see if he can catch every fish there is."

Lou stood off to the side while the tributes flowed, clapping occasionally, but mostly looking down, like a man forced to attend his own funeral. It was not clear if he would speak. Finally, after a whisper of encouragement and a gentle push from McCarthy, Lou stepped to the thicket of microphones. The crowd broke into loud, sustained applause—then fell silent as Gehrig delivered words that echoed off the walls of Yankee Stadium and into the annals of history: *Today, I consider myself the luckiest man on the face of the Earth.*

Instantly, sixty-two thousand throats roared in appreciation and agreement.

Gehrig spent the next few minutes pouring out gratitude: to the fans, the groundskeepers, to Joe McCarthy and Miller Huggins, to Jacob Ruppert and Ed Barrow, and his teammates, standing just a few feet away, many trying to control their emotions.

"When you look around," he said, "wouldn't you consider it a privilege to associate yourself with such fine-looking men as are standing in uniform in this ballpark today?" Again the crowd roared, as Lou sniffled and wiped his face with a handkerchief.

He saved the most personal tributes for last:

> "When you have a wonderful mother-in-law who takes sides with you in squabbles with her own daughter—that's something. When you have a father and a mother who work all their lives so you can have an education and build your body—it's a blessing. When you have a wife who has been a tower of strength and shown more courage than you dreamed existed—that's the finest I know."

The fans thundered one more time when he concluded: "I might have been given a bad break, but I've got an awful lot to live for."

Some of the most insightful observations about that July 4th come from a man on the far edge of the spotlight. Wally Schang spent eighteen years catching in the American League and played on seven pennant winners, including the 1923 Yankee squad that won the franchise's first World Series. In 1939, he was managing the Ottawa Senators in the Canadian-American League when Barrow invited him to New York. Schang wasn't sure why; he wasn't part of the '27 Yankees and had been Gehrig's teammate for only one full season and parts of two others. But the old catcher caught a train to New York and spent two days hanging around Lou and Yankee Stadium.

Overlooked by the New York media, Schang spoke about his trip to local sportswriters when he returned to Ottawa—and left perhaps the most complete witness account of what Gehrig, his colleagues, and friends were going through as the baseball world said goodbye to the Iron Horse:

> "You know, Lou was always a hustler. He ran out pop flies until the ball was caught. He wasted no time getting underway once he felt the crack of his bat against the ball. And he was willing and eager to try for anything within hailing distance of first base when he was in the field. I saw him this spring in the Yanks' early-season games at New York and Lou was slowing up. But no person could have made me believe at that time that Gehrig was due to stop completely within a couple of months."
>
> "I dropped into the dressing room before the [July 4th] game and he got up from in front of his locker to come over and shake hands. He shuffled a little in his walk and his speech wasn't exactly clear. That disease had hit him harder than I thought and harder than most people thought. He won't be able to play ball anymore, I believe . . . In many ways, Lou now resembles an old, feeble man. He has trouble getting his feet to function properly."
>
> "And don't think he won't miss baseball. The next day I was sitting beside him in the Yankee dugout. Joe Gordon was tearing around second base and Gehrig said, 'If I were only in that boy's shape I'd be glad to play for nothing.'
>
> "We all sat in boxes during the first ball game and when it was over we went down on the field . . . A band led us old-time Yanks to the flag pole in center field, directly in front of Miller Huggins' monument. Ruth pulled the rope raising the 1927 pennant and we then marched behind the band and took up a position back of the pitcher's box. Barrow went into the dugout and assisted Gehrig to home plate . . . I never heard anything just like the reception they gave Gehrig

when he walked out to the home plate. Gehrig came out from the bench and the cheer that went up was enough to make your hair stand on end."

"Gehrig got a lot of presents . . . They gave Lou some fishing tackle, loving cups, silver sets, a smoking stand, and other things . . . All kinds of silver, but you couldn't help thinking it wasn't much help to him. Gehrig doesn't want silver. He wants to play ball and he can't play anymore and that silver doesn't help any. He's got everything he wants but his health."

"The show was kind of a sad one and it lasted for about an hour. I figured that the crowd would start yelling 'Play ball!' any minute, but they didn't. The only yelling they did was for Gehrig and Ruth and the other ballplayers who were there."

"But it sure was sad. Pretty nearly everybody choked up. I know I did myself a couple of times and [Yankee batting practice pitcher] Joe Schulte, who is about the happiest guy in the world, said he couldn't feel worse if they were digging a hole for Gehrig and planting him in a pine box."

"Ruth helped some with his nonsense. Ruth's a kid who never will grow up. He was out there on the field with a handful of sandwiches and two bottles of beer and he kept kidding along until even Gehrig began to feel good. If it hadn't been for him and Barrow I don't think Gehrig would ever have been able to get up to the microphone and speak his piece."

"While it was all going on, Lou just stood there, a beaten, dejected man. Then . . . Gehrig stepped to the microphone and made a wonderful speech. Tears were blinding him as he thanked the fans, the Yankee club, baseball in general, his parents, wife, and mother-in-law for all they had done for him."

"Most of the old ballplayers on hand that day had gone through too much during their big-league careers to show any sentiment outwardly. But this was one time when no person could restrain his emotion. As Gehrig was addressing the big gathering, I looked around. Right down the line, the veterans of many big-league battles were plainly going through torture seeing one of their former teammates stumble along, his baseball career brought to an abrupt and tragic end."

"And the most dramatic moment of them all came just before the ceremony broke up. Several photographers were snapping Gehrig and Ruth was getting a great deal of attention as the Babe walked over to Lou. He put his big arms around Gehrig, smiled and offered words of encouragement. Some cameraman yelled, 'Hug him, Babe, give us a real picture." The Babe complied and the pressure of Ruth's arms finally broke through Gehrig's discouragement. He smiled broadly and the cameras grinded away."

The emotion and enormity of the day shook Gehrig to his core. He later told a reporter that he nearly "caved in" during the ceremony and broke down once he got back to the dugout. "I was still fluttery on that bench all during the [second] game," he said. The flutters apparently continued the next day, when Senators catcher Rick Ferrell stopped by the Yankee dugout to congratulate Gehrig. "I told him, 'Lou that was the greatest speech I ever heard.' He said, 'Do you really think so, Rick? I really appreciate that."

Ferrell said Gehrig then tried to light a cigarette but had trouble doing it because his hand was trembling. Ferrell thought the tremor was due to the disease—but it could have also come from Gehrig recognizing how much the baseball world appreciated him, even as the abilities that made him such a legend in that world were being snuffed out.

* * *

Gehrig continued to travel with the Yankees and make occasional appearances on the field. On July 11th, he carried the lineup card to the umpires as the All-Star Game was held at Yankee Stadium for the first time. Later that week he took part in a couple of pre-game warmups with his teammates, fielding ground balls and catching throws from the outfield. "Docs don't approve, but Lou can't resist," reported the *Daily News*.

Off the field, Lou found other ways to stay active. From time to time, he popped up at the 1939 New York World's Fair in Flushing Meadows. Photos taken that summer show him signing baseballs for kids, testing out a fishing rod, even playing umpire in a gag photo with World's Fair president Grover Whalen standing at the plate. When the Yankees visited Washington in early August, he went fishing off the coast of Maryland with Dickey, Senators manager Bucky Harris and sportswriter Grantland Rice. Rice told his readers three days later that Gehrig, apparently feeling good that day, reeled in a sixty-pound white marlin. "When Lou finally brought him back to the boat to be tagged and returned to the Atlantic, he wore a grin that refused to leave," Rice reported.

Underneath the smiles, however, Lou had to deal with some grim realities. One was the progress of the disease. He clung to any sign that his once-magnificent body was somehow fighting it off. A seven-pound weight gain in mid-summer provided one glimmer of hope; increased energy, probably from B1 vitamin shots prescribed the Mayo Clinic, provided another. But the gradual loss of muscle and functioning in his limbs was hard to ignore. Lou told Rice that his strength gave out easily. "Can you imagine it? The other night I was pouring coffee for some guests and had to quit at the fourth cup," he said. On Yankee train trips, teammates noticed Lou could barely hold the cards during games of bridge. His walking slowed and grew shaky. During the World Series in October, he stepped onto the field only one time, to say hello to Joe McCarthy's wife. A reporter wrote that he shuffled like an old man.

Lou was also facing the knowledge that once the season ended he'd need to find another line of work. Ed Barrow made it clear that while the Yankees would pay Lou his agreed-upon 1939 salary, and even give him a full share of the World Series money, the team did not require his services thereafter. The callousness offended both Lou and Eleanor, who felt the Yankees could be a little more generous under the circumstances. But rather than take their complaints to the press, Gehrig put out the word that he was looking for a new job. Some surprising offers materialized. One was for Lou to serve as a greeter at a new Manhattan nightclub. Another was for him to host a sports-themed radio serial entitled "Our Coach." The show was reported to be set for a premiere and looking for a sponsor in early October. But it never went on the air, for reasons unknown.

In the end, Lou accepted something less lucrative but more personally rewarding, a position as a New York City parole commissioner. Mayor LaGuardia first broached the possibility during the summer, after Lou told him the story about visiting Sing Sing prison with the Yankees in 1929. The mayor gave Lou some books about criminal justice to read, and the two met several times during the waning months of the baseball season. On October 11th, two days after the Yankees wrapped up their fourth straight World Series title, LaGuardia announced that Gehrig would join the city workforce. For a salary of six thousand dollars per year, Lou would review the cases of people in the city's criminal justice system and determine whether they could be released back into society. The move required the Gehrigs to leave Westchester County and relocate to a home within the New York City limits; Eleanor found a house in the Riverdale neighborhood, at the northern end of Manhattan, where Lou would live for the remainder of his life.

Lou told reporters he was proud of his appointment and would be fully prepared when he took office. In what sounds like a slap at Barrow, he added: "I am through with baseball and have severed my connections with the Yankee club."

Beginning that October, Lou drove or was driven each day to his office at 139 Centre Street in lower Manhattan, where he spent the day reviewing cases and meeting with prisoners. Sometimes, he visited the city prison on Riker's Island—the ominously-named Tombs—or a women's jail in Manhattan to talk with inmates who had filed parole applications. "He'd see them all—rapists, hookers, pimps, addicts," recalled Eleanor. "It was quite a shock to his noble and somewhat innocent soul, but he took it."

For many, such a radical shift in occupation might have been depressing, but Lou repeatedly told visitors and reporters he found his job fulfilling. "It came just at a time when I needed to take my mind off myself and become interested in some new field. This work is unbelievably interesting," he said.

Most days, Lou spent about seven hours at the office, then went home to eat dinner, read, and listen to the radio before an early bedtime. But even as ALS took its toll, Lou could still walk—slowly, clumsily, but on his own power—and got around to some surprising places. Always a lover of classical music, he attended all of the eight concerts that renowned conductor Arturo Toscanini broadcast from Rockefeller Center in late 1939. He never secured tickets for the Saturday night shows but had something better—a friend in NBC's manager of guest relations, Charles "Chick" Thurman. "[Thurman] is an old Gehrig fan and always sneaked him into the studio if there was an extra seat to be found," reported the *Radio and Television Mirror.*

Sometimes, Lou still had the energy to go in front of the microphones. On March 3, 1940, he appeared on sports announcer Bill Stern's show, talking about his transition from star athlete to spectator. Two weeks later, he made his first and only appearance on a genuine comedy program, the top-rated *Chase and Sanborn Show*, hosted by ventriloquist Edgar Bergen and his dummy, Charlie McCarthy. Bergen, the father of actress Candice Bergen, was a star on the national radio scene for two decades. If the notion of a ventriloquist performing on the radio seems odd, consider that audiences weren't tuning in to see whether Bergen's lips moved. They enjoyed the laughs generated when McCarthy, who Bergen infused with a wisecracking and mischievous wit, sparred with guests such as comedian W.C. Fields. In one characteristic exchange, Fields threatened to turn the dummy into a Venetian blind. "Oooh, that makes me shudder," Charlie retorted.

The recording of the show shows Gehrig sounding less robust than in the past but free of the slurred or slowed-down speech that affects many ALS patients. He had no trouble handling an opening segment that played off the fact it was St. Patrick's Day.

McCARTHY: "How will you be having your coffee, Mr. O'Gehrig?"

GEHRIG: "In a cup, Mr. McCarthy, and the name isn't O'Gehrig, its *Lou* Gehrig."

McCARTHY: "Well, it's got to be O'Gehrig, Only an Irishman could swing one of those wooden shillelaghs like you did for the Yanks."

Lou also took good-natured ribbing from the hosts. When Bergen announced their guest held the major league record for grand slams, McCarthy turned to Lou and said, "Wellll . . . pleased to meet you, Babe." When Bergen said Lou had played in over two thousand consecutive games, McCarthy quipped, "Whoa, he's in a rut!" Gehrig's sparring with the pair was nimble enough that it earned kudos from the nation's number-one Broadway and gossip columnist, Walter Winchell, who wrote, "L. Gehrig slammed a home run guesting on the McCarthy show."

Lou returned to the airwaves in early May, in a preview of the second season of the New York World's Fair. This time, however, ALS seemed to take a toll on his speaking ability, and he tripped up on several words despite reading from a script. There was also a heartbreaking exchange with a young boy who asked why Gehrig's old team was off to an uncharacteristically bad start that year. Gehrig replied that he wasn't in baseball anymore; the city of New York was his employer. The boy then asked in a halting voice, "But don't you think the mayor could lend you to the Yankees for a few games?" Gehrig might have been embarrassed by the way he came across, because two days later, on May 6th, a *Daily News* columnist reported that Gehrig had canceled all his upcoming public appearances, allegedly due to the severity of the medical treatment he was receiving.

Now and then, Lou would turn up at Yankee Stadium, where his former teammates welcomed him, razzed him, and did their best to ignore his physical condition. Sometimes it wasn't easy. Dahlgren recalled seeing Gehrig on opening day, 1940. "He toddled, not walked into the clubhouse, and I was so upset I went down the runway to look at the field," he said. But Lou followed him down the runway and asked for a cigarette. Dahlgren obliged, only to be horrified again when Gehrig had to grab the cigarette with his lips instead of hands, which had become largely immobilized.

In June 1940, Lou attended all three games of a series against the Indians. The Yankees were in an uncharacteristic batting slump, and the visitor didn't hesitate to needle his former teammates. "These aren't the Yankees I've been reading about in the paper," he joshed. "Six hits and seven hits a game. What's the matter with you guys?" During one game, he was photographed sitting in the dugout, watching the action, wearing a dark suit and tie. However, the Yankees sitting near him, including Joe McCarthy, look a little bit uneasy, something that longtime Yankee clubhouse man Pete Sheehy confirmed in an interview decades later. "It just killed us to see that big, strong guy in that kind of shape," he said. "I think Lou sensed he was making the guys feel uncomfortable because one day, he got up, walked out the tunnel and never came back."

* * *

In some patients, ALS progresses slowly, allowing them several years of relatively normal living conditions. Gehrig didn't fall into that category. "I think Lou Gehrig's ALS progressed pretty fast," says Dr. Richard Bedlack. "If we agree it started in the spring of 1938, after *Rawhide*, and he died in 1941, that's very fast. Fifty percent of people with ALS will do better than that. There's no evidence from his progression rate that him being so strong and physically fit helped him in any way. He didn't do better than the average person with ALS, that's for sure."

By the latter part of 1940, Gehrig had stopped going to games or radio shows or other public places. In hopes of arresting the disease, he tried experimental treatments like injections of histamine and ingestion of vitamin E pills, the latter under the supervision of the renowned Dr. Israel Wechsler, future president of the American Neurological Association. They had no effect. Medical tests confirmed he was continuing to lose strength and function in his limbs, and simple actions like swallowing and speaking became increasingly difficult. Despite doctors' warnings, he continued to smoke, with Eleanor or other helpers putting the cigarettes to his mouth.

Occasionally, he would still talk with reporters at the parole office and try to put on a good show. "I'm satisfied and the doctors are satisfied with my progress," he said in January 1941. "It'll take a long time to get well and all I can do is stick in there and slug and hope for the best." That April, in what may have been his last interview, he told a reporter from the International News Service that he still worked from nine to five every day. "That's a pretty good day, isn't it?" he said.

But in truth, his decline was accelerating. The INS reporter, Jack Henry, gave readers an honest picture of his diminished state. "He has lost weight. Gray strands streak his dark hair. The dimpled cheeks are rosy, but a pallor strange to the Gehrig countenance prevails. His powerful, swashbuckling motions are gone." Visitors to the Gehrig household—a mix of Yankee associates, sportswriters, and entertainers—saw the same deterioration.

Gehrig must have sensed time growing short, for in January 1941 he wrote again to Dr. O'Leary and begged for the truth about his prospects. "[I]t is getting a little more difficult each day and it will be hard to say how much longer I can carry on," he said. "I don't mean to be pessimistic but one cannot help wonder how much further this thing can go and I wish you would again drop a note as to your thoughts and percentage of making a proportional recovery.

He added: "Don't think that I am depressed or pessimistic about my condition at present. I intend to hold on as long as possible and then if the inevitable comes, I will accept it philosophically and hope for the best. That's all we can do."

He never got a straight answer from O'Leary, or anyone else.

The inevitable arrived on the evening of June 2nd. He had been housebound and mostly bedridden for weeks, and his breathing had become "slower and slower, like a great clock winding down," in the words of Eleanor. He spoke briefly that morning, then slipped into a coma.

With his wife, parents, mother-in-law, and a doctor at his bedside, he passed away that night shortly after ten P.M. "The most beatified expression instantly spread over Lou's face, and I knew the precise moment he had gone," Eleanor wrote.

Epilogue

In keeping with the man they honored, Lou Gehrig's funeral services were simple and modest. Eleanor allowed no more than a hundred people, all of them family and friends, to attend the short service at a small Riverdale church. At Eleanor's request, there were no speeches. "We will have no eulogy," the pastor said, "because you all knew him."

Afterward, Gehrig's body was taken to the Fresh Pond Crematory, the same facility where his sister Sophie was cremated thirty-five years before. Eleanor had the remains buried at Kensico Cemetery in the town of Valhalla and joined him in the grave over forty years later. Today, the spot is marked by a stone monument that simply reads, "GEHRIG." The monument has a typographical error: it says Lou was born in 1905, not 1903. No matter. Fans of the Yankee great still visit the site and leave baseballs or small American flags in tribute.

In June 1942, RKO Pictures released *Pride of the Yankees*, a respectful biopic with Gary Cooper as Lou, Theresa Wright as Eleanor, and Babe Ruth as his younger self. The movie told the story of the poor boy's rise to fame but at producer Sam Goldwyn's behest focused on the romance between Lou, portrayed a shy bumbler off the field, and Eleanor, portrayed as a near-perfect wife. The movie downplayed ALS; Lou didn't get sick until the last twenty minutes and was never seen struggling to walk or losing the use of his hands. The scriptwriters also took liberties with his famous speech, rearranging it so that the "luckiest man" line came at the end. Goldwyn knew what he doing; *Pride of the Yankees* was the seventh-highest grossing film of the year, and troops repeatedly called on Cooper to recite the speech when he toured U.S. bases in the Pacific during World War II.

Later depictions of Gehrig's life on television—a 1955 episode of the history series *You Are There,* a 1956 episode of the drama series *Climax* and a 1977 made-for-TV movie—concentrated primarily on his illness but also shied away from showing the worst physical effects of ALS. A new Gehrig film was reported to be in development in 2017; it will be interesting to see how the movie, if made, depicts the progress of the disease and Lou's efforts to cope with it.

Every so often after Gehrig's death—most often on the anniversary of when he ended his consecutive game streak—sportswriters would revisit his story and interview the people who knew him well. Many thought that if not for ALS, Gehrig could have played for several more years and rewritten baseball's record book. "There's no reason to believe he wouldn't have been hitting home runs when he was forty-five years old," said Joe McCarthy.

Forced to retire a decade younger than that, Lou still finished with four hundred ninety-three homers, second only to Ruth at that point in time. Gehrig remains high on baseball's all-time leaderboards a century after he made his debut. His most impressive number might be his OPS—on-base plus slugging percentage—a stat that wasn't even calculated in his era. Lou's 1.080 is the third-best in the sport's history, behind only Ruth (who else?) and Ted Williams.

Lou's accomplishments received a new wave of attention when the record that many thought unbreakable, his streak of two thousand one hundred thirty consecutive games, was finally topped by Baltimore Orioles shortstop Cal Ripken in 1995. Ripken, a two-time American League MVP, was credited with rejuvenating interest in baseball after the destructive 1994 players strike, and justifiably viewed his streak with pride. But he rejected any idea that he was Gehrig's equal as a player. "The strangest thing is all these comparisons to me and Gehrig," he said in one interview. "I think I'm a pretty good ballplayer in the scheme of things, but I'm no Lou Gehrig. What we do have in common is the love of the game and the stubbornness to be in the lineup."

Lou's contemporaries are now dead, the anniversaries now pass mostly unnoticed, and his records have all fallen (except for one: he still holds the Yankee team record for triples, with one hundred sixty-three). But Gehrig remains an icon, decades after he last stepped onto a baseball field. In 1999, fans were asked to pick baseball's All-Century team. Gehrig not only won the first-base competition but was also the top vote-getter among all players. For once, Lou beat the Babe. His popularity is also reflected in the high prices that collectors continue to pay for his bats, uniforms and other memorabilia. Several authenticated Gehrig game jerseys have fetched over a half-million dollars at auction. His 1937 Yankee home jersey sold for eight hundred seventy thousand.

Gehrig remains well-known among the ALS community, although not the focal point of attention he once was. "As time goes on, the association fades," says Brian Frederick, executive vice president for communications at the ALS Association in Washington, D.C. Today, the best-known athletes who came down with the disease are mostly football players, including former New Orleans Saints safety Steve Gleason, former Atlanta Falcons linebacker Tim Green, and former San Francisco 49ers receiver Dwight Clark, who blamed his ALS on concussions sustained during his career. The most famous ALS patient of the twenty-first century is the late British theoretical physicist Stephen Hawking. Hawking, a rare celebrity scientist, managed to live and to publish influential work for decades despite being diagnosed with ALS in his early twenties. When he died at age seventy-six in 2018, he was one of the longest-surviving ALS patients on record.

For many, however, ALS remains Lou Gehrig's Disease. Patients registering in the ALS National Registry see a picture of Lou on the website's front page. The University of Pittsburgh's ALS research institute is called the Live Like Lou Center. Columbia University's research center is named after both Eleanor and Lou. Some sufferers have gone a step further and refer to the disease itself as "Lou." Writer Dudley Clendenin was one. "I sometimes call it Lou, in his honor, and because the familiar feels less threatening," he said in a 2011 essay, not long before he died. When an ALS patient in his late thirties, Adam Smith, announced his diagnosis to family and friends in 2016, he did so a letter entitled "Me, You and Lou." Smith made it clear he did not like "Lou," the disease. "I was living a healthy life until Lou started hanging out with me," he wrote. "I'm angry thinking about Lou . . . Most of all, I'm tired and frustrated from Lou being a stage-5 clinger."

ALS remains a thankfully rare disease, affecting perhaps thirty thousand Americans at any one time. That's one reason progress toward a cure has been slow—more common diseases like cancer and Alzheimer's take the lion's share of public attention and research dollars. But scientists continue to plug away and develop new therapies. In late 2018, Boston-based researchers began a phase one safety trial of AT-1501, a drug that showed promising results when tested in mice and primates. The drug targets a protein, CD40L, which plays a role in inflammation. In ALS patients, the protein is produced in excess and may be a cause of neurodegeneration. The ALS Association donated one million dollars to help fund the trial.

Frederick believes the Ice Bucket Challenge, which raised one hundred fifteen million dollars for ALS research in 2014, injected new energy as well as money into the search for effective therapies. "There's definitely hope within the research community that we're on the cusp of a new treatment or a cure," he says. Those are optimistic words, not unlike the ones Lou Gehrig heard in 1939 and 1940 and 1941 as he fought his unsuccessful battle against the disease. The difference is that now, scientists have an infinitely greater ability to examine, analyze and understand the myriad processes of the human body. Sooner or later, researchers somewhere will hit upon a drug, an operation, or a gene therapy that can prevent or reverse ALS.

Then, when the disease becomes a hindrance instead of a killer, Lou Gehrig will be remembered first and foremost for what he was—one of the greatest baseball players who ever lived. As recently as 2016, writers at ESPN.com picked Gehrig as the best first baseman and the seventh best player overall in the game's history. The writers at BleacherReport.com gave him the same ranking a year later. Renowned baseball experts like Bill James, Joe Posnanski and Jim Jaffe have ranked him a bit lower, but still in the top twenty.

"If you look at Gehrig's on-field performance, his numbers are unreal," Major League Baseball's official historian, John Thorn, once said. "It's easy to think of Gehrig today as merely a medical case and a sad story, but he was one of the three best hitters in the history of baseball."

It's also easy to overlook his greatest performance, when he stayed in the lineup and helped the Yankees win a World Series, even as ALS ripped away the strength and skills that made him such an exceptional ballplayer.

Lou Gehrig ultimately lost his battle with ALS, but for one remarkable, unmatchable year, he fought it to a draw. Against a foe like ALS, that counts as a victory.

Notes

Page

Introduction

1 *"progressive imprisonment without parole."* Tony Judt, "Night," *The New York Review of Books*, January 14, 2010.

1 *"melts your nerves..."* Mitch Albom, *Tuesdays With Morrie* (Doubleday, 1997), p. 9.

2 *...noticed his right arm growing weaker.* Shaw described his early ALS symptoms in "Letter to My Younger Self," published on playerstribune.com, January 15, 2019.

2 *"Imagine what kind of constitution..."* Whitney Martin, Associated Press, June 21,1939.

3 *"Today, I consider myself..."* Newsreel footage of Lou Gehrig Appreciation Day, New York, Yankee Stadium, July 4, 1939.

Page

Lou Gehrig Crashed Here

5 *"The driver of one car was..."* The account of the accident is drawn from "Skidding Auto Knocks Lou Gehrig for Foul Into Newswoman's Yard in Jefferson City," *Knoxville Journal*, December 28, 1937; "Gehrigs Take to Road After Slight Wreck," *Knoxville News-Sentinel*, December 28, 1937; and a short Associated Press story from the same day. The *Journal* article was clearly written by Clara Park—she references herself in the article—but she was not given a byline, for reasons unknown.

6 *"He was perfectly built for power."* Grantland Rice, *The Tumult and the Shouting* (A.S. Barnes & Co. 1954), p. 284.

7 *"Hans the blue-eyed Dane."* Ibid.

7 *"I don't suppose I ever saw..."* Jim Murray, "Gibraltar in Cleats," *Los Angeles Times*, May 5, 1976.

8 *Lou had paid two thousand dollars...* Cancelled check published in The Barry Halper Collection of Memorabilia (Sotheby's, 1999).

8 *"I saw her coming down the highway." Knoxville Journal*, December 28, 1937.

8 *"He probably sprained his wrist..."* Ibid.

8 *"Somebody called Cowan Rodgers Jr."* Ibid and *Knoxville News-Sentinel*, December 28, 1937.

9 *"...the first baseman for the New York Giants."* Eddie Brietz, Associated Press, December 31, 1937.

9 *Lou pressed Ricie Stogner for damages.* Gehrig referred to this in a February 1938 interview with the News-Sentinel. He said he retained Clara Park's husband, Frank, to pursue reimbursement. "When I had a little accident in Jefferson City I just left matters in his hands and he looked after them," he said. At some undetermined point, he hired the Knoxville attorney as well.

9 *"Gehrig will be unable to attend."* This one line from a local newspaper, *the Jefferson City Standard Banner,* was included in a history of the city published years later. Oddly, the paper did not mention Gehrig's accident at the time it happened.

9 *Monroe would finally issue a ruling.* Most information on the case comes fromMonroe's one-page handwritten decision, found in the Jefferson County, Tennessee archives.

Page

Hollywood

10 *"I got in touch with..."* United Press, October 20, 1936.

10 *Leopard-spot caveman outfit.* Lou posed for the black-and-white photos in New York sometime that October and various shots appeared in newspapers in the days after the Tarzan-Sol Lesser story broke. Most papers published the more PG-rated pics, where Lou wore the full outfit and wielded a caveman's club or a stick. The steamier photos, where he wore only a pair of briefs and gave the camera his best come-hither gaze, can be found online.

11 *"screwy."* Gene Ward, "Gehrig Tries Out for Tarzan," *New York Daily News*, October 21, 1936.

11 *"I'm not an actor."* Henry Super, United Press, October 20, 1936.

11 *"a kick in the pants."* Henry McLemore, United Press, October 21, 1936.

11 *Custody of their only child.* The custody battle between Christy Walsh and his ex-wife is documented in articles published between 1935 and 1938 by the major wire services of the era and the *Los Angeles Times.* Walsh's efforts to win over Christy Jr. through sports didn't stop with baseball. In 1936, he asked Madaline for permission to take their son to the summer Olympics in Munich, Germany. Madaline balked and the matter wound up in the courts. The Los Angeles Superior Court eventually said father and son could go—but the ruling came in February 1937, eight months after the games were over.

11 *"I guess it's just instinctive."* Associated Press, April 21, 1936.

12 *Ties to George Herman Ruth.* Christy Walsh first detailed his relationship with Babe Ruth in his self-published 1938 memoir, *Adios to Ghosts,* written as he left the ghostwriting business. The most complete examination of the Walsh-Ruth dynamic can be found in Jane Walsh's book, *The Big Fella* (Harper, 2018).

12 *"When I was a young boy..."* The typed one-page letter, dated October 26, 1935 and addressed to "Master Christy Walsh Jr.," was sold at auction in 2012 for almost forty-two thousand dollars.

13 *"Who Is This Lou Gehrig?"* The headline actually appeared in several newspapers, somewhat incongruously, over photos of Lou and Philadelphia A's pitcher Jack Quinn. The caption noted that Quinn had struck out Gehrig three times in one game, but that a few days later, Gehrig hit his twenty-sixth homer of the season to pass Ruth as the league leader. The first event happened on June 26th, 1927, the second on July 1st.

13 *"There was a ready market..."* Christy Walsh, *Adios to Ghosts*, p. 35.

13 *A hefty ten thousand dollars.* Jonathan Eig, *Luckiest Man* (Simon and Schuster, 2005), p. 117.

14 *"...sat and played with a pussy cat."* The account of Lou's March 3rd, 1937 encounter with Christy Jr. and the aftermath is drawn from stories by the Associated Press and United Press, both on April 8, 1937.

15 *"Tickets to the game were scarce."* United Press, January 18, 1938. This article is also the source for details on Lou's January 1st, 1938 outing with the Walshes and the aftermath.

15 *"If my removal from his boyhood..."* Ibid.

15 *...and posed for photos with the players.* Associated Press photo, January 3, 1938.

15 *I'm not too good at riding horses.* Frederick C. Othman, United Press, January 4, 1938.

16 *"Maybe I won't have to kiss her."* Ibid.

16 *"I'm just a big lucky guy."* Joe Williams, "Suppose There Hadn't Been Any Baseball," *New York World-Telegram*, February 18, 1938.

16 *"...the boy dubbed Henry Louis Gehrig."* Sometimes, the name is reported as Heinrich but Gehrig's birth certificate, easily found online, confirms that his first name was Henry from birth.

16 *Low-rent, no-frills tenement building.* Details on 1994 Second Avenue come from various New York City records, particularly the Department of Buildings website. The tenement was apparently built in the 1880s, which is when references to the address first appear in official city journals. A state census conducted in 1905, when the Gehrigs lived there, found the building housed about fifty-five residents. Most of the adults were born in Germany or other European countries; most of the kids were born in America. The tenement remained in use until the 1960s, when safety violations began to mount. Inspectors declared it unsafe in 1967 and the city issued a demolition permit a year later. Why wasn't the building saved as a historic landmark? Possibly because for many years, Gehrig's birthplace was thought to be a building on East 94th Street. His sister Anna was born at that address, but by the time Lou arrived a year later, the Gehrigs had moved.

17 *Eight to ten dollars a week.* Harry T. Brundidge, "Lou Gehrig Gives Baseball Full Credit For Rescuing Parents and Self From New York Tenement District," *The Sporting News*, December 25, 1930.

17 *"Lou's family was just plain poor."* Eleanor Gehrig and Joe Durso, *My Luke and I* (Signet, 1977 paperback edition), p. 29.

17 *...when they met in 1901.* Date of the meeting comes from Eig, *Luckiest Man, p. 4.*

17 *The baby died in September.* September 5th was the exact date, per New York City records found on ancestry.com.

17 *Photos of the long-demolished structure.* The pictures are available through the New York City Municipal Archives Online Gallery.

17 *She had suffered from convulsions.* Eig, *Luckiest Man,* p. 7.

17 *...the loss of two other children.* New York state has birth and death certificates for Anna and Sophie Gehrig, but neither exist for the other Gehrig child. He may have been stillborn, or lived only a few days. Gehrig appears to have mentioned this brother only once, in the 1930 Brundidge article. The boy and his year of birth are also mentioned in "The Life of Lou Gehrig," a twenty-nine page biography that Fred Lieb wrote for the *1942 Baseball Register* (The Sporting News, 1942). Lieb didn't cite a source for the info, but given that he was friends with Gehrig's parents, it's reasonable to conclude they gave him the information.

18 *"We were a sickly lot..."* Brundidge.

18 *...a robust fourteen pounds at birth.* This figure, cited frequently in Gehrig biographies, appears to originate in Lieb's 1942 profile of Lou. Presumably Lieb got the factoid from Christina and Heinrich.

18 *"I believe in food..."* Hortense Saunders, Newspaper Enterprise Association syndicate, August 6, 1927.

18 *"...never played hooky or missed a day."* Gehrig and Durso, *My Luke and I,* p. 34.

19 *He played soccer...* Information on Gehrig's high school soccer, football and baseball exploits comes from *My Luke and I* and numerous articles published in New York-area newspapers during 1919 and 1920, when Lou attended the High School of Commerce. Gehrig was apparently quite good at soccer; an October 12, 1919 *Brooklyn Standard Union* article credits him and two teammates with "impenetrable defense" in a 2-0 win.

19 *"He can hit a ball harder..."* James Crusinberry, "New York Prep Nine, Sans Suits, Bats, Sure Stars," *Chicago Tribune,* May 23, 1920.

19 *...cooking meals at the Sigma Nu Theta.* Niven Busch, "The Little Heine," *The New Yorker,* August 2, 1929.

19 *In one not atypical contest...* "Fordham Fails to Hit Gehrig, Lion Wins 8-2," Columbia Spectator, May 16, 1923.

20 *batting average was .444, with seven homers.* These are Lou's 1923 statistics as given throughout the years by Columbia University.

20 *"I needed the money badly..."* Harry Grayson, Newspaper Enterprise Association, May 27, 1938.

20 *"...feeble hitting."* Marshall Hunt, "Ruth and Meusel Down Senators, 8-5," *New York Daily News*, June 3, 1925.

20 *"It was Gehrig's first home run..."* Grantland Rice, "The Sportlight," October 4, 1932.

21 *"Some people thought Lou was jealous..."* Gehrig and Durso, *My Luke and I*, p. 141.

21 *"...Gehrig lived in Ruth's shadow."* Fred Lieb, *Baseball as I Have Known It* (Grosset & Dunlap, 1977), p. 202.

21 *"Mom makes a home comfortable enough..."* Busch, *The New Yorker*, 1929, and "Gehrig Won't Spend Salary," *The Morning Call* (Allentown, PA), January 10, 1928.

22 *"...to break down his inbred inferiority complex."* Lieb, *1942 Baseball Register.*

22 *"Curious how Gehrig..."* Frank Graham, "Setting the Pace," *New York Sun*, February 6, 1938.

23 *"If I ever want to commit suicide..."* Film historian John Bengston has said Gehrig's cameo and all of Ruth's scenes were likely shot on September 15, 1927 in New York.

24 *"The toughest part about this whole business..."* Unbylined article, "DiMag Goes Hollywood," *San Francisco Chronicle*, August 5, 1937.

24 *"histrionic all..."* Associated Press, March 5, 1937.

24 *"I believe we will hit a home run..."* Jack Guenther, United Press, March 3, 1937.

24 *"that personal magnetism..."* Jack Miley, "Alas, Poor Yorick!" *New York Daily News*, March 6, 1937.

24 *"He had a tremendous personality."* Gomez interviewed by Rod Roberts, April 1, 1983. The entire interview is on the National Baseball Hall of Fame website, oral histories page.

25 *"Because Gehrig was quiet..."* Thomas Meany, *Baseball's Greatest Players* (Grosset & Dunlap, 1953), p. 104.

25 *"Lou didn't lead by being talkative..."* Faye Vincent, *The Only Game in Town* (Simon & Schuster, 2006), p. 64.

25 *"Modesty is the main thing..."* Christy Walsh, *Adios to Ghosts* excerpt, *The Hammond (Ind.) Times*, January 16, 1938.

25 *A movie called The Trail Blazers.* Guenther, United Press, March 3, 1937 and "Gehrig to Star with Dick Allen," *Los Angeles Times*, March 5, 1937.

26 *"Lou never had more fun..."* Wilson, *Knoxville News-Sentinel*, February 6, 1938.

26 *Done largely at the Morrison Ranch.* "Cast Enjoys Birthday Fete," *Los Angeles Times*, January 30, 1938.

26 *"...more fun than the World Series."* Jack Guenther, United Press, January 25, 1938.

26 *"no mike or camera fright."* Article bylined as J.H., "Gehrig Tells of His Experiences as an Actor," Portsmouth (N.H.) Herald, April 26, 1938.

26 *"Mrs. Gehrig razzed me..."* United Press, January 29, 1938.

27 *...evidence of Gehrig's early symptoms.* Dr. Edward J. Kasarkis and Mary Winslow, "When Did Lou Gehrig's Personal Illness Begin?" *Neurology,* September 1, 1989.

27 *Klawans concurred with Kasarskis.* Dr. Harold Klawans, *Why Michael Couldn't Hit and Other Tales of the Neurology of Sports* (W.H. Freeman and Company, 1996), p. 255.

27 *...concluded that Gehrig functioned normally.* Melissa Lewis and Paul H. Gordon, "Lou Gehrig, Rawhide and 1938," *Neurology,* February 20, 2007.

28 *"like an overgrown kid..."* Donald Kirkley, "Screen—Lou Gehrig," *Baltimore Sun,* April 20, 1938.

28 *"surprising poise..."* Stanley Frank, "Gehrig Gives Creditable Performance," *New York Post,* March 24, 1938.

28 *"tosses off his lines..."* Wanda Hale, "Gehrig Makes Debut in Globe's New Film," *New York Daily News,* April 25, 1938.

28 *"He has both the personality and the voice..."* Film review, *Variety,* April 6, 1938.

29 *"People think I'm modest..."* Jack Thale, "Premiere Here Honors Gehrig," *Tampa Bay Times,* March 24, 1938.

Page

First Signs

30 *Interview and a late breakfast.* This account of Wilson's chat with the Gehrigs comes from two articles he wrote for the *Knoxville News-Sentinel*: "Gehrig Stops Off to Eat and Roar with Laughter Over His Movie," February 5, 1938, and "Gehrig: Sportswriters Will Run Bill Terry Out of Town if He Starts to Slip," February 6, 1938.

30 *"... muscles in his hair."* I'm giving Lefty a pass on this one. This quote is widely attributed to him but I can't find any reference to it during his lifetime. The earliest seems to be a column by the *New York Times'* Ira Berkow soon after the pitcher's death in February 1989. The quote does sound like something he'd say, and I have no reason to think Berkow or another writer made it up. Assuming he said it, I think it originated long after his career was over, when he was a frequent after-dinner speaker at sports banquets.

30 *"I asked him about the movie..."* Wilson, *News-Sentinel,* February 5, 1938.

31 *"Joe's a great kid."* Ibid.

31 *Demographers detailed the stark reality.* William D. Witnauer, Richard G. Rodgers, Jarron M. Saint Onge, "Major League Baseball Career Length in the Twentieth Century," National Center for Biotechnology Information, 2007.

32 "*At the end of the season.*" Fletcher interviewed by Brent Kelley, March 17, 1992. The entire interview can be found online in the Oral Histories Collection of SABR, the Society for American Baseball Research.

32 *five-figure salaries.* Information on salaries comes from baseball-reference.com.

32 "*It was really, really rough in the Depression...*" Lopez interviewed by Rod Roberts, February 22, 1988. Hall of Fame website, oral histories page.

32 *...one team owner immune to the Depression.* Information on Ruppert drawn from *The Colonel and Hug* (University of Nebraska Press, 2015), by Steve Steinberg and Lyle Spatz.

34 "*Lou is not the sort that holds out.*" Joe Williams, *New York World-Telegram*, January 9, 1932.

34 "*You know I've got a new manager now.*" Associated Press, February 14, 1935.

34 "*I am only asking what I believe...*" Associated Press, February 12, 1937.

34 "*There isn't a man on the team.*" Associated Press, February 11, 1937.

34 "*Why do you think they want you...*" Scotty Reston, Associated Press, March 10, 1937.

35 "*Wait till you see me riding...*" Jack Smith, "Lou Here to Meet Ruppert," *New York Daily News*, February 8, 1938.

35 "*I certainly expected to see some beer...*" Joe Williams, *New York World Telegram*, December 18, 1931.

35 "*The ascending note is the motif...*" Will Wedge, "No Luck in Ruppert Confabs," *New York Sun*, February 9, 1938.

36 "*Why should I take the same...*" Kevin Jones, "Gehrig Asks 41 G's, Ruppert Offers 36," *New York Daily News*, February 9, 1938.

36 "*There's the two-gun man, boys.*" Ibid.

36 "*Lou Gehrig was offered thirty-six thousand...*" Ralph McGill, "Colonel Ruppert Doesn't Even Go to Brewery With Gehrig Case," *Atlanta Constitution*, March 11, 1937.

36 "*As a rule, baseball's holdouts...*" Francis J. Powers, *Chicago Daily News*, February 20, 1938.

36 "*When one considers the years...*" George Barton, "Sportographs," *Minneapolis Star-Tribune*, February 11, 1938.

37 "*If ever a ballplayer deserved...*" Braven Dyer, "The Sports Parade," *Los Angeles Times*, February 16, 1938.

37 "*The chances are Gehrig can...*" Will Wedge, "Gehrig Demands Salary of $41,400 for 1938 Season," *New York Sun*, February 8, 1938.

37 "*Let's assume Gehrig will be...*" Lester Rodney, "On the Scoreboard," *The Daily Worker*, February 9, 1938.

37 "*I went more than halfway...*" Alan Gould, Associated Press, March 9, 1938.

37 *"The next move is up to Colonel..."* International News Service, March 10, 1938.

38 *"a long summer of hibernation."* *New York Post,* March 13, 1938.

38 *"I can't see anybody but us..."* James Dawson, "Ruppert Assails DiMaggio's Stand," *New York Times,* March 14, 1938.

38 *"After eight months..."* Ibid.

38 *He struggled in batting practice.* James Dawson, "Ruppert Impressed by Yankees' Performances in First Inspection of Camp, *New York Times,* March 15, 1938.

39 *"Very good, Mr. Gehrig!"* Rud Rennie, "Gehrig Takes Scream Test Upon Camp Arrival," *New York Herald Tribune,* March 16, 1938.

39 *George Selkirk riding a mule. New York Daily News* photo, published March 18, 1938.

39 *"his legs didn't feel so strong or springy."* Gehrig and Durso, *My Luke and I,* p. 163.

39 *He tried taping a piece of rubber...* James Kahn, "Champs' Averages Misleading," *New York Sun,* March 26, 1938.

40 *"not the first exhibition game he has missed..."* Rud Rennie, *New York Herald Tribune,* March 26, 1938.

40 *"Hollywood hands."* Sid Feder, Associated Press, April 3, 1938.

40 *"It's highly plausible something was going on."* Author interview with Dr. Richard Bedlack, February 2019.

40 *"he can't clout a ball as solidly..."* James Kahn, "Gehrig Pleased Over Choice on All-Time Team," *New York Sun,* March 30, 1938.

40 *"approaching form."* Associated Press, April 1, 1938.

41 *"he's not driving the ball..."* Stanley Frank, "Yankee Slump is No Real Cause for Alarm," *New York Post,* April 4, 1938.

41 *"It was quite mild at first."* Grantland Rice, "The Sportlight," August 10, 1939.

41 *"Gehrig's contributions were..."* Stanley Frank, "Yank Bats are Dynamite," *New York Post,* April 13, 1938.

41 *"The consistency of his hitting..."* James Kahn, "Gehrig's Heavy Hitting Brightens Outlook for Yankees," *New York Sun,* April 14, 1938.

42 *"I got to do something about..."* Hugh Bradley, "Two-Gun Lou Okays Blue Background at Ebbets Field," *New York Post,* April 16, 1938.

42 *"producing only soft, looping fly balls..."* There are several quotes that turn up in many a Gehrig biography, article and website, and the one attributed to James Kahn—usually starting with "I think there is something wrong with him; physically wrong, I mean,"—is among the most frequently cited. Only one problem: he never wrote anything like that. I searched the archives of Kahn's paper, the *New York Sun,* and while Kahn certainly chronicled Gehrig's decline as it happened in 1938 and 1939, he never wrote that he saw Gehrig meeting the ball squarely and producing only soft fly balls. In fact, the earliest

reference to the Kahn quote seems to be in Eleanor's memoir, published in 1976. So where did the quote come from? At the time of this writing, it's unclear. But I'm searching.

Page

A Slow Start

43 *wet, gray, windy afternoon in Boston.* This account of conditions at Fenway Park that day is drawn from: Gerry Moore, "Sox Drub World Champs, 8-4," *Boston Globe*, April 19, 1938; John M. Flynn, "Red Sox... Turn Back Yankees 8-4," *Berkshire Eagle*, April 19, 1938; and a Paramount newsreel from the game, found on the Getty Images website.

43 *"When is DiMaggio going to join the club?"* Paramount newsreel.

44 *"Get a horse, Lou!"* John M. Flynn, "The Referee's Sporting Chat," *Berkshire Eagle*, April 19, 1938.

44 *"Two thousand wonderful games."* Recording of Fred Hoey from WNAC radio broadcast, April 18, 1938.

44 *...not into a slump but a drought.* Gehrig's 1938 game logs on baseball-reference.com

45 *"I hope he's ready to play Saturday."* Sid Mercer, International News Service, April 20, 1938.

45 *"Lou doesn't look good at the platter."* Bill McCullough, "Poor Showing in Hub Clouds Yanks' Opening," *Brooklyn Daily Eagle*, April 21, 1938.

45 *"Yankees' opening-day festivities."* This account drawn from: Jack Smith, "Yankees Win," *New York Daily News*, April 23, 1938 and the "Diamond Dust" column in the same edition; "Morris Refuses to Pass Stadium Pickets," *Daily Worker*, April 23, 1938; and Associated Press, April 22, 1938.

46 *Lou belted a four-hundred-foot drive.* Jack Smith, "Nats Rip Yanks," *New York Daily News*, April 25, 1938; Associated Press, April 24, 1938.

46 *"[F]ans are beginning to wonder..."* Gayle Talbot, Associated Press, April 25, 1938.

46 *"...this one is the worst ever."* Unbylined article, "Poor Physical Condition Clue to Gehrig Ills," *Brooklyn Daily Eagle*, April 25, 1938.

47 *"It's not uncommon during the first year..."* Author interview with Dr. Richard Bedlack, February 2019.

48 *"I got a hanging curveball..."* Frates in YouTube video, "Pete Frates' Story," published on December 20, 2013.

48 *"...I was striking out a ton."* Casey Sherman, Dave Wedge, *The Ice Bucket Challenge: Pete Frates and the Fight Against ALS* (ForeEdge, 2017), p. 5.

49 *"Lou Gehrig now inspires me every day."* Pete Frates, "My Journey from Baseball Star to ALS Patient, 75 Years After Lou Gehrig," bleacherreport.com, July 2, 2014.

49 *"Yankee captain is down in the mouth."* Unbylined article, "Mishap Hands Knickerbocker Lease on Life," *Brooklyn Daily Eagle,* May 2, 1938.

49 *"He will be no fit company for man..."* John Lardner column, April 23, 1938.

49 *"But if he had a bad day..."* Art Rosenbaum, "DiMaggio: Gehrig One of a Kind," *San Francisco Chronicle,* May 24, 1995.

50 *"...searching for a good sharp knife."* James Kahn, *New York Sun,* April 29, 1938.

50 *"Lou is down in the dumps."* Unbylined article, "Yankees Expect Jolting Joe to Get 'Em Rolling," *Brooklyn Daily Eagle,* April 30, 1938.

50 *"Let Lou hit his way back."* James Kahn, "DiMaggio Nudges Gehrig Aside in Shakeup of Yankees," *New York Sun,* May 8, 1938.

51 *"Yeah, the Yankees are having trouble..."* Gordon Cobbledick column, *Cleveland Plain Dealer,* May 4, 1938.

51 *"He ain't a-going to get better."* "Nats On Par With Cream of East," *Washington Evening Star,* May 3, 1938.

51 *"don't become discouraged..."* Eig, *Luckiest Man,* p. 247.

52 *"I carried a picture of Lou in my binder."* Interview of Dahlgren by Cincinnati Reds announcer Claude Sullivan, 1965. The recording can be heard on the website of the Kentucky Digital Library.

52 *"...he wants to be protected."* Letter from George Weiss to Yankee scout Joe Devine, April 21, 1937.

52 *"I never did think for a moment..."* Sullivan interview, 1965.

52 *....a really bad pitcher.* Walkup told interviewer Rick Bradley shortly before he died: "I wish I had gotten with a better ballclub. I believe if I had got with a good ballclub I would've been all right." Interview can be heard online through SABR's Oral Histories Collection.

53 *Lou beat it by a hair.* Associated Press photo, May 3, 1938.

53 *"...almost tore off George McQuinn's leg."* Harold Wecke, "Yankees Beat Browns 5-1," *St. Louis Post-Dispatch,* May 3, 1938.

53 *"I was holding my right arm too stiff."* Hugh Bradley, "Holding Right Arm Too Stiff Caused Gehrig's Slump," *New York Post,* May 12, 1938.

54 *"He's as fast as any other pitcher."* John Lardner, North American Newspaper Alliance, August 6, 1937.

54 *"...making me jump out of my skin."* Bob Feller with Bill Gilbert, *Now Pitching: Bob Feller* (Carol Publishing Group, 1990), p. 21.

54 *"I'm sure [catcher] Rollie Hemsley..."* Jack Cuddy, United Press, May 14, 1938.

55 *A home movie taken by a fan.* The moment is part of ninety-second clip entitled "Yankees Baseball with Joe DiMaggio and Lou Gehrig" that can be found on YouTube.

55 *"By the time he reached the plate."* Frank Graham, "Setting the Pace," *New York Sun,* May 13, 1938.

55 *"a lot of doubleheaders for the Yankees."* *New York Times*, May 18, 1938.

55 *"How can they be the same old Yankees..."* Associated Press, May 24, 1938.

56 *...three thousand kids rushed the field.* "Yankees Wallop Butler; Youngsters Halt Battle," *Pittsburgh Sun-Telegraph*, May 17, 1938.

Two Thousand

Page

57 *Lou... blasted the ball, on the fly.* Jack Smith, "Tribe Beats Yankees, Rout Pearson in 4th," *New York Daily News*, May 23, 1938.

57 *only to be stabbed by a sharp pain.* "Hudlin Pitches for Tribe Today," *Cleveland Plain Dealer*, May 23, 1938.

58 *"Charley horse."* Associated Press, May 22, 1938.

58 *"Crick in the back."* *Cleveland Plain Dealer*, May 23, 1938.

58 *Doc Painter... treated Gehrig with heat lamps.* James Kahn, "Lame Back Menaces Gehrig," *New York Sun*, May 23, 1938.

59 *"Oh, he pulled a muscle..."* Charles P. Ward, "With Pollyanna in Reserve, McCarthy Sticks by Yanks," *Detroit Free Press*, May 25, 1938.

59 *"... made up his mind on Tommy Henrich."* Eddie Brietz, Associated Press, May 26, 1938.

60 *"If you don't play..."* Ira Wolfert, North American Newspaper Alliance, September 20, 1941. The story of Eleanor urging Lou to end the streak at 1,999 was dramatized in the 1942 movie *Pride of the Yankees* and was recounted in *My Luke and I*. I chose to cite this telling of Eleanor's story because it seems to be the very first time it appeared in print.

60 *"You can't be serious..."* Ray Robinson, *Iron Horse: Lou Gehrig in His Time* (W.W. Norton, 206 paperback edition), p. 235.

60 *"Lou, I want to congratulate you..."* The film clip of McCarthy addressing Gehrig can be found on the Getty Images website. It was used in a newsreel retrospective of Gehrig's career, released after his death.

61 *"The darn thing's gotta end some time..."* Lester Rodney, "2,005, Or How About a Week Off, Lou?" *The Daily Worker*, June 14, 1938.

61 *What has he to gain..."* "Letters to the Sports Editor," *New York Times*, June 4, 1938.

62 *"No fuss please..."* George Kirksey, United Press, June 1, 1938.

62 *"If I'm out of even an exhibition..."* Bill McCullough, "Yanks Back in Flag Stride," *Brooklyn Daily Eagle*, June 1, 1938.

63 *"stiff as a steel beam."* Despite Lou's less-than-stellar broadcasting skills, he became a frequent guest on radio shows as the '30s wore on. In addition to the shows mentioned throughout the book, he appeared on singer Rudy Vallee's variety program in October 1932, singer Kate Smith's season premiere in October 1937, and a program called "MGM Good News of 1938," broadcast from Hollywood while Lou was in town

making his movie. He was also on many local radio shows, usually for interviews.

63 "*Why don't you have dinner...*" Hubbell and Gehrig appear in a three-minute segment unrelated to that night's play, a baseball drama starring comedian Joe E. Lewis. The whole one-hour program is on YouTube.

64 "*A big bowl of Wheaties.*" This is one of those stories about Gehrig that appears in nearly every book about him, but rarely with the precise details. I was able to establish the correct date, program and announcer through contemporary newspaper reports. There is no known recording of the show, and reports vary to some degree on exactly what Bond and Gehrig said, but I think the version presented here seems most likely.

64 "*Lou Gehrig Plugs Wrong Breakfast Food.*" *Tampa Tribune*, August 1, 1937.

64 "*Play Baseball Lou! Stay Off Radio!*" *Pittsburgh Press*, July 31, 1937.

64 "*That's a reaaal load off my mind...*" Recording of "Ripley's Believe It or Not," October 9, 1937. The whole show can be found on YouTube.

65 "*Our scene opens in the Yankee dugout...*" There are two known copies of the script for the May 31, 1938 "Believe It or Not": one signed by Ripley and Gehrig, and one in the Doug and Hazel Anderson Storer Collection at the Wilson Library of the University of North Carolina. Doug Storer was a radio producer who worked on the Ripley program.

66 *...sold for four thousand seven hundred dollars.* Hunt Auctions website, results from August 6-7, 1999 auction.

67 *Gehrig fell while making a throw... New York Daily News*, June 9, 1938.

67 "*unleashing thunderous applause...*" W. Vernon Tietjen, "Hitting of Almada Helps Browns Beat and Tie Champions," *St. Louis Star and Times*, June 20, 1938.

68 "*Gehrig catapulted his two hundred five pounds...*" Eugene J. Whitney, "Hemsley's Bunt Proves 3-Run Hit," *Cleveland Plain Dealer*, June 23, 1938.

68 "*They just jump up in the air...*" Charles P. Ward, "Ward to the Wise," *Detroit Free Press*, August 20, 1938.

68 "*yells, screams, whistles, hand-claps...*" Gordon Cobbledick, "Indians Smash Yanks Twice," *Cleveland Plain Dealer*, June 23, 1938.

70 "*Umpire Bill Summers halted the game...*" Doc Holst, "Tiger Notes," *Detroit Free Press*, June 25, 1938.

Page

All-Star

73 "*We're going to play to win...*" Dave Anderson, "Babe Baptized the All-Star Game," *New York Times*, July 6, 1983.

73 *"The American League has never regarded..."* Associated Press, July 6, 1935.

73 *"...the Giants' ace enhanced his comfortable..."* While no longer a household name like Gehrig, Hubbell was nearly his equal in terms of fame during the mid-1930s. The two shared the cover of *Time* magazine ahead of the 1936 World Series and as noted, appeared together on *Lux Radio Theater.* In a 1971 episode of *All in the Family,* Mike Stivic and Archie Bunker are talking about baseball players. "I bet you've seen a lot of the great ones," Mike says to the older Archie. Archie replies: "Yeah, seen 'em all—Ruth, Gehrig, Hubbell."

74 *"Lou outpolled his nearest rival..."* "Final Returns in All-Star Baseball Poll, *Chicago Tribune,* June 25, 1933. The Trib conducted the official voting for the first All-Star Game.

74 *...good first basemen in this era.* Bottomley, Kuhel, Bonura and Trosky never made an All-Star Game roster, despite many fine seasons. Foxx got picked for the AL squad nine times but started at first base only twice.

75 *"He's all washed up."* Lawrence Ritter, *The Glory of Their Times* (William Morrow & Co, enlarged 1984 edition), p. 310.

76 *"How many runs has Gehrig batted in?"* Charles P. Ward, "Where's Hank Greenberg? All-Star Game Fans Ask," *Detroit Free Press,* July 8, 1935.

76 *"What we want to do..."* "Harridge Answers Critics of All-Star Team," *Detroit Free Press,* July 5, 1935.

76 *"I'll tell you one thing..."* Hy Hurwitz, "What About It?" *Boston Globe,* July 5, 1938.

76 *"I was picked for the All-Star team..." Hank Greenberg: The Story of My Life* (Crown Publishing, 1989), p. 97. Greenberg would eventually play in two All-Star Games. He might have played more, but missed four and a half seasons due to World War II.

77 *"No, nein, non, nit."* J.C.I, "The Old Sport's Musings," *Philadelphia Inquirer,* June 28, 1938.

77 *"Gehrig is batting only .275..."* Bob Ray, "The Sports X-Ray," *Los Angeles Times,* June 27, 1938.

77 *"Columbia Lou has been the worst..."* Gordon Graham, "Graham Crackers," *Lafayette Journal,* June 27, 1938.

77 *"Without having interviewed them..."* Gordon Cobbledick, *Cleveland Plain Dealer,* June 28, 1938.

77 *"Mr. McCarthy should not be blamed."* Associated Press, *July 2, 1938.*

77 *"When the 1938 All-Star Game came..."* Greenberg, *Story of My Life,* p. 97.

78 *"We're going to let you hear the noise."* Recording of 1938 All-Star game, Mutual broadcast, available on YouTube. There appears to be no film of the actual game, just brief clips of the warmup in which Gehrig does not appear.

79 *"Being in there day in day out..."* Morton Moss, International News Service, July 3, 1938.

79 *Bang-bang play in the third.* Jack Smith, "Yankees Tie for First, Smack Nats 10-5," *New York Daily News*, July 5, 1938.

80 *"a female camera addict..."* "Youth Sleep in Line for All-Star Tickets," *Cincinnati Post*, July 6, 1938.

81 *"You can't see what you call the spin..."* Gehrig interview with radio station KROC, Rochester, Minnesota, August 22, 1939.

81 *"We'll catch the Indians..."* Moss, International News Service, July 6, 1938.

81 *"That exhibition of pitching..."* Edward T. Murphy, "Cincinnati Filled with Baseball Notables," *New York Sun*, July 6, 1938.

81 *"Here's Lou Gehrig coming up."* Recording of '38 All-Star Game, Mutual broadcast.

82 *"Oops—he threw it away!"* Ibid.

82 *"He hits a long fly ball..."* Ibid.

83 *"There wasn't much noise..."* Lou Smith, "Nationals Take All-Star Honors, 4-1," *Cincinnati Enquirer*, July 7, 1938.

83 *"Many Fans Wondering..."* Stanley Frank, "Gehrig Holding Bag in Decline of Yankee Power, *New York Post*, July 12, 1938.

84 *"Gehrig Smacks Critics in Eye..."* Stanley Frank, "Gehrig Smacks Critics in Eye With Stellar Performance, *New York Post*, July 13, 1938.

84 *"I'm glad they got beat..."* Bob Hogan, "Trosky: Glad They Got Beat," *Iowa City Press-Citizen*, July 7, 1938.

Page

Reversal

95 *"The Yankee pitcher was Spud Chandler."* Milton Gross, "The Yankees' Angry Ace," *Saturday Evening Post*, July 13, 1946.

95 *The throw bounced off Lou's glove.* Charles P. Ward, "Tiger Notes," *Detroit Free Press*, July 18, 1938; and "Iron Man Injured," *Brooklyn Daily Eagle*, July 18, 1938.

96 *a fracture in the thumb.* Associated Press, July 19, 1938.

96 *...soldiering through his troubles.* Frank Graham, "Setting the Pace," *New York Sun*, July 20, 1938.

98 *"I am for the immediate removal..."* Henry McLemore column, January 29, 1942.

98 *"McCarthy should be criticized..."* Lester Rodney, "On the Scoreboard," *Daily Worker*, July 21, 1938.

99 *"If he continues to go through hitless games..."* Edward T. Murphy, "Yankees Fight to Protect Slim Lead with Gehrig Hurt," *New York Sun*, July 20. 1938.

100 *"Even with a broken thumb..."* J. Roy Stockton, "Extra Innings," *St. Louis Post-Dispatch*, July 27, 1938.

100 *The Yankees were grooming Ed Levy.* Associated Press, July 31, 1938, and Jack Cuddy, United Press, August 11, 1938.

100 *"I'm going to be the greatest..."* Associated Press, March 3, 1939.

101 *Lou won the first base position in a landslide.* Associated Press, August 1, 1938.

101 *"I hope it does not sound untruthful..."* *The Sporting News,* August 11, 1938.

102 *...a mid-game fistfight.* Associated Press, July 10, 1937.

103 *"I'm a policeman in Dayton..."* Associated Press and United Press, July 30, 1938, and "Jake Powell Is Suspended for Radio Remark," *Chicago Tribune,* July 31, 1938.

103 *"insulted twelve million Negro citizens..."* "Powell Insult Gets Boot of Judge Landis," *Pittsburgh Courier,* August 4, 1938.

103 *"unethical and disparaging remarks."* International News Service, July 30, 1938.

103 *"something that he did not mean."* "Powell Glad to Apologize," *Pittsburgh Courier,* August 4, 1938.

103 *"the longest home run ever made at this park."* "Lou Gehrig of Yankees Brings Stars to Harlem," *New York Age,* October 19, 1929.

103 *"The only important man present vetoing..."* Jimmy Powers, "Colored B.B. Players—OK," *New York Daily News,* February 8, 1933. Incidentally, many books and articles on Gehrig quote him as calling for the integration of baseball. One quote, found on the Columbia University website, has him saying, "I have seen many Negro players who belong in the big leagues. I don't believe there's any room in baseball for discrimination." While writing this book, I searched for the origin of that alleged quote, or its variations, without success. As far as I can tell, Gehrig never said anything like that to New York dailies, the out-of-town papers, the magazines, the black press, or even to the *Daily Worker,* which crusaded for integration and took note whenever a star voiced support for allowing black players in the big leagues. According to researcher Larry Lester, the *Daily Worker* did quote Gehrig on the subject, but not until July 1942, a year after his death. I wasn't able to search the archives of every New York paper, and it's possible the original quote is still out there, waiting to be discovered. But for now, I shy away from reporting Gehrig's comments as fact.

105 *"Gehrig won the ball game..."* Gordon Cobbledick, "Yanks Shut Out Indians, Lead by 5½," *Cleveland Plain Dealer,* August 8, 1938.

106 *"He is the menace of old."* Rud Rennie, "Yankees Down A's, 4-3, 9-2," *New York Herald Tribune,* August 15, 1938.

107 *showered the Yankee outfielder with boos...* Associated Press, August 17, 1938 and the *New York Times* article mentioned in the text.

108 *switched to a lighter bat...* United Press and Associated Press, August 13, 1938.

108 *"He returned the style of hitting..."* Rennie, *Herald Tribune,* August 15, 1938.

108 *"I don't know what did it..."* Associated Press, August 22, 1938.

108 *...a temporary reversal of his ALS symptoms.* Richard Bedlack, Timothy Vaughn, Paul Wicks, Jamie Heywood, Ervin Sinani, Roger Selsov, Eric Macklin, David Schoenfeld, Merit Cudkowitz and Alex Sherman, "How Common Are ALS Plateaus and Reversals?," *Neurology,* March 1, 2016.

109 *"It's possible this disease..."* Author interview of Bedlack, February 2019.

110 *"You know, something happened in that game..."* Donald Honig, "Out of Reach of All the Glory," *The Atlantic,* May 1971.

110 *"bounced on the front porch..."* Jack Smith, "Yanks 14 Hits Lash Athletics," *New York Daily News,* August 20, 1938.

111 *"Gehrig is hitting the ball again..."* Grantland Rice, "The Sportlight," August 17, 1938.

111 *fishing off the coast...* Fred Fletcher, "Outdoors," *New York Daily News,* August 24, 1938.

112 *"giving him the kind of a hand..."* Irving Vaughn, *Chicago Tribune,* August 24, 1938.

Page

Singles Hitter

113 *"Gehrig, Joe DiMaggio and George Selkirk agreed..."* Information on the home run contest comes from "Brownie Notes," *St. Louis Post Dispatch,* September 18, 1938; "Yanks, Though Beaten Twice by Browns, Clinch Tenth Pennant," *St. Louis Star-Times,* September 19, 1938; and "Selkirk Wins $100 in Hitting Contest," *New York Daily News,* September 19, 1938.

115 *"We were playing a midseason series..."* Joe Williams, "When McCarthy Learned Gehrig Was Slipping," *New York World-Telegram,* February 7, 1945.

115 *"Can He Reach .300?" Daily Worker,* August 29, 1938.

116 *"Somewhere in the creeping mystery..."* Gehrig and Durso, *My Luke and I,* p. 167.

116 *"If Lou Gehrig Can Belt..."* Eddie Brietz, "Sports Roundup," Associated Press, August 30, 1938.

117 *"Gehrig may not be smashing home runs..."* Harold Burr, "Gehrig King of Baseball's 100-Run Men," *New York Post,* September 6, 1938.

117 *"Sure it makes me feel good..."* Bill McCullough, "Mark Breaking Pleases Gehrig," *Brooklyn Daily Eagle,* September 6, 1938.

118 *"...the only Yank who could fathom Dutch." The Sporting News,* September 15, 1938.

118 *"staged a one-man celebration."* Associated Press, September 9, 1938.

118 *"Psst! Did you hear?"* Gus Uhlmann panel, *New York Post,* September 10, 1938.

118 *"He has a better constitution..."* This quote from Gomez popped up as a column filler in dozens of newspapers across the U.S. during late September and early October 1938. But it's hard to tell where and when it originated. The earliest publication I can find occurred September 18, 1938 in, of all places, a small Illnois newspaper, the *Decatur Herald Review,* in a column by sports editor Howard V. Millard. It seems doubtful that Millard would get the quote directly from Gomez, so there may be another source.

119 *"Ruin stared Eisenstat in the face..."* Charles P. Ward, "Eisenstat Aids by Halting Foe in a Relief Role," *Detroit Free Press,* September 16, 1938.

119 *"Ruth, when he hit a hard ball..."* Gehringer interviewed by Rod Roberts, July 26, 1985. Hall of Fame website, oral histories page.

119 *"...about the middle of the 1938 season."* Auker quoted by Dr. Edward J. Kasarkis and Mary Winslow, in their article "When Did Lou Gehrig's Personal Illness Begin?" *Neurology,* September 1989.

119 *"You could see something was off..."* Richard Lally, *Bombers* (Crown, 2002), p. 19-20.

120 *"Several reasons have been advanced..."* Charles P. Ward, "Ward to the Wise," *Detroit Free Press,* September 24, 1938.

121 *"Home run far into the Washington bullpen." Washington Post,* September 28, 1938.

121 *"Gehrig Falls Below .300," The Sporting News,* October 6, 1938.

123 *"Brown retreated to the clubhouse..."* Waner's account of Brown's despair after giving up the fateful homer is in *The Glory of Their Times,* 1984 edition, p. 364.

124 *"I'll tell you, that Gehrig..."* Herman interviewed by Rod Roberts, August 8, 1990. Hall of Fame website, oral histories page.

Page

World Series

125 *"There isn't much betting."* Gayle Talbot, Associated Press, October 4, 1938.

125 *"If the Yankees didn't win..."* Sid Feder, Associated Press, October 5, 1938.

125 *"We were overmatched."* 1990 Herman interview by Rod Roberts.

126 *"The winnings?"* Johnston D. Kerkhoff, International News Service, October 4, 1938.

127 *"Jimmy Foxx gave it to me."* John Kieran, *New York Times,* March 21, 1941.

128 *"The ball sailed out high and far..."* James Crusinberry, "New York Preps Down Lane Tech In Hitfest 12-6," *Chicago Tribune,* June 27, 1920.

128 *"Lou was in good spirits."* The account of the Yankees' departure for Chicago comes from "Slugging World Champions on Way to Chicago," *Chicago Tribune*, October 4, 1938, and an Associated Press story, also October 4.

128 *"tight as a drum."* Gehrig interview with radio station KROC, Rochester, Minnesota, August 22, 1939.

128 *"They were relaxed and arrived at Wrigley..."* United Press, October 5, 1938.

129 *"Team followers were surprised..."* Charles P. Ward, "Cubs Send Lee Against Yank Power Today," *Detroit Free Press*, October 5, 1938.

129 *"selling seats on her rooftop."* Associated Press, October 5, 1938.

129 *"almost invisible throughout the competition,"* Eig, *Luckiest Man*, p. 260.

129 *"a hollow imitation of his halcyon years."* Ray Robinson, *The Iron Horse* (W.W. Norton, 2006 paperback edition), p. 241.

129 *"the way you hustle, young man..."* Lally, *Bombers*, p. 19.

130 *Lou slipped into an odd skipping motion.* His trot down to first base and his run from third to home can be seen in a newsreel film from game one, available on the Getty Images website. His run from first to third can be seen in *Baseball 1938*, a one-reel summary of the season produced by Castle Films, a company that produced silent 8 mm movies for home use. A low-quality clip is available on You Tube.

130 *The throw... beat him by several steps.* Castle Films reel.

130 *"The tip-off on Gehrig came..."* Charles P. Ward, "Ward to the Wise," Detroit *Free Press*, October 11, 1938.

130 *"...one of which struck the wrist."* "Co. Clerk Injured by Batted Ball at World Series Game," *Dixon Evening Telegraph*, Oct. 6, 1938.

131 *"Lou yelled bloody murder..." The Sporting News*, October 13, 1938.

131 *"...the spectacle of Lou Gehrig."* Damon Runyon column, October 6, 1938.

131 *"It was the worst decision called on me..." The Sporting News*, October 13, 1938.

132 *"throwing mostly slowballs."* Mutual radio broadcast of game two, October 6, 1938. This is one of four surviving broadcasts from the '38 series, along NBC's coverage of games one and two and CBS coverage of game four. Why three different networks? Until 1939, baseball's powers allowed any radio station or network to air the series (and the All-Star Game) as a kind of public service. Starting in '39, the series went to a single network, with Gillette as the sponsor. The Mutual and CBS broadcasts from the '38 series can be found on YouTube. The NBC broadcasts are in the Library of Congress Recorded Sound Research Center.

132 *Gehrig, running smoothly.* Game two newsreel footage.

132 *"Gehrig says something to Hartnett."* Game two Mutual broadcast.

133 *"Gehrig went in kind of hard."* Ibid.

133 *Lou milled around on the edge...* Game three newsreel footage.
133 *...running smoothly and with adequate speed.* Ibid.
133 *"He reached out with his gloved hand..." The Sporting News*, October 13, 1938.
134 *"Somebody started the rhythmic clapping..." The Daily Worker*, October 10, 1938. This can be heard on the CBS broadcast of game four.
134 *...lining a single past Collins.* Game four footage from Castle Films reel. Cavarretta said Gehrig's hits in the series had no oomph but this single was hit fairly hard, getting past a leaping Collins and allowing Joe DiMaggio to go from first to third.
134 *"And so, the world champions for 1938..."* Game four CBS broadcast. As an aside, Mel Allen at this time had yet to develop the intense, staccato broadcasting style he became known for. His 1938 voice was considerably more mellow.
134 *impromptu chorus.* James Dawson, "McCarthy Calls Yankees Best Ever as Victors Celebrate With Song," *New York Times*, October 10, 1938.
134 *"a big kiss on the cheek."* Castle Films reel.
135 *"Old Rawhide really went to the corral..."* Cy Peterman, "Strictly Sports," *Philadelphia Inquirer*, October 11, 1938.
135 *"But did you see him hustle?"* Bill McCullough, "Joe McCarthy to Plan for '39 in December," *Brooklyn Daily Eagle*, October 12, 1938.
135 *"So they say my legs are gone."* Grantland Rice, "The Sportlight," October 8, 1938.
135 *"Half asleep, I answered the phone."* Fred Fletcher, "Outdoors," *New York Daily News*, October 11, 1938.
136 *"He ordered two of the lightest possible rods."* Ibid.
136 *"I feel there is a greater market..."* Harold Heffernan, North America Newspaper Alliance, October 11, 1938.

Page

Citizen Lou

138 *...the need for the United States to be well-armed.* Audio of Roosevelt speech to the Herald-Tribune forum, October 26, 1938. The speech can heard through the website of the FDR Presidential Library and Museum.
139 *The NBC microphones were on.* I do not mean to imply I have heard a recording of Gehrig's speech. The Library of Congress holds recordings of several speeches from the forum – including those of Eleanor and Franklin Roosevelt, Katherine Hepburn, Fiorello La Guardia and several less well-remembered figures. Unfortunately, Gehrig's speech is not among them. While his speech was apparently broadcast, it's not clear whether or not a recording exists. I did hear some of the introductions delivered by Mrs. Ogden Reid, which is why I am able to describe the nature of her voice.

139 *"No program on sports could be complete..."* Transcripts of the remarks by Reid, Gehrig and everyone else who spoke at the forum are in *America Facing Tomorrow's World: Report of the Eighth Annual New York Herald Tribune Forum on Current Problems,"* a book-length compendium of all the speeches given during the October 25-27, 1938 event.

139 *"the Yankees went up to Sing Sing..."* Ibid. The account of the game comes from "Babe Ruth Gives Saddest Crowd of Boys in World 2 Happy Baseball Hours," *Brooklyn Daily Eagle*, September 6, 1929.

141 *"Gehrig in Unfamiliar Role."* The package of headline, photo and caption was distributed by the now-defunct Central Press Association and appeared in a handful of papers on October 27 and 28, 1938.

142 *"die Juden* and other minority groups..." Gehrig and Durso, *My Luke and I*, p. 157.

142 *Lou told reporters he had stopped in Munich.* Jack Cuddy, United Press, February 13, 1935, and "Home From World Tour, Gehrig Expected to Ask $35,000 Salary from Yankees," *New York Times*, February 14, 1935.

142 *... relatives in the town of Baden Baden.* Jack Cuddy, United Press, February 12, 1935.

142 *...Hitler and Italian dictator Benito Mussolini.* Burt Thomas, "Dividing Up the World," *Detroit News*, May 16, 1938. This somewhat bizarre cartoon, which played on the ethnic roots of Gehrig and DiMaggio, also appeared in newspapers in St. Louis, Tampa and Waco, Texas.

143 *He did pick Schmeling.* "Yankees Vote for Louis 17-10," *New York Sun*, June 22, 1938.

143 *"No catastrophe in modern times..."* "Night of Stars to Aid Appeal for Refugees," Jewish Telegraphic Agency, July 27, 1934.

143 *Jack Benny, George Gershwin, George Burns.* "Theatrical Stars Aid Jewish Cause," *The American Israelite*, September 27, 1934, and "Elite of Stage, Screen, Radio Join Big Show," *The Central Jersey Home News*, September 23, 1934.

143 *President Roosevelt chimed in....* White House statement, November 16, 1938.

144 *Among those who signed on...*The list comes from pre-event stories that appeared in many New York-area newspapers. Gehrig's participation was announced in advance, in "Night of Stars Benefit Tonight," *New York Daily News*, November 16, 1938.

144 *"Star-Spangled Banner followed by... Hatikvah."* This account of the event is drawn from "Several Show Biz Groups Enlist in Refugee Succor," *Variety*, November 23, 1938 and "Mayor Indicts Nazis at Benefit," *New York Daily News*, November 17, 1938.

144 *"I'm glad to be in a country..."* "Lou Knows," *The Daily Worker*, July 4, 1939.

144 *"speaking as an American of German descent..."* *Variety*, November 23, 1938.

145 *"It's a pleasure to be here..."* "Night of Stars Is Seen by 20,000," *New York Times*, November 16, 1939.

145 *"a but-lah for their New Rochelle manse!"* Walter Winchell column, December 6, 1938. Winchell's column printed the rebuttal from Eleanor four days later.

145 *Gabrielson was destined to be...* Harry Grayson, "The Payoff," Newspaper Enterprise Association, September 30, 1938.

145 *a sportswriter touted Frank Milani...* Sid Feder, Associated Press, October 28, 1938.

146 *Fred Collins and Johnny Sturm.* Drew Middleton, Associated Press, December 29, 1938.

146 *"...so Dahlgren sits in the shade."* Ed R. Hughes, "Dahlgren's Job an Easy One," *San Francisco Chronicle*, December 5, 1938.

146 *"Foxx made a strong comeback..."* Unbylined article, "Gehrig Visions Renewed Vigor in '39 Season," *New York Daily News*, November 13, 1938.

146 *"There'll be a different Gehrig out there..."* International News Service, December 10, 1938.

147 *"...only a bad season for Gehrig."* Leslie Avery, United Press, February 2, 1939.

147 *"He's as strong and powerful as ever..."* Phip Harris, "It Occurs to Me," *Tampa Bay Times*, January 22, 1939.

147 *"...Gehrig isn't through yet."* Grantland Rice, "The Sportlight," January 25, 1939.

147 *"Lou would miss a curb..."* Associated Press, April 30, 1974.

148 *six thousand people in the U.S. are diagnosed.* "Facts You Should Know" page, ALS Association website.

149 *"He was completely sold on the gall bladder deal."* Associated Press, April 30, 1974.

149 *"You hit or you don't."* Harry Grayson, International News Service, January 16, 1939.

149 *"As far as Lou was concerned..."* Lieb, *Baseball as I Have Known It*, p. 199.

149 *Mary counseled Gehrig.* Ibid, p. 203.

150 *"Lou hadn't been too well..."* Ibid, p. 208.

150 *"When all's said and done..."* Howard Whitman, "Ruppert Makes Up With Babe – Dies With Smile," *New York Daily News*, January 14, 1939.

150 *"I have been an admirer of the Colonel..."* *Brooklyn Daily Eagle*, January 13, 1939.

151 *"There won't be any real change..."* Gayle Talbot, Associated Press, January 18, 1939.

151 *"a bat boy's salary."* Garry Schumacher, International News Service, January 30, 1937.

152 *"I'll play one hundred fifty-four games..."* Hy Turkin, "Gehrig, Accepting Pay Cut, to Leave Early for Camp," *New York Daily News*, January 26, 1939.

152 *"a type of public enemy in our great country..."* Recording from January 26, 1939, held in the Marr Sound Archives at the University of Missouri-Kansas City.

152 *fundraising party hosted by Jack Dempsey.* Associated Press photo, January 29, 1939.

153 *"Lou looked well..."* Lieb, *Baseball as I Have Known It*, p. 208.

153 *...reported hunting in the Everglades.* Eddie Brietz, "Sports Round Up," Associated Press, February 24, 1939.

153 *fishing in the Miami area.* Fred Fletcher, "Outdoors," *New York Daily News*, February 25, 1939.

153 *Lou ... turned the rod over to Eleanor.* Ibid.

153 *"Watch Der Gehrig..."* Fred Fletcher, "Outdoors," *New York Daily News*, February 27, 1939.

154 *noted that his leg muscles were sore.* Associated Press, February 28, 1939.

Page

ALS

155 *One of the few existing pieces of film...* The twenty-second clip can be seen on the Getty Images website.

155 *"He responded the way you'd expect."* Gehrig and Durso, *My Luke and I*, p. 168.

155 *"He stayed out there so long..."* Gayle Talbot, Associated Press, March 9, 1939.

155 *McCarthy... played Henrich at first.* Phip Harris, "It Occurs to Me, *Tampa Bay Times*, March 23, 1939 and Jack Smith, "Yankees Rip KC Farmhands 14-4," *New York Daily News*, March 23, 1939.

156 *"He would miss the first eight or nine pitches..."* Dave Anderson, *New York Times*, August 6, 1979.

156 *"I have a vivid memory..."* Bob Harig, "The Iron Legacy," *St. Petersburg Times*, August 27, 1995.

156 *"You could never imagine this big, strong fellow..."* Ibid.

156 *"I will not play Gehrig unless..."* Jack Smith, "Gehrig Given Ultimatum," *New York Daily News*, March 30, 1939.

157 *"Gehrig CAN Run."* Caption for AP photo published in *New York Daily News*, April 5, 1939.

157 *"His legs were wobbling..."* Flem Hall, "Pitchers Show Poise Against Yankees," *Fort Worth Star-Telegram*, April 6, 1939.

157 *"... Lou has lost the glow of youth."* W.N. Cox, "Breaks of the Game," *Norfolk Virginian-Pilot*, April 14, 1939.

158 "*...there was Lou. He looked awful.*" Milt Browning, "Ferrell Recalls Gehrig: Can it be 50 Years Ago?" *Greensboro News and Record*, July 6, 1989.

158 "*I am improving every day.*" Unbylined article, "Gehrig Quit? Not as Long as He Can Walk," *Chicago Tribune*, April 29, 1939.

158 "*When you're down on yourself...*" James A. Kahn, "Iron Man Unburdens Himself," *New York Sun*, April 26, 1939.

159 "*I'd do it just the way I have.*" Henry McLemore, United Press, April 25, 1939.

160 "*Why doesn't he quit?*" Gehrig and Durso, *My Luke and I*, p. 169.

160 "*Three times yesterday...*" Bill McCullough, "Dimag Mishap Spells Dry Dock for Gehrig," *Brooklyn Daily Eagle*, May 1, 1939.

160 "*get in there.*" Babe Dahlgren, "Gehrig's Last Day," *Sports Illustrated*, June 18, 1956.

160 "*You couldn't figure out what happened...*" Harig, *St. Petersburg Times*, August 27, 1995.

160 "*I just can't understand.*" James Dawson, "Buoyant Gehrig, Long String Ended, Puzzled Over His Batting Decline," *New York Times*, May 4, 1939.

160 "Don't try to get me thinking..." Joe Williams, *New York World-Telegram*, May 17, 1939.

161 "I'm not cheering for him..." Bob Broeg, "Baseball Flashback by Cameraman Babe Dahlgren," *St. Louis Post-Dispatch*, April 4, 1965.

161 "When I barely knocked the ball..." Hy Turkin, "Hail and Farewell," *New York Daily News*, July 4, 1939.

161 "When he took off his clothes..." Eig, Luckiest Man, p. 310.

162 "*Gentlemen, we have bad news.*" Whitney Martin, Associated Press, June 21, 1939; Stanley Frank, "Gehrig's Spirit Unbroken," *New York Post*, June 22, 1939; Arthur J. Daley, "Infantile Paralysis Terminates Gehrig's Playing Career," *New York Times*, June 22, 1939.

162 "To whom it may concern..." Ibid.

162 "*This story is beyond belief.*" Grantland Rice, "The Sportlight," August 22, 1940.

163 "*I urge that you keep pushing ahead.*" Jonathan Eig, "A Legend's Last Letters," *Wall Street Journal*, March 29, 2005.

163 "*I thought I had him fooled...*" Ira Wolfert, North American Newspaper Alliance, September 20, 1941.

163 "*And I guess we signed autographs...*" Bill Dickey interviewed by Rod Roberts, April 27, 1987. Entire interview on Hall of Fame website, oral histories page. A variation on this story has Lou saying the climactic words to *Herald Tribune* writer Rud Rennie. However, Dickey makes no mention of Rennie. It's possible that both Dickey and Rennie were on the scene and heard Gehrig utter the premonition of his own death.

163 "*Well doc, how am I doing today?*" Wolfert, September 1941.

164 *"prototype of the best sportsmanship..."* The quotes from LaGuardia, Farley, McCarthy and Ruth are drawn from newsreel footage of Lou Gehrig Appreciation Day, July 4, 1939.

165 *"When you look around..."* Newsreel footage, July 4, 1939. As Jonathan Eig and others have noted, only four lines of Gehrig's speech are known to have been recorded. When I started this book, I held out hope that the full speech might exist somewhere, maybe in an overlooked film canister or misplaced radio transcription disc. I scoured the internet and checked with various sound and film archives in hopes that somebody had the full speech and just didn't realize it was "missing." Among the places I looked: the Hall of Fame, the Library of Congress, the National Archives, the Smithsonian, the Marr Sound Archives at the University of Missouri-Kansas City, the Paley Center for Media, websites with old-time radio content like archive.org, too many others to list. Doak Ewing, a collector of old-time baseball footage and the owner of Rare Sports Films, Inc., said on his website that he had an episode of the 1950s CBS television program "You Are There" that contained parts of the speech. Alas, the alleged recording was a fake. A well-done fake, I should add; whoever voiced Gehrig for the episode captured his accent, inflections and pacing to near-perfection, and the producers even put realistic-sounding Yankee Stadium echo on the voice. But it wasn't the real Lou, and the search goes on.

166 *Schang spoke about his trip to local sportswriters.* The Schang quotes come from two sources: Jack Koffman, "Along Sport Row," *The Ottawa Citizen*, July 8, 1939, and Walter Gilhooly, "In the Realm of Sport," *The Ottawa Journal*, July 8, 1939. Schang apparently gave a separate interview to each man. I used quotes from both articles to assemble the old catcher's account of the event.

168 *"I was still fluttery on that bench..."* Halsey Hall, "Gehrig Coming Along Fine," *Minneapolis Star-Journal*, August 24, 1939.

168 *"Lou that was the greatest speech..."* Browning, *Greensboro News and Record*, July 6, 1989.

168 *"Docs don't approve..."* Hy Turkin, "Yanks Wallop Tigers," *New York Daily News*, July 16, 1939.

169 *Gehrig... reeled in a sixty-pound white marlin.* Grantland Rice, "The Sportlight," August 10, 1939.

169 *"...had to quit at the fourth cup."* Ibid.

170 *radio serial entitled Our Coach.* Jo Ranson, "Radio Dial Log," *Brooklyn Daily Eagle*, October 7, 1939.

170 *"I am through with baseball..."* "Mayor Gives Gehrig Parole Board Post," *New York Daily News*, October 12, 1939.

170 *"He'd see them all..."* Gehrig and Durso, *My Luke and I*, p.19.

170 *"This work is unbelievably interesting."* Dillon Graham, Associated Press, January 30, 1941.

171 "*...always sneaked him into the studio.*" Dan Senseney, "Coast to Coast," *Radio and Television Mirror*, February 1940.

171 "*...the name isn't O'Gehrig, its Lou Gehrig.*" NBC, "Chase and Sanborn Hour," March 17, 1940. Full recording can be heard in the Library of Congress Recorded Sound Research Center.

172 "*L. Gehrig slammed a home run...*" Walter Winchell column, March 30, 1940.

172 "*But don't you think the mayor...*" NBC, "New York World's Fair Sports School," May 4, 1940. Full recording can be heard in the Library of Congress Recorded Sound Research Center.

172 "*He toddled, not walked...*" Bob Broeg, "Baseball Flashback by Cameraman Babe Dahlgren," *St. Louis Post-Dispatch*, April 4, 1965.

172 "*These aren't the Yankees...*" George Kirksey, United Press, June 2, 1941.

173 "*It just killed us to see...*" Earl Gustkey, "He's Been Managing the Yankees for 52 Years," *Los Angeles Times*, October 17, 1978.

173 "*...Gehrig's ALS progressed pretty fast.*" Author interview with Bedlack, February 2019.

173 "*...the doctors are satisfied with my progress.*" Graham, Associated Press, January 30, 1941.

174 "*That's a pretty good day, isn't it?*" John Henry, International News Service, April 9, 1941.

174 "*It is getting a little more difficult...*" Joe Burris, "A Signature Collection," *The Baltimore Sun*, May 2, 2005.

174 "*like a great clock...*" Gehrig and Durso, *My Luke and I*, p. 177.

174 "*most beatified expression....*" Ibid.

Page

Epilogue

175 "*We will have no eulogy...*" International News Service, June 4, 1941.

175 *Fresh Pond Crematory.* United Press, June 4, 1941.

175 *...at producer Sam Goldwyn's behest.* Information on movie, besides viewings, comes from Richard Sandomir, *The Pride of the Yankees* (Hachette Books, 2017).

176 *Gehrig film in development.* Dave McNary, "Authorized Lou Gehrig Biopic 'The Luckiest Man' in Development, *Variety*, June 21, 2017.

176 "*There's no reason to believe...*" Ed Feinen, United Press, May 1, 1959.

176 "*The strangest thing is all these comparisons...*" Pat O'Brien, "Ripken's Streaking to History," *New York Daily News*, July 11, 1995.

177 *...the top vote-getter among all players.* Ronald Blum, Associated Press, October 24, 1999.

177 "*As time goes on, the association fades.*" Author interview, March 2019.

177 "*I sometimes call it Lou...*" Dudley Clendinen, "The Good Short Life," New York Times, July 9, 2011.

177 "*I was living a healthy life until Lou...*" ALS Association Official Blog
178 "*There's definitely hope...*" Author interview, March 2019.
179 "*It's easy to think of Gehrig today...*" John Thorn podcast interview, 2014

Index

About the Author

Dan Joseph is a journalist, author and incurable baseball fanatic. By age ten, he memorized most of the Baseball Encyclopedia. He spent one summer buying six packs of baseball cards per day, searching for the elusive Don Robinson. In college, he'd climb to the roof of his dorm, trying to pick up faint radio signals of Pittsburgh Pirates games. He's more rational now; he holds a day job, has a family of his own. But at random moments, he'll plunge into deep study of Mickey Rivers or Eddie Joost or Manny Sanguillen, and can't be reached for hours.

CPSIA information can be obtained
at www.ICGtesting.com
Printed in the USA
LVHW031830050919
630059LV00005B/796/P

9 781620 062326